Rough and Plenty

Life Writing

Wilfrid Laurier University Press's Life Writing series celebrates life writing as both genre and critical practice. As a home for innovative scholarship in theory and critical practice, the series embraces a range of theoretical and methodological approaches, from literary criticism and theory to autoethnography and beyond, and encourages intersectional approaches attentive to the complex interrelationships between gender, class, race, ethnicity, sexuality, ability, and more. In its commitment to life writing as genre, the series incorporates a range of life writing practices and welcomes creative scholarship and hybrid forms. The Life Writing series recognizes the diversity of languages, and the effects of such languages on life writing practices within the Canadian context, including the languages of migration and translation. As such, the series invites contributions from voices and communities who have been under- or misrepresented in scholarly work.

Series editors: Marlene Kadar, York University
Sonja Boon, Memorial University

Rough
and
Plenty

A MEMORIAL

Raymond A. Rogers

WLU PRESS

WILFRID LAURIER
UNIVERSITY PRESS

LAURIER
Inspiring Lives.

Wilfrid Laurier University Press acknowledges the support of the Canada Council for the Arts for our publishing program. We acknowledge the financial support of the Government of Canada. This work was supported by the Research Support Fund.

Canada   ONTARIO ARTS COUNCIL   CONSEIL DES ARTS DE L'ONTARIO
an Ontario government agency
un organisme du gouvernement de l'Ontario

Canada Council   Conseil des arts
for the Arts   du Canada

Library and Archives Canada Cataloguing in Publication

Title: Rough and plenty : a memorial / Raymond A. Rogers.
Names: Rogers, Raymond Albert, author.
Description: Includes bibliographical references.
Identifiers: Canadiana (print) 20190162570 | Canadiana (ebook) 20190162627 | ISBN 9781771124362 (softcover) | ISBN 9781771124386 (EPUB) | ISBN 9781771124379 (PDF)
Subjects: LCSH: Rogers, Raymond Albert. | LCSH: Fishers—Nova Scotia—Biography. | LCSH: Fisheries—Nova Scotia. | LCSH: Fishers—Nova Scotia—Economic conditions. | LCSH: Fisheries—Economic aspects—Nova Scotia. | LCSH: Fishery closures—Nova Scotia.
Classification: LCC HD9464.C23 N87 2020 | DDC 338.3/72709716—dc23

Front-cover photo is from iStockphoto and shows the Atlantic coast of Nova Scotia. Cover design by Heng Wee Tan. Interior design by Daiva Villa, Chris Rowat Design. Title-page photo (page iii), showing the author aboard the *Whitestreak*, by Laura Jane McLauchlan.

© 2020 Wilfrid Laurier University Press
Waterloo, Ontario, Canada
www.wlupress.wlu.ca

This book is printed on FSC® certified paper. It contains recycled materials and other controlled sources, is processed chlorine free, and is manufactured using biogas energy.

MIX
Paper from
responsible sources
FSC
www.fsc.org   FSC® C103567

Printed in Canada

For
Laura Jane McLauchlan

Such, however, is the change in style of living and dress, and so considerable is the failure in all their crops, that with all their other advantages they do not seem to me to have all the rough and plenty they had long ago, or to be as far removed from poverty as then. They live now more luxuriously, but more from hand to mouth, and therefore the changes from what may appear to be plenty to poverty and want, are likely to be more rapid than formerly, when any particular cause for such changes occur.

— *Roderick Stewart, Napier Commission witness, 1883*

Contents

List of Photographs

Acknowledgements

Thanks first to all to those in Atlantic coastal communities for their generosity and know-how. Thanks also to the Faculty of Environmental Studies at York University who gave an out-of-work fisher a chance at a second career. More specifically, I am very grateful to Siobhan McMenemy, senior editor at Wilfrid Laurier University Press, for her encouragement and advice throughout the publication process, and thanks as well to managing editor Robert Kohlmeier, for his editorial input. Thanks also to Clare Hitchens, Marian Toledo Candelaria, and the rest of the WLUP staff for their expertise in the production process, as well as the two anonymous reviewers for their excellent advice on improving the manuscript. Closest to home, I am in a state of total insolvency in terms of what I owe Laura Jane McLauchlan, and our son, Lauchlan Rogers.

Within, within, you birds of tin
The coin of the realm has done you in,
No *visage*, no *roman*
No hot little crucible to carry you along.
You don't want to hear from me.

Without, without, you're blasted about
The land when the master has turned you out,
Until nothing remains, only a domain
Where you and your tyranny become the same.
You don't want to hear from me.

Prologue

In the spring of 1940 in Little Harbour, Nova Scotia, a family is listening to news about the war on the radio when Grandmother calls from upstairs, saying she can see a light on the water from her bedroom window. "It is waving back and forth in a horrid place." The family goes outside, and sure enough, in the haze of fog, there is a light off the Madd Rocks.

As they prepare to go down to the wharf below the houses, two strangers come up through the alders and cross the yard. They ask where they are and if there are any local boats about that might be big enough to tow their vessel out of the surf. Calls are made to Lockeport, as well as to others in Little Harbour who might be of help to the stricken vessel.

More community members join the group as they make their way down the hill to the wharf. One of the strangers describes their situation. "It's the *Douglas and Robert* we are on. She's a salt banker, making our way into Lockeport. She's only three or four years old, and loaded to the hatches after a long trip on the Grand Banks. Fog began to move in when the wind died and the sun went down. We reefed the sails and started the engine to jog in a ways further. We were trying to reach harbour before dark, but we slowed down once we lost sight of the lights on land. We stopped to check the depth of water with the sounding lead. Twelve fathoms. 'Let her run for five more minutes and I'll check 'er again,' says Captain Tanner. 'I imagine we will have to anchor off the harbour until daylight.'

"The skipper had come back out on deck and was pulling on his oil pants for the next sounding when the vessel shudders. Then that terrible rolling up and laying down on her side. Things as they shouldn't be. Everything familiar, and everything wrong, all at once. Then the rush of attention, care and know-how, the skipper shouting over the barking of the

Newfoundland dog. We shifted as much weight as we could to the stern. We rowed out anchors and dropped them in deeper water, started up the old one-lunger, and tried to winch ourselves off the rocks. And when that failed, the skipper sent us off in the dory for help."

Tow ropes are lowered from the wharf and three boats cast their moorings and steam out over Middle Ground to the south'ard of the Can Buoy where the vessel lays. The three boats idle up to the vessel in the dark. A dory rows out to take the tow lines back aboard. The Captain shakes his head when he sees the boats, knowing they are far too small to have any purchase. Engines roar and lines snap, to no avail. The very qualities that make a vessel sleek and efficient in the aquatic world work against it when it meets the land. All its capabilities are elsewhere, and its vulnerabilities come to the fore.

"Start emptying the hold overboard to lighten her," shouts the Captain. Soon salt cod are floating in the waves and washing up on the rocks. There is some talk of bringing the fishing boats alongside and loading the catch into them, but there is just enough surf to make that too dangerous, given how shoal the water is, and how many rocks there are. And so throughout the night, despite the casting off of its payload, the *Douglas and Robert* begins to settle in the surf, its wooden skeleton collapsing slowly under its own weight, and the oppressive air that pushes down on it from above.

"The tide is still going. Better wait till morning, when it's up again." The Captain's arms slacken at his sides and he drops the junk of rope he has in his hands. "Maybe we can get a bigger boat from Lockeport to pull us off when the tide is up. I'll stay with it as long as I can." The crew members climb down into the dories, leaving aboard only the skipper and dog, who stands next to the main hatch and barks into the night. They row out to the waiting boats, and after tying the dories fast to their sterns, the three boats steam back into

Little Harbour, where the crew is billeted around to whoever has a spare couch or bed.

In the slate grey of the next morning, it has already begun to breeze up from the east'ard, and with each wave the vessel shifts farther up onto the rocks, until it begins to turn sideways in the surf. There is no steamer to be found in Lockeport, and in any case trying to tow the vessel off the rocks now would probably tear it to pieces. As the day lightens, the tide starts to fall again. The deck is now at a sickening angle. Finally, the Captain crawls down over the rail into the surf. The spars are beginning to lie down and salt fish are spilling out through a breach in the hull. While a short time before, they had all been full of commands and invective, the crew stands together now as mere witnesses, looking out. The Captain turns to his mate and says, half to himself, "If I owned Little Harbour and I owned Hell, I'd rent out Little Harbour and live in Hell."

Throughout the day, the wind continues to blow. Word spreads and a crowd gathers. The salt cod are now coming ashore everywhere. By evening, the winds are gale force and it isn't fit to be outdoors. Those who have kept watch out near the vessel can no longer hear or see the dog, who could not be persuaded to come ashore even when it was still fit to do so.

The following morning, the owner of the vessel comes down from Lunenburg with a bus. He berates the Captain and the crew as they gather together with what remains of their kit bags. "You weren't where you thought you were, and this has all ended so badly, after such a good trip. Coming in at night on a falling tide? My. My. My. My. My. My."

By the time the wreckage of the *Douglas and Robert* has been picked over, local people have a good supply of salt fish put away for the winter. In time, the vessel is blasted to rubble by a series of severe storms, until only a few gaunt remnants remain, half submerged among the rocks and sand.

Figure 2   The deadeye pulley block. Photo by Lauchlan Rogers.

I hold a piece of the *Douglas and Robert* in my hand now, found on a walk amid the Madd Rocks at low tide, just inside of where the vessel ran aground. The remnant is a deadeye pulley block used to tighten the ropes that once trimmed the sails. The block is made of lignum vitae, one of the hardest woods on earth, and one of the few species of wood that doesn't float. The block has the look of a skull, with its two remaining eyeholes and what looks like a partial jaw where a piece of the block broke off during its long vigil in the surf. The iron band that once encircled it is also gone, although rust marks remain.

During walks along this shore, I have at times gathered pieces of coal from the *Brantford City*, a streamer that also met its fate on the Madd Rocks. The rocks are so named not because they are deranged but because they are intertidal and therefore especially treacherous: they are visible only part of the time and shoal enough to be dangerous all of the time.

This stretch of coastline leading out to Hemeons Head is called the Western Shore, as it marks the western boundary of the entrance to Little Harbour. It is an especially rough stretch to walk, as it is made up of rocks and boulders. Above the shoreline, stunted cat spruce gradually give way to overgrown fields as you move farther out onto the headland. In one of those fields, close to the collapsing bank, stands the solitary gravestone of Donald McDonald. The inscription reads:

In
Memory of
Donald McDonald
Who departed this life April 9
A.D. 1881 Aged 85 Years A Native
Of the Island of Lewis
North Britain

My home is nearby, one of the few that remain out here on the headland, and as other homes gradually disappeared into the undergrowth, I came to regard Donald as my nearest neighbour. And out of neighbourly interest, I wondered how he got here from Lewis, an island in the Scottish Hebrides, and why he is buried at this place on the shore. These were idle thoughts at first, but eventually I came to see that our fates were entwined although our lives were separated by a century.

I grew up in Manitoba and came to Nova Scotia in my mid-twenties during the 1970s, riding around the province on a bicycle. I bought the piece of land I have now on Hemeons Head with traveller's cheques while I was on my bike. I lived in a tent as I built my house and then went fishing. This was all brought about because the only act I seemed capable of at that point in my life was "living under a log." Before coming to Nova Scotia, I had been a child-care worker in group homes and wilderness camps in Manitoba. This employment in the front-line trenches of care is known to be stressful. Its practitioners are poorly paid and the burnout rate is high. I was grinding my teeth at night and had a hard time sleeping. It was difficult to make sense of the world when continually faced with the suffering of young people who are wards of the state. This situation is made worse by the fact that large numbers of wards in these care facilities are Indigenous. This makes it impossible to separate family breakdown from colonial tyranny. On top of that, a great deal of social work is conservative in nature: Stop hurting yourself and fit in. This kind of advice was meagre gruel at best, given the complicated lives that await Indigenous youth in Canada.

The membrane between myself and the world was increasingly frayed and porous, as I over-identified with those around me. And it all got to be too much. The simplest solution at the time seemed to be to get away from these pressing realities while I tried to grow a new layer of skin. A friend had been on a recent trip to Nova Scotia and had said how beautiful it was, and how relaxed the people seemed to be. This made coming here, where I knew no one, seem like a very good idea.

As it turned out, I enjoyed living rough. I discovered that I have a great love for carpentry, as well as a strong aptitude for it. So it wasn't so much that I needed a new skin: I needed a new context in which to live, one that was not so confounding and discordant. I realized that character armour is essential only when dealing with situations that have ceased to make sense or that are full of adversity. As unlikely as it sounds, the North Atlantic at night in thick fog was a salve to my spirit, less conflictive and political, more elemental and habitable. When out in the North Atlantic at night by yourself, one's first response might be to hunker down and close ranks. That is exactly the wrong thing to do in the face of so much dread and uncertainty. The most useful response is to open up and take in every nuance, to fully inhabit that world so as to respond to it in ways that keep you alive and help you catch fish.

Although I was working hard to create a new life on Hemeons Head, the industrial realities that surrounded that world were increasingly encroaching upon it in ways that threatened ecological collapse. So as my own life began to take shape, the world around me was going to pieces. In trying to "leave history," as I hoped to do when I came to Hemeons Head, I was now face to face with historical forces that eroded the livelihoods of the fishing communities along this shore, and thrust these fishers and their families into a historical transformation that eventually marginalized and dispossessed them.

But dispossession was the furthest thing from my mind as I began to make a life for myself as a fisher in Little Harbour. I embraced my new life in reliving the pioneer experience that was such a large part of the Canadian psyche. I cleared the land and began to build my house. For five years I lived without running water. Life was simple. In due course, I bought the *Whitestreak* fishing boat and used it for a number of years before I built a new boat, out of fibreglass, and named it the *Laura Elizabeth*. My arrival in this new way of life coincided with a near collapse of the fish stocks in the early 1970s, followed by their complete collapse in the late 1980s and early 90s. The debts I incurred building the new boat put me in a tough place. The banks were emptying my accounts to pay my debts for the boat and Revenue Canada was threatening to garnishee any money I made. When I left Nova Scotia to find temporary work, I felt I was hanging by a thread, a thread that I began, over time, to weave back into a stronger fabric that connected me to the rough and plenty of the community I had left, as well as to the world of earlier inhabitants such as Donald McDonald.

In my gradual transformation from a fisher to an academic with a specialization in political economy and environmental history, I came to understand that the marginalization of local people such as those in Atlantic coastal communities

improvement is disrupted by an alternate version of history that may explain both Donald McDonald's history and my own. I remembered how one of McDonald's relatives told me that he wanted his grave to point back toward Lewis. This allegiance to the past helped me as I struggled to understand what had happened to fishers in my community and, as it turns out, to many Scottish crofters like Donald McDonald.

The path I take in exploring these parallels has led me to eyewitness accounts of the nineteenth-century Scottish crofters as well as to my own lived experience as a fisher in Nova Scotia and as a worker on a hydroelectric dam in Long Spruce, Manitoba, and indeed as a sorter of beaver pelts for the Hudson's Bay Company in London. The vast majority of the dialogue in the book comes either from the nineteenth-century historical record of first-hand accounts or is recalled from my own lived experience. For the purposes of knitting the narratives together, I have on occasion created dialogue that serves the unfolding of the story. I have endeavoured to tailor these narrative links in ways that are in keeping with the historical record and my own life experience.

Although the worlds I am describing are fraught with marginalization and dispossession, they are also predominantly male. This is especially true of the historical record from the nineteenth century that relates to the crofter experience. So in my search for first-hand voices to include in my narrative, I have made every effort to include the voices of women wherever possible, and to emphasize that what is happening in the narrative affects whole communities, as well as to avoid the mock heroism of patriarchal voices unless they are being very clearly critiqued. This work combines a historical biography of Donald McDonald and my own autobiography as an example of life writing whose aim is to "resist and reverse the literary and political consequences...[of] 'depersonalization' and unrelenting 'abstraction'" where economic marginalization is replicated in the forms in which that marginalization is discussed (Marlene Kadar 12). Similarly, Julie Cruikshank, who situates her research within the resistant voices of Indigenous women in an approach that includes the work of critics such as Harold Innes, Mikhail Bakhtin, and Walter Benjamin, writes: "Each [of these writers] was concerned about the diminishing role of oral storytelling in the world, and each deplored the consequences when this form of communication becomes marginalized by more powerful knowledge systems. Each insisted that narrative is grounded in material circumstances of everyday life and is capable of addressing large questions about human behaviour" (2005, 61).

The central goal of this work, then, is to use first-hand perspectives to convey the experience of dislocation, not just the consequences of it, and also to provide a memorial to the tenacity, capability, and grief of those who lost their ways of life in the name of "progress" and "improvement," in what Michael Taussig refers to as a residual history of "collective representations of ways of life losing their life" (17). But memorial is also used in another sense: as a "statement of facts addressed to a government and often accompanied by a petition" (Merriam-Webster), which is the precise way that the crofters used the term when making their case to the Napier Commission (1883) against expulsion from their traditional homelands.

The curse for an advocate who has failed—as we have in the east-coast fishery and as the Scottish agitators did in large part in the nineteenth century—is that one is called upon to become a historian reassessing one's failures, and to identify the causes of the social injustice and environmental degradation that have become history's judgment: in other words, to go forward by going backward when under threat, as the porcupine does. In a world where capital abhors all communities but itself, remembering becomes a form of advocacy, a hope that presenting other pasts may lead to other futures. I can remember saying to myself as I was doing this research,

"Don't write with your face, write from somewhere farther back." This work is my "farther back." For all its grief, it is meant to provide ballasted hope for those who might feel increasingly rudderless and adrift in the powerful currents of the present. It is important to tell yourself a story that makes you strong. Despite all of its grief and suffering, this story— a kind of inoculation against the banalities and savagery of modern life—is one that I hope can give you strength.

~~~~~~~~~~

There are two frames that organize the work: one connects the stories of Donald McDonald's life and my own life as our fates were linked in this landscape/seascape in southwest Nova Scotia. The other is more formal and historical and has to do with the dispossession that is central to entrances into modernity for particular groups; that dispossession is reflected in the way the three sections of the book are set out to convey the increasing enclosure of the commons. For the purposes of this work, fishers and crofters share a broad definition: they are both small-scale artisanal, largely subsistence members of decentralized rural communities. Property rights are informal and largely held in common. In the case of the crofters, they are the descendants of the Scottish clans who had inhabited the Highlands and Islands for generations but who became "redundant populations" standing in the way of large-scale forms of sheep farming and agriculture. Similarly, as small-scale artisanal participants in an increasingly industrialized fishery, the inshore fishers came to be seen as inconsequential and inefficient; when the fish stocks began to collapse there was a consensus that there were "too many boats chasing too few fish," and inshore quotas were cut. This forced the artisanal fishers out of the industry. The privatization of fish quota became an industry-funded downsizing strategy that rewarded those with the deepest pockets.

The characterization of crofters and fishers as being out of step with the times gains clear definition only when the

opposite appears—that is, when large-scale industrial opera-
tors embark on enclosing the commons so that resources, as
private property, are made more easily subject to profit and
accumulation. The enclosure of the commons and the for-
malization of private property rights is a central feature of
the world of progress and modernity, and is, at the same time,
a process that is devastating for local communities, whose
members became strangers by staying in the same place. The
three sections of this book convey the gradual encroachment
of these forces on their lives.

In charting the increasing enclosure of fisher and crofter
communities within modern economic relations—outlined
at the start of each section with a History from Above over-
view—this work contains three main sections that chronicle
the intensifying threats to the "rough and plenty." In each
section, the first-hand narrative draws parallels between the
world of the fishers and the world of the crofters. The first section, entitled "Hemmed-In Communities," presents narratives
of a "day in the life" of fishers in Little Harbour, Nova Scotia,
in the mid-1970s and crofter communities in the Isle of Lewis
in the early nineteenth century, as they live their lives and
reflect on the changes they see occurring around them. The
rough and plenty still informs how life is lived on a daily basis,
but it is clear that forces are gathering to threaten their lives.

The second section, "Remittances Home," draws parallels between the lives of migrant crofters and migrant fishers,
both of whom leave home in order to support the diminishing
prospects of the communities they are attached to. Crofters
of the eighteenth and nineteenth centuries go to the "Nor'
Wast" by signing on as "wintering servants" for the Hudson's
Bay Company, and east-coast fishers go "out west" to toil as
labourers on a hydro project in Western Canada on the Nelson River near Hudson Bay in 1976.

The third section, "Outbreaks of Unrest," chronicles the
strife-ridden resistance by fishers and crofters as they fight

CHAPTER I

Shelburne County, Nova Scotia, Mid-1970s

History from Above

In the aftermath of World War II, a powerful international distant water fleet made up of many industrialized nations took advantage of a range of technological advances such as radar, sonar, hydraulics, refrigeration, polypropylene rope, and diesel engines—not to mention a great many surplus ships—and set out to mine the marine world. The unforeseen consequence was, in some large areas, the collapse of fish stocks. This ocean-going juggernaut reached the northwest Atlantic off Canada's east coast in the 1960s, and over-exploitation by this fleet led to a severe drop in fish catches between 1968 and 1972. At the time, any regulation of this fishery was voluntary, since it was taking place on the "high seas," in international waters. Because of the complaints of coastal states, there was a series of United Nations International Law of the Sea Conferences in the 1970s that aimed to limit the activities of this predatory fleet. One of the few outcomes of this process was the extension of coastal zones over which nations had control from three miles to twelve miles. As an indication of the international dimensions of exploitation during this period, Canadian fleets were catching only twenty per cent of the fish off its coast. It is into this world of dwindling catches and predatory fleets that the inshore longline fishers from Little Harbour venture into the night.

History from Below

I was not the first wayward soul to arrive in the land of the Mi'kmaq and make my home here. The territory in the vicinity of Little Harbour, as in most of Shelburne County, were annexed by Europeans in the 1780s after the American Revolution. An earlier wave of Plantation settlers had come from the Boston States to provide an English presence in Nova Scotia in the aftermath of the expulsion of the French Acadians. The arrival of the British Loyalist later in the eighteenth century expanded this settler presence dramatically, as did subsequent waves of displaced Scottish Highlanders throughout the nineteenth century.

In preparation for the arrival of the Loyalists, surveyors walked the land, laying out fifty- and hundred-acre lots for its decommissioned soldiers and for the refugees from revolution. Many of those who came from New York with the Port Roseway Associates in the mid-1780s were wealthy, and built homes in what became known as Shelburne—or, more accurately, their slaves and indentured servants built the houses—with grand plans for Shelburne to be the new capital of Nova Scotia. But the majority of those who were discharged on these shores were not wealthy. They were conscripted soldiers, as well as freed slaves from the American South who had fled behind British lines, and had fought against the revolution, on the promise they would be granted freedom when the war was over. With the battle lost, the "freedom" for these Black Loyalists came in the form of wresting a livelihood from the rocky and marginal land in Birchtown, to the west of Shelburne. Those who were given lots in the Little Harbour area near my home were former soldiers from the British army. Their names are no surprise—Murray, McDonald, Malcolm, Matthews, Nicolson, McLearn, Grant, Kilmartin, McKinney, Lawlor—as many of them were conscripted Highland Scots who were coerced by the Lairds to sign up and fight in colonial wars from Quebec to Africa, Asia, and the Caribbean.

The stone walls found in the stands of cat spruce on the headlands in the vicinity of Little Harbour are the King's lines, marking the edge of lots laid out for the benefit of his "loyal subjects." And so the meandering map of navigable rivers, and the loose assemblage of camping sites and burial mounds of the Mi'kmaq were usurped by a grid of the King's measure and occupied by those exiled to the tattered edges of empire.

More recent changes in settlement patterns on Hemeons Head were brought about not by grand colonial schemes but by incremental changes in technologies and their accompanying relations. The original habitations in this part of Nova Scotia were predominantly on the headlands because transportation along the coast was by water. This close proximity also made the rowing of small skiffs and dories out to the fishing ground less arduous. Only the larger ports such as Shelburne and Liverpool needed anchorage for schooners. What most of these settlers required was access to the sea near their homes, along with a woodlot further inland where there was a good mixed stand of hardwood and softwood to provide lumber to build their houses as well as firewood to keep them warm in the winter.

This settlement pattern began to change when gasoline engines were installed in fishing boats in the 1920s and 30s, initially with one-lunger single-piston engines and later with modified automobile engines. Internal combustion increased the size of the boats, both to accommodate the weight of the engine and for safety reasons, as fishers could now go out farther and had to deal with rougher weather and, at times, larger catches. Because of the increase in size and weight, the boats could no longer be hauled up makeshift slipways at the end of the day, as dories had been, and instead required sheltered harbours in which to moor. Wharves began to be built in the bays away from the open ocean. At the same time, the newly expanding road system joined the heads of these harbours farther inland. This led settlements to gradually migrate away from the open headlands and up into the protection of the harbours, connecting them as well to the services that became available along these new roads.

Little Harbour is well named. Even now, after large armour rocks were set out along a ledge on the inside of middle ground and the wharf extended on the inside of them, the protection for boats is precarious in the pitch and wail of storms. This new wharf accommodated the expansion in the number and the size of boats fishing out of Little Harbour, reflecting the general expansion of the fishery in the 1950s and 60s, as well as for the freezer and fish-buying stations that were set up to supply the fishers with bait and to buy their catches.

The large shoal-water banks off the coast of Nova Scotia provide excellent habitat for cod and haddock—the main commercial species—as well as cusk, hake, and halibut. This habitat is especially advantageous to inshore fleets because of the makeup of the accompanying ocean currents. The warm Gulf Stream travels northeast up along the edge of the continental shelf a hundred or so miles offshore. Inside of it, the Labrador Current flows down from the Arctic to Newfoundland and then south along the coast of Nova Scotia, before mixing with the Gulf Stream on Georges Bank, where powerful tides move in and out of the Bay of Fundy. The plant and animal life that this mixing sustains makes Georges Bank one of the most productive fishing areas on earth. What is crucial for the inshore fleet is that in the summertime the Gulf Stream tends to move up onto the banks and closer to shore, and because ground-fish like cod and haddock are cold-water fish, schools of them shift farther onshore in search of the colder water. Historically, this made large amounts of fish available to the inshore fleet during the nicest stretches of weather in the year.

Up until the early twentieth century, the fishing grounds close to shore were reached by rowing a dory, or using a small sail when possible, where two fishers, working together, would either handline or set a couple of tubs of trawl line with baited hooks every seven feet or so. These same dories were used to haul lobster traps by hand in the wintertime. Otherwise, fishers went out as hands on offshore salt bankers such as the *Bluenose* or the *Douglas and Robert*.

The adaptation of the gasoline engine to smaller boats created an inshore fishing fleet that could make a living from home, returning each day from the grounds, and as a result, created a large number of small fishing villages along the coasts of Nova Scotia. But the inshore fleet was only a minor part of a rapid modernization of the fishing industry in Atlantic Canada. The expansion of the fishery was far more evident in the development of the large offshore dragger fleets that eventually rendered the salt bankers obsolete. The qualities that made these habitats so productive made them attractive to the Russians, the Japanese, the Germans, and the Spanish dragger fleets, which in turn led to the destruction of these schools of fish.

~~~~~~~~~

It is into this world of powerful forces and precarious fish stocks that I first arrived on Hemeons Head. The land I bought is called the Hill Field and, as the name suggests, it is on a rise that is surrounded by wetlands and bog. Although the field has not been used for fifty years, there are still areas where grass grows and the stone wall that surrounds the field is visible here and there in the undergrowth.

The field had belonged to Sarah Ringer, whose family home is up the road a ways, occupied now by her son Robert and his family. Sarah is the daughter of Gideon Hemeon, whose house once stood out on the end of the head surrounded by the ocean on three sides, and she is also related to Donald McDonald. Her family spent their lives fishing off these shores and Gideon Hemeon built boats in a shop in the sou'west cove of the head, where you can still see the remains of the slipway where he launched his boats.

The house I built in the Hill Field was modest. It was a one-person house, eighteen feet by twenty-two feet with a ten-by-eighteen loft. In time, it became a very cozy home, with lots of south-facing windows and a wood stove to keep me warm in winter. But in those first years, between learning to fish and inhabiting a drafty construction site, I felt as if I were living in the elements. There was very little ease, except for the comfort in knowing that the life I was living was my own.

It is the most unusual of things to do: to choose to arrive in a place thousands of miles from your childhood home, a place where you know no one, and begin to make a life, a voluntary migrant as it were. And for a time, the people of Little Harbour were not sure what to make of me. This became clear one evening when Robert Ringer stopped by, as he did from time to time, with his dog Bobby to have a chat while I was working on the house.

Robert climbed out of his Chev truck and Bobby jumped down from the box wagging his tail while I was gathering up scraps of cuttings from a day's work. "I was just having a yarn with Harold, you know, at the cottages back up the road, and he said that he thinks you are an undercover Mountie looking for dope boats coming ashore. He said you're a big fella from out west and you're building a house where you can see all around. Gotta be a Mountie. Why else would he be out on the bleak stretch of shore all by himself?"

"That's a new one on me, Robert. What did you say?"

"Well, I said, 'You never can tell. Maybe he is.'"

That is how life goes: just when your life starts to make sense, you become incomprehensible to the people around you. Without trying to explain my background to Robert, I denied that I was a Mountie, and in any case I guess there are worse things to be mistaken for.

That fall I worked as a lobster crewman with Frank Decker, and by the time I bought Murray Swim's old boat the following summer, the lack of comprehension had gradually turned

into acceptance. Murray had retired from fishing a number
of years before I arrived in Little Harbour and the *Whitestreak* had been across the road among the weeds, covered in
a tarp. Murray had built the *Whitestreak* himself, with help
from Vernon Murphy, and although it had not been used for
a number of years and required a great deal of work to get it
seaworthy again, it was also seen as a boat that was well built.
Nonetheless, most of the local fishers were not optimistic that
I would get the engine going again after it had sat untouched
for so long. The lifters were stuck and I had to roll the engine
by hand just to supple it up, bending the pushrods in the process. But in time the Olds 455 roared to life and never gave me
grief in the five years I used it.

On the rare occasion when I took a break from my various labours, I walked the headland and begin to familiarize
myself with the natural history as well as human history of my
new home. Earlier in the century, mine would have been one
of many homes along this stretch of road.

For the settlers on this coast, advancements in technology
in the early part of the twentieth century not only changed life
on the water, they also changed the way of life on places such
as Hemeons Head. Until car use became widespread, sheep
roamed freely most of the year. Combined with the large
amount of firewood that was cut annually, the foraging of
the sheep created park-like vistas of forest and field. In those
earlier days, if you had a garden and did not want your fresh
green shoots eaten down to the root, you had to build a fence
to keep the sheep out. The few gates that did cross roads were
no great inconvenience to slow-moving ox carts, nor were the
herds of sheep that fed along the ditches.

The arrival of the automobile altered these relations. With
the faster-moving cars, many sheep were killed as they wandered along the road, causing discord between neighbours.
Gates were deliberately left open so as not to inconvenience
motorists, thereby causing damage to crops when animals

took advantage. Eventually, it was agreed that grazing animals had to be fenced in rather than fenced out.

Sheep gradually disappeared from the land, as the expense of fencing was seen as onerous, while a great many other settlers did not have enough cleared land to support their herds, having counted on the run of the commons to provide the forage. At the same time, there was a general increase in the availability of wool and cotton garments in the new stores that were opening, and for the first time, people had some money to spend. Any fencing that was carried out led to more severe divisions in the landscape. Some fields were heavily foraged, while other areas became overrun with alder and cat spruce, until only the most stubborn stone walls and markers were still visible.

Aside from other neighbours such as Robert and his family nearby, there is also Molly, farther inland, who has become a friend and who, at eighty-five years of age, lives by herself in a well-kept home. She spends her days gardening in the summer, preserving in the fall, and knitting and hooking rugs in the winter. I stop by one day while she is thinning her carrots. As we are talking, a car full of young people roars by on the gravel. "How can they stand it?" Molly says. "Young people tear around like idiots and never put their hands in the earth. What kind of a life is that?"

Robert is in the process of tearing down the home next to Donald McDonald's grave. From time to time, I can hear him and his two sons as they strip the roof of shingles and pull boards from the walls. They are going to use the wood to build a shop next to Robert's house so he has a place to work on his lobster traps during the winter.

I walk over one day to see how they are getting along. They have returned the house to the bare frame on the inside, the wooden pegs and notched-in numerals showing how the frame was first constructed on the floor of a barn in Rockland over the course of a winter, before being moved by ox cart and erected on this rock foundation. I walk across the round log floor beams and go out the back door that faces the water, admiring how solid the frame remains even now. Robert joins me as we look out over the water to Black Rock.

"At one time, this was the home of Alphonso and Nessie Nickerson, relations of mine, and we used the mark of 'Phon's house over the rock' when we followed the hard bottom by looking back at the house from our boat and lining it up with Black Rock, then dumping traps while steaming toward Point-to-the-Island Shoals, where Black Point to the west'ard would just be visible outside of Ram Island." Ram Island is situated a mile off the end of Hemeon's Head and for 150 years sheep were kept on it. Robert points with a left hand that is missing parts of two fingers from an accident on an offshore dragger. Until that accident, it was said, Robert could pick up just about any musical instrument around and play any tune that came to mind.

The use of marks—landmarks—was something that was becoming increasingly familiar to me: "Green Rock over the Brunch" and "Louis Head Church steeple over Raspberry Head" were examples of features on the land that fishers made use of to orient themselves on the water. Directly below the Hill Field is lobster ground that uses the mark "Shanties over the rock" when setting traps parallel to the Western Shore along the nine-fathom edge of the mud. The shanties were on Ram Island and were used during lobster season. In the early part of the century, fishers lobstered out of dories and hauled their traps by hand. The areas outside of Ram Island along the breakers and ledges are excellent lobster bottom, so the shanties were built on the island and were used by the fishers during the week to save having to row home after a long day. Only on Saturday night did they make the trip up the harbour to spend Sunday with their families, returning to the island on Sunday night. The shanties were built above "landing cove" on the east side of the island, where the gradual slope of the rising ledge provided a ready-made slipway for hauling the dories up out of the surf.

One fine day in spring, Frank Decker hauled the boat around and headed to the nor'east from Black Rock, looking back over his shoulder to line up the rock with where the shanties used to be. "Let her go," he shouted to me back in the stern. I dumped the first trap over the rail, and this gradually pulled the other four traps one by one off the stern. I then threw the buoy for the other end of the string overboard, and walked up into wheelhouse behind Frank, to begin banding the lobsters we had just taken out of the traps.

"Where are the shanties?" I asked.

"What shanties?"

"You said we were setting the gear accordin' to 'shanties over the rock,' and I don't see any shanties."

"It's the lobster shanties on Ram Island."

"I don't see 'em."

"My goodness, sonny, they've been gone for fifty years now."

Of all the places where they might be, these were the marks that guided you to places where the lobsters could be, more often than not. Across the shifting expanse of the green-blue world, these are the lines where experience taught you to go—the lines that connected the world on top of the water with the depths, making the world beneath knowable. These are the marks that are disappearing from the land and therefore, at the same time, making the depths less knowable in the ways they had been in the past.

Standing with Robert in the newly opened frame of the house, there is a view down across the field to where it gives way to an eroding bank of strewn rock next to the shore. I can make out Donald McDonald's tall white gravestone near the edge of the grass, leaning into the wind. In the area surrounding the gravestone there are a number of fieldstones set in the earth on their edge. And below the bank next to the grave, large boulders are gradually rolling out of the ordered

Figure 3   Donald McDonald's gravestone on Hemeons Head.
Photo by Lauchlan Rogers.

sediments of the earth, and becoming part of the loose assemblage of a rocky beach that is moving inward toward Donald's resting place. These are not sharp and jagged rocks but rounded and water-worn as they emerge from the earth. This is not the first time these stones have been assailed by wind, rain, and grinding surf. They are more battle-weary now than newborn, as they meet the elements again. The straight-sided and fluted gravestone seems almost a vanity set against the uneven shapes emerging below it, although the incongruity lessens as the gravestone leans toward the encroaching bank, as if falling in line for the eventual slide into the waves.

I could imagine now lining up the nearby barn, which used to be next to the road, with Donald's gravestone here by the shore, and believe it would trace a line back to the Isle of Lewis, connecting the dual stories of the path travelled up here in the elements now, and the one that goes further back and further down, tethered to the rough and plenty of the past, and guided by the marks of what used to be, as a way to know this disappearing world. Presence and absence. Me here now and Donald gone. Donald's grave remaining as I move on. The past is here, in pieces, as is the future. The lines we draw are always changing, based on the marks we create to navigate the course of our days.

By folding my life in among those I lived with, and Donald's in among the Scottish crofters from his community, I hope to tell a larger story about historical changes that bind the two of us together. Attachment and grief. If life is a combination of looking backward and living forward, up until now I have focused on looking back over time at the historical contexts that link the fishers and crofters. The rest of the narrative focuses on living forward in the moment so as to better convey the experience of being in these communities in the time when they are disappearing.

The Voyage into the Night

Roll over on the cot and listen to the quiet in the air. Rise up and sit. The muscles rehearse now and the mind imagines the night ahead as I dress and make my way outside in the near sundown. Backing the truck out onto the gravel road, I turn north for the harbour. I pass a couple of cars out for a drive near sunset, stopping to have a yarn, engines going and windows down. Go by the Temperance Hall and roll up the hill next to the church and store, and then down the hill again to the wharf. Step out and take in the quiet ease as the sun goes down. Chat with another fisher, leaning on the box of the truck. "Probably going to shut in thick, my guess…this time of year." Then turn and dip toward the door of the bait shed, feel my toes in the ends of my slippers. Crash through battlements of the night ahead as I cross the wide threshold and yank on the heavy iron handle of the thick insulated door. The cold air from the freezer turns to fog as it rolls past my ankles and out across the concrete floor, greasy with mackerel fat. Drag out the baited tubs of trawl and

Figure 4   Boats in Little Harbour. Photo by Ray Rogers.

stack them together along one wall. Everyone has their spot. I set out seven tubs—the ones painted dory buff—so they will give up some in the warmth before they are taken out on the back of the truck after midnight and lowered aboard the boat.

Outside the door of the bait shed, gulls caw and flutter over the cardboard and plastic in the burn pile next to the armour rock, picking out the mackerel heads thrown there with the empty boxes of bait. The sou'west breeze has flunked out and the harbour has settled into a quiet evening of falling tide. The lines to the boats all droop in their duties, slack and snoozy. Moored in a line perpendicular to the wharf is a row of Cape Island–style boats. There's the *Diane and Christine*, and then the *Lydia B*, and then *Sheldon and Sisters*, and then *Karl and Jackie* and *Whiz Kid II*, and then *Miss Rebecca*, and then the *Barbara J* and the *White Streak*, and then the *Bobby and Berty, Whitewave II*, and *Kid Dynamite*.

The bows of the boats are pointing out to the mouth of the harbour, their sterns toward the slipway, so as to take the storm surges when they come. The outside of the main wharf faces east to the open ocean and shoulders the storms, and even now with the adding of armour rock, it is better for the boats to be moored in a line away from the wharf so as to protect them from the heavy undertow that curls around the armour rock during rough seas with waves pouring over the wharf in a pulsing waterfall.

But the gulls are not headed seaward tonight, cresting on the wind. Instead, they are eating mackerel heads or poking around in the sand flats out on the bar, sociable and contrary. And the boats are nosing alongside each other. Every once in a while, there is the *erch* of a fender made from an old car tire, as it is squeezed between the dry oak ribbands when two boats rub together. There is ease in the world, a warm transparency through which we float. Tonight, says the old fella, "you could sail to the West Indies on a pen board." There is not the surge of waves but rather their periodic collapse on the sand beach, as they run out of momentum and fold back into the space they thought they had left behind.

Home now again. Pack a lunch, bring in some wood. Pad around the half-built structure. Lay low. Back on the cot for a while. "Well, that boat wouldn't float in a sea of tar. When it was across the road, you could throw a cat through every crack. Maybe it has soaked up some since going back in the water, but my God, it spent seven years high and dry in the weeds. Hard to believe it would ever be a boat again.... This is no place for women. I can see that you love it here, but look around. What is there to do for someone like me. I'm sorry, but, as beautiful as it is, I cannot see a future for myself here."

I am still lying there awake when the alarm goes off three hours later. Up I rise for real this time. Pull on extra layers of warm clothes. Look out the window to the Western Shore. "Sure enough. Thick dungeon of fog." Do I have everything? Lunch, cotton gloves, pocket watch, jar of water. What was warm and radiant earlier in the evening is now cold and damp. Run the windshield wipers, and turn on the heater to clear the window for the drive around the beach.

There is the haze of headlights and the bang of tailgates dropping as others load their gear onto the backs of their trucks for the short trip out onto the wharf to the hoist in the haul-up shed where the trawl can be lowered aboard the boats. With the fog as thick as it is, the lights on the wharves are barely visible, and the navigational light at the end of the wharf appears as a diffused ball. There is the loosening of stern lines and then the climb down the wharf ladder for the crawl across the boats. While the other boats have closed-in wheelhouses that cover the engine and provide shelter from the elements, with bunks and a table down forward in the cud, the *Whitestreak* has only an old-fashioned sprayhood, which is a tent-like upside-down V that covers the front half of the boat as far back as the engine, but leaves me out in the elements as I stand at the wheel or haul gear. "Why, sonny, she'll catch a lot less wind that way and it will be easier to stay up on your gear."

I duck under the sprayhood and set my lunch under an old oil jacket. I pull the two pairs of cotton gloves out of my back pocket and set them by the compass. Sliding back the wooden engine cover, I flip on the twelve-volt light bulb. There it is: the Oldsmobile 455 four-barrel that I brought back to life after so many years. Pull out the dipstick and check the oil, check the coolant level in the expansion tank, and then turn the valve on the fuel line coming from the gas tank bolted to the rail beside the engine. Switch off the light, say a prayer in the darkness, and turn the ignition key. A couple of rolls and the engine roars to life.

As engines start across the harbour, the world changes. It's all seaward now. Turn on the deck lights, and shove back the fog a bit. First the all-round light at the apex of the sprayhood that is meant to be visible to other boats and to shine down on the compass. Then the stern light that is taped to the stay wire of the riding sail comes on above the trawl chute and lights most of the deck.

There is now only one boat ahead of me that still needs to lower its gear aboard. I crawl back over the stern deck next to the punt and lift the galvanized hook from the ringbolt and drop it into the water. It takes the stern lines down with it as it goes, leaving only a buoy and line that is tied to the hook, so it can be gaffed when I comes back in. "Oh, that I shall return." The boat slides forward as the weight of the heavy chain holding the bow sinks into the water. I then climb up around the hauler and out along the sprayhood to the bow, sucking exhaust fumes as I go, and lift the bow hook from the ringbolt on the stem and drop it into the water, along with its buoy and buoy line. "I am adrift now, no longer attached to earth." Making sure there are no lines under the stern that can get caught in the propeller, I come back to the wheel, put the boat in gear and turn toward the wharf, idling along as I wait for the last boat to move off from under the derrick. I reach in under the sprayhood and turn on the CB radio.

"Where are you bound for tonight, Mert? I imagine you are quite a ways off now. Over."

"That's right, Arthur. I'm about twenty minutes outside the Groaner. I'm bound for the eastern end of the 45-Fathom Ridge, Art. Same place as the other night. Over."

"You're an old dog. Hard to get ahead of you. We're just going by the Can Buoy. At least I think that's it on the radar. Man, it's some thick. I guess you'll be setting to the east'ard, will ya, Mert?"

"That's right, Arthur. Over"

"If I can find your high flyer on the radar, I imagine I'll set from your end to the west'ard, probably. We'll see how it looks when we get out there. I'll give you a shout in an hour or so. Over."

"Good enough, Art. Over and out."

"Yeah, over and out for now, Mert. *Miss Rebecca*. I guess

that's you ahead of me on the radar, is it, Bud? Over."

"I guess it's me, Art. Man, that's some thick. Can't see the bow of the boat."

"Yeah, I figured that must be you, Bud. I saw you leave the wharf ahead of us there. Where you bound for tonight, Bud? Over."

"I'm going to try the edge of the ground tonight, Art. Haven't had much luck anywhere else, so I figured I'd give that a try, if I can find it. Over."

"They're some scarce. That's for sure. I guess it doesn't matter where a fella sets these days. They're just not bitin' or they're just not there. Hard to tell. Good enough then, Bud."

"If they don't want to bite my hooks, then fuck 'em. That's what I say, Art."

"Good enough, Bud. Over and out."

"I'll tell you where they are, Art. They've all gone to market. That's where they are."

"I guess that's you, is it, Dale? Over."

"That's right, Art. They've all gone to market. Just like those four-legged ones with the curly tail."

"Yes, I guess they have, Dale. Where you bound for tonight?"

"I'm about ten minutes outside the Groaner and I'm bound for deep water, Art. East'ard of Lockeport Ridge somewhere. Guess I'll set a couple of strings. Try my luck."

"That used to be the home of 'em, Dale. Maybe you'll load up. You never can tell. Over."

"At this point, I don't think it matters too much where you go, Art. It's the same everywheres. Looks like someone up ahead on the radar. I best pay attention before I run somebody down. Catch ya later."

"Good enough, Dale."

And so it went as Arthur worked his way through all those on their way out into the night. I listen as I take a couple of turns around the derrick line and lower the seven tubs of gear from the wharf to the boat deck. Knowing where everyone else is going is necessary if we are to keep clear of each other's gear. Up and down the ladder a couple of times to move tubs off to the side, before lowering the last of them aboard. Climbing down the ladder, I untie the short becket that had been wrapped around the wharf fender to keep the boat close.

"*Bobby and Berty, Karl and Jackie.* I guess you're heading out to the south'ard are you, Robert? That's what you said on the wharf. Over."

"*Bobby and Berty* back. That's right, Arthur. I'm halfway between the Can and the Groaner. Over."

"That's good, Robert. We won't reach you with our gear then. You'll be well clear there. Over."

"I should be the western boat. And I shouldn't reach off to where you are. Over."

"Good enough, Robert. We'll hear you later. Over and out."

"*Whitestreak, Karl and Jackie.* Come in, Ray."

"I hear ya, Art. I'm just leaving the wharf. Over."

"Good enough, Ray. I figured you would be coming out about now. We'll talk to you later, then. I guess Joe is not going tonight. Over."

"Joe's gone to the city. Thanks for the call, Art. Over and out."

I idle out around the end of the armour rock and gradually leave the aura of the outside wharf light. Swing wide to miss Ol' Chris that lurks just off the end of the wharf. Arrange the pocket watch on top of the steering box just below the compass. Look down at the red blink of the flasher sounder registering one fathom of water. Point the bow of the boat east-southeast (120 degrees). If it were daylight, I would be aiming the boat at the Can Buoy three-quarters of a mile away at the mouth of the harbour. Instead, I look at the watch again to get the exact time and then at the compass to lead me on. I rev up the engine to running speed (about 2000 rpm) and head off into the night. Look back one last time to see the wharf light fade into the fog, and then turn back to face the dark. Watch the compass. Watch the watch. Watch the compass. Watch the watch. After about a minute the sounder deepens it off to three fathom. At two minutes and a half, the bottom begins to shoal up on Middle Ground to less than a fathom when the tide is low, as it is now. "Maybe I am running ashore." An important quality for a fisher is to have no imagination at all. Otherwise you die a thousand deaths. The potential for things to go wrong is so varied and multi-faceted that it can overwhelm you. So your spirit must be a solid thing in a world that is always at risk of dissolving into insubstantiality.

The sounder begins to deepen off again after I cross Middle Ground. After four minutes of going east-southeast, the sounder reads four fathom. At five minutes, the *Whitestreak* is in the range of the Can, which is a large steel drum with a radar reflector on top of it, but no light. I have in the past run the Can down in the night and do not want to again feel the sudden smash as the boat catches the edge of it and then hear the Can chew its way through a noisy and threatening passage along the length of the rail, as if it might reach in and pull me with it over the side as the boat carries on without me.

Slow down and idle along for a minute or so while in the range of the Can. When I think I am safely past it, I turn the boat to the southeast and stream for another five minutes in the direction of the Groaner, which is a larger buoy that has both a green blinking light and a wave-activated foghorn. The Groaner is the outside fairway navigational buoy that identifies the inside edge of safe passage for boats travelling along the coast, as well as marking the outside entrance to Little Harbour. Beyond it to the southeast, there are no other fixed hazards, just one's own failings, other boats, and the elements.

After running for the five minutes, I slow down again, although not as much this time, since the Groaner's light gives some notice, even in the fog. After watching for another minute or so, I rev the engine back up and begin to steam southeast for the next hour or so, until the sounder registers thirty-eight to forty fathom of water.

I am the last of the Little Harbour boats to leave the Groaner. Six other boats are spreading out ahead of me on a range of courses from south to southeast. I prefer to be the last boat, because—unlike the other boats—I have neither an autopilot nor a radar. As I am steaming off to the fishing grounds, I need to work back in the stern, getting all of my gear arranged before I set it. Because I don't have an autopilot, the boat tends to wander off course in a meandering fashion as I work in the stern. On foggy nights like tonight, I can't see if there are other boats nearby. One night a couple of years ago, I left the Groaner five minutes ahead of the *Barbara J*. Fifteen minutes later, when I was returning to the wheel to bring the boat back on course, I looked at the compass and saw I was heading due east. Because of my wanderings, the *Barbara J* had caught up with me, evident now as its broadsides emerged out of the fog. Very quickly, I hauled to the northeast just in time to steam through the wake of the *Barbara J*, missing its stern by about thirty feet. Joe was back aft at the time working on his gear, and I will always remember the look on his face as he took in what might have happened.

So at least for now, of all the things I have to think about as I steam offshore, I don't have to worry about running anybody down or being run down, at least until I reach the shipping lanes twelve miles off, when I could end up in the path of a Russian trawler or a coastal freighter, if there are any in the area.

Cod and haddock, along with cusk, hake and halibut, are demersal fish, or bottom feeders. Their movements on the ocean bottom are influenced by the presence of food, which in turn is influenced by the geological makeup of that bottom.

The thing I desire is the thing I cannot see, but can only infer. I therefore follow the marks of the things that may influence the migration of schools that I can identify. I can only know the fish itself when it lands on the deck of the boat, but by then it is in a health crisis and there is not much useful information that can be gleaned about its behavior when in its own habitat. The fish I catch have air bladders that allow them to regulate their buoyancy in the depths. When they are towed to the surface on a hook, their bodies don't have time to adjust to the changes in pressure and they blow up like a balloon by the time they get to the water's surface. As you stick the gaff in them, there is a distinctive hissing of air as they deflate. So we are cursed with acquainting ourselves with the fish only when we kill them.

But there are other things beyond watching them die that I am able to know. Edges are where the fish tend to be. I need to find the edges between hard bottom and soft bottom, and try to stay just on the hard bottom so my bait remains on the hooks longer than it would in the mud. But to stay on the edges I need to know what the tide is doing. And so it goes: the endless vigilance that is required. My technological window is a compass and a watch and a flasher sounder. Between the swirl of experience and the murk of the deep, I make my way.

Amid all the worry, and all the tasks, and all the other skills and work that are required to get out to the fishing ground and back again, along with the boat upkeep between times, after all that there is the accumulation of knowledge that takes years to acquire, and that, and at the best of times, combines with a special awareness in those who know where to go to find the fish. For the rest, it's follow the crowd and at the same time try to stay out of each other's way.

Beyond the Groaner is a large area of hard bottom that deepens gradually and is called, appropriately enough, the Flatground. After steaming for forty-five or fifty minutes, I have gradually deepened it off to thirty to thirty-five fathom, when there is a sharp drop in depth to forty fathom. This is called the Fall-off of the Flatground. Ten thousand years ago this would have been a cliff at the ocean's edge. At the bottom of the Fall-off is a strip of sand that used to be the beach, until the massive ice sheets began melting. Set gear in this strip and expect to haul up old clam shells that are still lying on top of the sand. So for the next fifteen minutes of steaming, there is broken bottom with humpy patches of hard bottom mixed in with soft sandy areas that at one time felt the warmth of the sun.

After I cross this broken bottom, it hardens up again and shoals up to what is called the 45-Fathom Ridge running parallel to the shore. It is a very narrow ridge, and outside of it are miles of muddy bottom, so it is a tricky place to set gear, especially if the tide is running strong. Farther to the west'ard, this ridge turns south and becomes Lockeport Ridge, which is perpendicular to the shore and is the high point of a range of hard bottom that eventually deepens off to ninety fathom on the eastern side of Roseway Bank, which, in turn, rises up to fifteen fathom as a large flat sandy shoal that would have been an island ten thousand years ago. Banks such as Roseway and LaHave reach out farther offshore and, although they have traditionally been excellent fishing areas, are beyond the range of the inshore boats. In recent years they have been prime fishing areas of the international dragger fleet.

Beyond the Flatground, there tends to be more fish, but they are gathered in increasingly intermittent ridges that are harder to find, and there is a much greater chance of setting gear in the mud. The safer bet for setting your gear on hard bottom is to stay closer to shore, but the chances of catching some fish in these lean times are not very good. And slinging three thousand hooks into the mud leads to a day full of recrimination as each muddied hook comes back whispering, "You are a fool."

The sounder now deepens off quickly to thirty-eight fathom and I take the boat out of gear. Pause as the engine quiets, take a deep breath, and look around. "What's to see? I'm up here with all my gear, and you're down there without a care."

Angling in the Darkness

"*Whitewave II*. Have you started to set yet, Mert?"

"Yeah, I just got one tub out, Art."

"I won't bother you, then. You're busy. I think I see your

western end here on the radar. I'm a good berth to the west'ard of your high flyer and I'll set up from there."

"Good enough, Arthur."

"I'll call ya after we get the gear out. That's some thick. Over and out."

"*Miss Rebecca, Karl and Jackie.* Come in, Bud. I guess that's you to the west'ard of me, is it, Bud?"

"Yeah, that's right, Art. I'm still steamin' for another ten or fifteen minutes. I've changed my mind and decided to go to the west side of Lockeport Ridge, so I won't be in your way. I think I see Dale up ahead of me on the radar, and he told me on the wharf he was going to the eastern side of the ridge in the deep water, so we'll be well clear of each other."

"Good enough, Bud. Yeah, we'll be well clear of each other, then. Over."

"I was thinking of going off to the shoal water of Roseway, but I see a couple of objects on the radar that look like big boats. Probably those goddamn Russians dragging up every last one. Bastards."

"Yeah. Good enough, Bud."

"Maybe I should go out there and start World War III, get in their way just to fuck 'em up."

"Maybe so, Bud. Maybe so. Over and out for now."

"Send those bloody Commies back where they belong."

"You better watch it, Bud. They might take you back with them."

"I guess that's you, is it, Dale? Over."

"That's right, Bud. I see two or three of them up ahead of me. I imagine it's the Ruskies. I hear their crews are mostly women. They would make mincemeat out of a guy like you. They'd be dancing a jig on your ass before they got to Sable Island."

"If this was over in the States, we'd have those bastards on the run. That's for sure."

"I'm just getting ready to set here, Bud. I steamed off well to the eastward out into the mud, dropped down to a hundred fathom for a time. I've hauled her back to the westward now and she's just started to harden up. I see you on the radar to the nor'west of me. So I'll catch you later."

"Okay, Dale. Over and out."

After following the conversations on the radio, I have a good idea where everyone is setting their gear, so I continue steaming southeast-by-south for a short time beyond the Fall-off of the Flatground, where I plan to set my gear over the broken humpy bottom between the Fall-off and the inside reaches of Lockeport Ridge, ending up to the west'ard of Art. There had been some haddock around and they tend to like this kind of broken bottom. Andrew and Milton are setting on the outside range of the Flatground, so I have to watch for them now, although they should be to the east of me some.

"Gull Rock Lighthouse. *Georgina Darlene*. Come in, Tommy"

"That you, Bursey?"

"That's right, Tommy. How are you makin' 'er? Over."

"Not bad, Bursey, although I'm the only person I know who can get all broke up laying in bed. Over."

"I hear ya, Tommy. Listen, the Coast Guard wants me to give you a call about shift change. They said you aren't fussy about coming off on the helicopter. Over."

"That's right, Bursey. There no bloody way I'm getting aboard that soup can. I want shift change in the skiff as usual. Over." Most fishers only have a CB radio, but because he is a harbour pilot leading large draggers in and out of Lockeport harbour, Bursey has both a CB radio and a VHF radio and has been talking to the Coast Guard. He is also an old drinking buddy of Tommy's, and the Coast Guard has called him because they hoped he might be able to reason with Tommy about the advantages of modern helicopter flight.

"Coast Guard figures it is going to be too thick for the skiff in the morning, plus they have some parts for the backup generator they need to bring out and they are too heavy to jackass aboard the skiff. Over."

"I don't give a shit what it's like, I ain't crawling into that egg beater. No way." Gull Rock is one of the last lighthouses on the coast to have keepers. The two keepers work thirty days on and thirty days off. Tommy had taken the job as part of his plan to dry out and get off the rum. Thirty days on Gull Rock is no problem because the lighthouse is a couple of miles off the coast near Lockeport, and so there was nothing in temptation's way. Plus the work isn't very demanding: maintenance on the light and a little painting, as well as listening to the radios for distress signals. His partner Vernon has been with the Coast Guard for thirty-one years, and so keeps all the bases covered. It is the days off that are a struggle, knocking around town with time on his hands. Sometimes it works out, and sometimes it doesn't.

"Coast Guard just came back to me and they want me to tell you that they have a mechanic aboard the helicopter, if anything goes wrong. Over."

"By the liftin' Jesus, the mechanic better be the Six Million Dollar Man if he is going to fix that bucket of bolts before it hits the water. Tell them no bloody way, no how. I'll swim ashore if that is what it comes to, but I am not climbing into that death trap. They can take Vernon off with them, but I'm staying."

"I'll let 'em know. I'll tell them to go ahead, and I'll come and get you myself, first chance I get."

"Thanks, old son. I'd appreciate that. Over."

"Talk to you later, then. Over and clear."

"Over and clear."

I lower the long length of the high flyer into the water and carry its eighty-fathom-long coil of line near the steering wheel and drop it on the deck. A high-flyer buoy is made up of a sixteen-foot-long pole cut from a small cat spruce, with a weighted piece of pipe on one end and a radar reflector on the other, and with a foam buoy in the middle. This arrangement creates a marker that stands up in the water, making it visible on radar screens and with the naked eye from a considerable distance. This allows fishers to find their gear in the fog as well as to avoid other fishers' gear.

I grab the end of the line next to the high flyer and make sure there is no slack rope under the side of the boat that could catch in the propeller, and then put the boat in gear. Running the line through my hand to make sure it doesn't snarl on the way out, I idle away from the high flyer, watching it disappear into the night. When the line has run out, I walk back to the twenty-pound anchor sitting on top of the trawl tub next to the chute and heave it overboard.

Since the anchor is tied not only to the high-flyer buoy line but also to the first tub of gear, it begins to pull the ground-line with the gangions and baited hooks over the stern of the boat as it descends to bottom. I go back to the wheel, put the boat in gear, and rev the engine up to about 1200 rpm. As I steam away from where the anchor was dropped, the baited trawl is pulled out of the tub through the horns of the chute and over the stern on its way to bottom.

The sounder is still deepening it off beyond the Fall-off. After about four minutes, I go back in the stern to see how much gear is left in the tub. I then go back to the wheel, run for another thirty seconds before idling down the engine. I watch as the last of the line from the first tub goes out over the chute, and then yank the empty tub out from under the chute and shift the second tub back as the top of its coil is pulled overboard.

The sounder bounces up and down—39...40...38 fathom—as the second and third tubs run out. At the end of the third tub, I throw a middle buoy over the side that is tied around the ground-line. The middle buoy is a five-gallon keg that has seventy fathom of line wound around it. As the gear sinks in the water, the buoy line gradually unwinds off the keg as it rolls slowly on top of the water. The middle buoys provide one more route to the gear—besides the end buoys—in case the ground-line parts off as it is hauled back. Because the gear is anchored on bottom, there are many opportunities for it to catch under rocks. Ideally, the boat spends all its time directly above the gear, but with the continual buffeting from wind and tide, the boat may easily "drift off the gear" and drag it across bottom at the same time as the gear is being hauled up. This increases the likelihood of "getting hung up on bottom" as well as of losing fish that are pulled off the hooks by the obstacles in their way. So the precaution of a middle buoy is in recognition of one's own incompetence and the vagaries of wind and tide.

"*Whitestreak, Karl and Jackie.* Come in, Ray. I figure you're busy setting, but I just wanted to let you know that I can see a large dragger or freighter on the radar heading to the west'ard in our range. It is just to the east'ard of me now, and I think that's you to the west'ard of me setting off, so keep an eye out for it. I just got my gear out. We'll talk to you later."

"*Whitestreak* back. Thanks, Arthur. I'll keep an eye out. I have a little less than two tubs left. So I should have the gear out by the time it gets here. Over and out."

The boat continues south-by-east over the hummocky, broken bottom as the fourth and fifth tubs go out over the stern. Another middle buoy is thrown after the fifth tub. As I near the end of the seventh tub, I begin to make the rise of the inside of Lockeport Ridge. I slow the boat down, and make sure the end of the seventh tub is tied to the fifty-five-pound boat anchor, and that the anchor line is tied to the bow painter. Take the boat out of gear, lift the anchor to the rail, make sure that anchor line is clear of any snarls. Look back over the stern to see the ground-line stretched out with the gangions and baits hanging off it, the strain of it coming now on the end of the anchor. I lift the ground-line out of the horns of the chute and heave the anchor clear of the boat. The anchor line coil begins to jump as the line follows the anchor to bottom while the ground-line disappears below the surface of the water. Grab the anchor line, hold onto it and stop its descent, take the strain on it and go up to the wheel and put the boat in gear. Steam to the southeast to make sure the anchor line and ground-line don't snarl up in each other as they descend. Hold on until the line stretches out, letting go when the strain is too great. Swing the boat around to the western side of the line, so the boat will drift to the west'ard in the tide, and away from the anchor. "It's a two-man job with one man's pay, if you are lucky."

The anchor reaches bottom, and the line now moves in slow hitches over the rail as the pull of gravity ends and the drift of the tide takes over. Tug on it a couple of times to make sure it is running out to the east'ard, and not arcing around under the boat toward the propeller. I lean over the side of the boat and listen now for the deep throb of a large diesel engine. I also scan the fog for any sign of lights, although two-hundred-foot freighters have precious few of them. No sound but my own engine and no lights either. Watch and listen as I clean up the boat, rinsing and stacking the empty trawl tubs that were thrown around in the process of setting, sweeping up the baits that flew off the hooks and landed on the deck, and finally, setting up the slatting pen next to the fish pen.

When the anchor line has all but run out, I reach down and tie a bladder buoy into a bite of the anchor line, and flip the buoy over the side. The buoy is there in case I need to untie the boat from the gear. It is also there as a buffer that lessens the chances of the boat dragging the anchor and parting off the ground-line. The force exerted by the boat on the anchor would first have to submerge the buoy to create a straight pull on the line. I stand there watching the last of the line pay out and come tight, the buoy barely visible now in the pale glow of the mast headlight. The boat swings slowly around from "side to" the tide, and heads up into it as the anchor line comes tight.

I turn off the engine and listen. Sure enough, there it is. RRRrrrRRRrrrRRR.... Look at the compass. Low notes are not very directional. This is why sirens, horns, and whistles on wharves are high-pitched. Stare into the wet. First out on one side of the spray hood and then the other. Go back in the stern and listen. I cup my ears and turn slowly in a circle. I look again at the compass and decide the churning throb is to the east'ard. So it is still coming. The *Whitestreak* has a radar reflector on top of the sail spar, but I have been told by others that I don't show up very well on the radar. It is probably because the sprayhood is less prominent than a full windshield with a radar stand on the roof. And because the freighter is so much higher out of the water, its radar is probably scanning over top of my boat, even if I had shown up when the freighter was farther away.

"*Whitestreak, Karl and Jackie*. Come in, Ray. Over."

"Yeah, I gotcha, Art."

"I see on the radar that the freighter is between us. It went by just outside me and I am on the inside edge of the 45-Fathom Ridge. I make it to be about a quarter mile to the east'ard of you. Over."

"Thanks, Art. I got the gear out and I've turned off the engine so I can listen for it. I hear it coming. If it gets too close, I'll start her up and have the bait knife ready to chop the anchor line. Over."

"I imagine it sees ya and will go by outside. With all the boats around, you'd think they'd shift outside a berth or two, just to be clear of us. Give us a shout and let us know if ya need anything. Over and out."

"Good enough, Art."

RRRRRrrrRRRRRRRrrrRRRRR...gets louder as the fog wets my eyes. "In the face of danger, open up. Do the most vulnerable thing in the most difficult moment. That is how to survive." The anchor line has now come tight and the boat has headed northeast up into the tide, so it is facing the approaching freighter head on. Listen to its engine. Stare at the compass. It stays on the nor'east heading as it gets closer. I think about turning off the mast headlight so I can see farther into the dark, but that would make me less visible to the freighter.

The full-throated sound gets louder. Start the engine and maybe put the boat in gear, but where to go? Then there is a sudden rush of water above the thumping of the diesel engine. A giant rusted bulb is ten feet to starboard, and its wake is breaking over the rail and shoving the *Whitestreak* sideways. Then the boat swings back in and I put out my hand to fend off the large wall of rusted steel as it grinds along the ribbands. Wake water continues to pour over the rail as the boat scrapes against the freighter's hull. From somewhere above me in the steel face, bilge water streams down as I stand at the wheel. Diesel stink. The passing of the rusted face of the freighter seems to go on forever, as if it is a wall that is cutting me off from the rest of the world. Finally there is the churning violence of the huge propeller that is half out of the water. Its heavy, slapping spray cleanses me with its saltiness. I am now at the very centre of a vortex and about to be chopped to pieces. The *Whitestreak* rolls up on its side to the point where I have to grab hold of the hauler as the wake of the freighter shoves me sideways into a sudden calm. The *Whitestreak* is then swung around by the freighter as the anchor line catches on the freighter's rudder gear, almost pulling the bow under. For a brief time, I am being towed along in the churning wake of the freighter, until the blades of its propeller chop the anchor line off.

Suddenly released, I am not so much floating in a boat on the ocean as I am adrift in my existence. Draw a breath, and lean down and turn the lights back on. As I do this, I can again hear my own engine idling. My God, it still working. I go back to the wheel. The pump is running, the smell of diesel rises from the hose end as the bilge water spills over the rail on the port side. "Am I sinking?" I pull up the deck hatch and listen to the pump hum. It gurgles as it sucks out the last of the bilge water. There is no onrush of water and the pump stays quiet. I crawl out onto the bow and retrieve what's left of the parted end of the bow painter and anchor line. There is about two fathom of the frayed anchor line tied to the end of it. I put the boat in gear and idle back to the east'ard in the faint hope of finding the bladder buoy still attached to the anchor line. Make a couple of slow circles, careful not to go too far, idling along in the sudden stillness of the night. Finally, there is the bladder buoy just off the bow, flattened but still floating. If it is not attached to the anchor line, I will have to steam back along where I think the gear is and try to spot one of the middle buoys, or the high flyer on the inside end of the gear. There would be little hope of seeing them in the dark, and if I idle here until morning, the tide will have taken me away from my gear before daylight.

I idle up and gaff the flattened bladder buoy, lift it aboard, and take a strain on it. It returns the favour, much to my relief. Still attached to the world, it pulls on my grateful arms, stretches my thankful muscles. Bend the line down over the rail and stand on the bladder. Retie the painter into the anchor line, and let it run out over the rail again, after snapping on another bladder alongside the flattened one. The rumbles of the freighter grow fainter now in the west. "I am still here."

Waiting in the Night for the Fish to Bite

"*Karl and Jackie. Miss Rebecca.* Come in, Art."

"I hear ya, Bud. Over."

"I don't know what's wrong with the bastard, but it died on me. I have been trying everything for twenty minutes and I can't get the prick to go."

"You say your engine quit, Bud? Over."

"That's right, Art. It's just like you threw the switch. Bang, she died. I was back in the stern sweeping up baits after getting the gear out and thump, she quit. I got to be careful now. I've ground her so much the battery is getting down."

"What have you tried so far? I know you have the Chev 292 same as mine. Over."

"I checked first to make sure she was getting gas. I undid the gas line next to the engine, and there was lots of gas there.

So I undid her on the other side of the fuel pump to make sure that was working, and as I rolled her, gas was coming out. So gas is getting to the carburetor. Then I checked the coil, and made sure she had spark. I pulled off one of the plug wires and rolled her, and there was plenty of spark. So she's got spark and she's got gas, so the fucker should go. But I've ground her and I've ground her, and no dice. Over."

"Not sure what it could be, Bud. But come to think of it, I remember the time Wesley and I were fishing down by what they call the Stonewall, way to the eastward. It was the fall of the year and there were big steak cod around. Each one as big as a man. We were hauling along on about our third tub, and just like you say, Bud: bang, she quit. Well, we fiddled for quite a good long while, and come to find out, the points had stuck together. We happen to have the point file aboard, and sure enough there was this piece of carbon there holding the points together. I look the ripper and pried them apart, and then took the file and filed the points smooth again. I thought I'd try filing first, rather than put the old ones back on, although I had them down forward. You know how fussy they can be trying to get the gap right. And there was quite a slop on. It had breezed up from the sou'west by then. Anyway, we turned the key and away she went. So maybe give that a try, Bud. Could be your points are stuck together. Over."

"I'll give that a try, Art, and give you a call back. Over."

"Good enough, Bud. I'll stand by. I think I have an old set of points down in the cupboard that I could run over to you if you need 'em, Bud. Over and out for now."

"Arthur, you got enough parts down forward to do a complete engine rebuild if you had to. Over."

"Maybe I do, Dale. Maybe I do. You never can tell. I've had three of those 292s now, so there's lots of parts and pieces around, that's for sure. I know I have a couple of alternators in a plastic bag under the bunk. You never know when it might knock off charging. I guess you got your gear out, do you, Dale? Over."

"That's right, Art. I finished up here outside the Hake Hole. Just getting cleaned up and gonna turn in for a while. According to the radar, there's draggers ploughing the shoal water of Roseway flat. I imagine it's the Russians. There won't be a haddock left in the world. Over."

"I don't imagine there will be, Dale. Not at this rate."

"*Karl and Jackie, Miss Rebecca. Over.*"

"I get ya, Bud. How did you make out?"

"I had the distributor cap off, Art, and had a look at the points. They seem fine. I also cleaned up the terminals in the cap. But no go. Just grind, grind. Any other ideas? Over."

"Well, there was another time, Wesley and I were lobstering out off the shoal water of Bantam in the spring of the year. We tried fishing a few times that spring but there wasn't much around, so we decided to put some traps out in May to see if we could make up a month's work. I think we only had about a hundred traps out, from Bantam to Black Rock. Same thing happened, she just died. We didn't have a lot of sea room outside the breaker, so Wes threw the anchor and tied her fast while I took off the engine box cover and had a look-see what was going on. I frigged around with all the things you have done, Bud, and no go. Come to find out it was the condenser. I tried everything else, and I thought to myself, 'Well it's every once in a long while that the condenser gives up on ya, and I'd tried everything else. Tell me, Bud, did ya change it the last time you did a tune-up? I know sometimes I don't. Over."

"Come to think of it, I didn't change the condenser when I changed the points. I think it's still in the box down in the cud. I'll have a look. Over."

"If you don't have one, I believe I have one somewhere in the tool box and I could run it over to ya. Over."

"I laid my hand right on it, Art. I'll change it and let you know."

"Give that a try, Bud. The only other thing I can think is that there might be a crack in the distributor cap. I've heard tell of that happening to Andrew once just like that."

"*Diane Christine* back, Art. Yep, that happened to me alright. Sloppy day too. First week of lobstering. Damn near froze my fingers off before we got it sorted out. But accordin' to, she was quite corroded up inside the cap from the moisture. I cleaned up the terminals and gave her a good shot of WD-40 to try and dry 'er out. She wouldn't go until I'd hauled the coil wire off the cap and cleaned up the end of wire. Man there was some white stuff in the top where the wire goes in. Away she went. It was after dark by the time we got the gear hauled that day. And cold. Man, I was half froze to death. Over."

"*Karl and Jackie, Miss Rebecca*. Over. I changed the condenser and she took right off first hitch, Art. Thanks for the help. Over."

"That's good, Bud. I'm glad you got her going. You never can tell. Anyways, I'm glad she's working. Let me know if you have any more trouble. Over."

"I'm just going to let her run. To hell with it. No way I'm turning that bastard off again tonight. She needs to charge up anyway. I already had the hydraulic belt on, thank Christ, so to hell with it. Let her go."

"Well, I'm glad you got her goin', Bud. So we'll hear you later. Over and out.

"Thanks again, Art. You're the doctor."

"I wouldn't know about that, Bud. Anyways. Over and out for now."

"You're the doctor all right, Art. You're a hard man to fool when it comes to those 292s, Art. Over."

"I guess that's you, Mert. I've had three of them from Steel and Engines in Liverpool by now. Well you've had 'em too, Mert. They're hard to beat as far as a gas engine goes. Some say the diesel is more dependable, and maybe so. But as far as a gas engine goes, they're hard to beat. I was talking to Walter McDonald when I was down in Liverpool last time. He's the man for a 292. Borg-Warner transmissions too, especially those 2.57-to-1 reductions. He swears by them. I still have the old engine I took out of her up in the shed. Every once in a while I start her up and she sounds as good as ever. She was in the *Karl and Jackie* when I got her. But I had run her for seven years, so some things were bound to begin to wear out after a while. I don't know why I took her out, really. Before that the *Lorraine G* had a 292 as well, along with the small engine for hauling gear. That one is in the back of the shed somewhere under some gear. I took the water-cooled manifold off it when the first one in the *Karl and Jackie* cracked."

"They haven't let us down yet, Art, and you never spared the ponies when you ran 'er either. Over."

"I guess I didn't in them days, Mert. I take it easier now. But you know, I don't believe runnin' them hard hurts them any. They'll start burnin' oil just as likely if you run 'em easy. That old engine, why she would only use about a third of a quart of oil on a day's running even at the last of it."

"I run this one hard too, Art, and she's never let me down. Well, I got her cleaned up and geared up for the morning, Art, so I'm going to turn in for a while. I'll give you a shout after daylight if there is not too much skip on. Over and out."

"Good enough, Mert. I'm going to turn in too just now. I've been frigging with changing the paper on the sounder, although I don't really need it for hauling back the gear. Over and out for now. *Whitestreak, Karl and Jackie.* I guess that freighter went by all right did it, Ray? Over."

"That's right, Art. She came quite close and had me worried for a few minutes. But all's well. Over."

"That's good, Ray. I figured it would be. Over and out for now."

"Thanks for the call, Art. Over and out."

"*Lydia B., Karl and Jackie.* You got your gear out, do you, Milt? Over."

"*Lydia B.* back. I guess I do, Art. Although good chunks of it went out in a ball. I don't know what Danny was thinking when he baited it. Man, what a mess it will be when I haul it back. The snarls, the snarls. Well, I won't be clearing them out here, that's for sure. He can do it when I get back in. Chuck it in the tub just the way it comes aboard and let him deal with it. That's the only way he'll learn. Over."

"I guess you're right there, Milt. I'll had a little hicker there on the third tub myself. I'll give you a call after we get some gear back in the morning. Over and out for now."

"Good enough, Art. Over and out."

I stand on the deck with only the mast headlight on. The shadows in the fog do not materialize into anything else, but merely project out into the night my small, creaking world held together by five hundred board feet of lumber. The pump kicks in. I look at my watch so I can keep track of how much time it takes for the leak to lift the automatic mercury switch in the bilge. I sit on the lid of the fish pen and wait. Nine minutes pass before the pumps cuts in again. There is a seam seeping somewhere, but it won't kill the battery before daylight comes.

Crawl under the sprayhood now and lie down beside the engine box. The front of the wooden engine cover is open and the warmth coming off the engine cuts the dampness. Pull out an old orange life jacket and use it as a pillow. Lying among the wrenches and spare parts, I look back through the inverted "V" of the sprayhood opening, past the dual exhaust pipes and the steering box to all my friends: the spar cut from the cat spruce behind the outhouse, the fish pen made from tongue-and-groove left over from boarding in the roof of the house, the spare high flyers and bladder buoys found during walks on Black Point Beach; the replaced stern boards made from spruce that had been stored in the barn that Murray helped with after he sold me the boat; the new hackmatack timbers milled out for me by Amos Hagar, along with the new planking where the fresh water had weakened and rotted the old ones along the water line next to the hauler. There are also the four new knees that attach the new floor beams to the hull that were cut from the exposed roots of spruce trees that were upended in a storm two years before.

As I lie there, I feel the boat gradually swing around as the wind shifts, and I sense new warmth in the dark air. And then I see a light over the stern. I sit up and go out on deck. It is not another freighter. It is only Venus. The fog has lifted and the sky is now full of stars, with the blurry band of the Milky Way crossing from northeast to southwest. I scan the water and count the lights of a dozen fishing boats. There is a hint of dawn now in the sky over the bow. I stand there for the next fifteen minutes, taking in the recently arrived balmy breeze. As the sky lightens, the boats and the stars gradually dissolve into the invisibility of day.

As the Day Gets Up

"*Whitewave II*. You got woked up yet, Mert? Over."

"I've just fried up some bacon and eggs, Art. I'll be dropping on in a few minutes. Man, that's some change in the weather. Gonna be a fine day, I believe. Over."

"It sure looks like it, Mert. I guess I'm ready to drop on myself. We'll see what takes place. Over."

"Send me over a plateful, will ya, Mert? Over."

"I guess that's you, Dale. I figured you'd still be laying on the end."

"That's the only place a fella should be on a morning like this. Laying on the end."

"That's right, Dale. You want to steam over, I got a couple more eggs here if you want 'em. Over."

"I guess I'm hell and gone from where you are now, Mert. I'm just hauling up the anchor line. I ended up in ninety fathom of water, so I'll be half the morning getting the rode back. Over."

"I guess you will. Over. You'll lay right on where you are. That's the home of 'em. Well, I better get at this breakfast 'fore it gets cold. I'll hear you later, Dale. Over and out."

"Good enough, Mert. Over and out. I doubt if it's the home of 'em. According to the sounder, I got the last tub down in the mud. I'll be hauling slime eels and snot for the first while at least. I suppose you got a couple of tubs back by now, do you, Art?"

"No, Dale, I don't. I was getting ready to haul in the buoy line and come to find out I forgot to put the hydraulic belt on. So I frigged with that and I just got the high flyer aboard. I didn't bother to anchor up. I've just been jogging up on the gear every once in a while, keeping an eye on the high flyer on the radar. That freighter went by some close, you, so I figured I'd keep an eye on her and just jog here next to the gear. Over."

"Most of the time I think those fellas put her on autopilot and turn in. They don't pay any attention to us, and why they don't run a course further outside, I don't know. Over."

"That's right, Dale. You can never be sure they see you, 'specially when they get close like that. Their scanners are so high up. They probably have it set on sixteen mile or something. Over."

"They'd run you over and never know it, or care for that matter. Here comes the anchor finally, Art, so I'll let you go."

"Good enough, Dale. You'd daresn't chance it, as thick as it was. If it was clear and they could see your lights that would be one thing, but with it as thick as it was, you have to wonder. We'll hear you later, Dale, when the day gets up a bit. Over and clear."

"*Miss Rebecca, Karl and Jackie.* I guess everything is working fine, Bud? Over."

"Everything's fine but the fish, Art. I've got two tubs back and I might have a hundred pound. I don't know where I ended up finally. The bottom looked broken when I set, but I must be right up on top of Lockeport Ridge. Every bait is coming back as if it never got to bottom. Over."

"You got an early start, Bud. You'll probably pick some up as you haul along. So we'll hear you later. Over and clear."

"I said to hell with it and dropped on early, Art. Get the hell in out of here. Over."

"We'll see what takes place, Bud. Well, I best get busy if I am ever going to get back to the wharf. Over and out for now."

I slide the hauler belt onto the front pulley of the engine and, with a big screwdriver, pry the other end of the belt onto the pulley at the base of the hauler. That done, I start the engine, and there is an extra rumble now that the hauler is engaged. Most fishers have hydraulic haulers, but I have the old-style car transmission with a pulley on either end. The front pulley is connected to the front pulleys on the engine and is always turning. When I put the transmission in gear, the back pulley has a belt on it that turns the hauler that lifts the ground-line up off bottom, pulling it in over the roller on the rail and into the boat. When I take the transmission out of gear and, in effect, put it in neutral, it will run backwards under the strain of the trawl. To stop this from happening, there is a break on the shaft of the hauler made of a cogged wheel with a metal dog, or flap, that will clink along if the hauler is pulling the gear in, but will jam in the cogs if the hauler tries to go backwards. So it's *clink, clink, clink, clink, clink* all day long as the trawl is hauled aboard, marking the progress toward home.

I have already connected the three-foot-long steering arm to the steering wheel. This allows me to steer the boat while standing at the rail hauling the gear. There is also an extra set of controls for putting the engine in and out of gear from the rail as I haul along. Putting the boat in gear now, I steer in the direction of the bladders on the anchor line. When I have created enough slack in the anchor line for it to be lying alongside the boat, I drop the line into the sheaves of the hauler, which are like two steel dinner plates with their bottoms bolted together and set on their edges like a wheel on an axle. The line is dropped into the "V" between the two turning plate bottoms and is squeezed enough to be pulled along by the rotation. At five o'clock on the turning plates, a brass "finger" that is the shape of that "V" forces the line out of the sheaves so that it coils in the trawl tub that is set under the hauler.

I haul along to the good bladder tied alongside the flattened one, unhooking the swordfish clips from the bite in the line and continuing to haul along, and periodically putting the boat in gear when the line stretches out ahead. I idle along until the ground-line aims straight down into the water. *Clink, clink, clink.* With a fifty-five-pound anchor, I need at least a three-to-one ratio between the depth of water and the length of rode I am using, so as to make sure the boat doesn't drag the anchor. So for the first few minutes, all I am hauling is slack line until I get close to two-thirds of it back. Then I can feel the line coming tight as the anchor breaks clear of bottom. This morning the anchor lifts without much complaint, which is surprising, given that the freighter must have dragged it some. There is now the strain of pulling up the anchor, as well as the attached ground-line with, I hope, the accompanying fish. At this point the belts begin to slip and so I have to pull on the line myself to help the hauler along. Finally, I hear the clunk of the anchor as it hits the side of the boat and I reach down and heft it up over the rail. After carrying the anchor to the offside of the boat, I drop the ground-line of the fishing gear onto the hauler sheaves. I place an empty trawl tub under the hauler and run some of the ground-line into the bottom of it, leaving the anchor tied on for now in case the gear jumps off the sheaves, and I lose it over the side.

I pause and raise my arms to the sky. The day is getting up now and the stiffness in my muscles is easing. I am still attached to my gear and there is a path before me. Pull on a pair of white cotton gloves, and touch the muffler briefly for the warmth. Aim the boat back toward shore. There are actually two trips back: one path is on the ocean bottom where the gear is, and the other is on top of the water. The two paths separated during the night as I set the gear off the stern, as it followed the anchor to bottom. One path is full of noise and activity up here in the elements, the other is dark and quiet, with unpredictable offerings. For good or ill, I will reunite these two paths on the journey toward home. Whatever there will be on the line has already been decided, and all there is for it now is to haul the gear back in one piece. The voyage out has all the uncertainty and wagers in it. The voyage back is one of efficiency and acceptance, and the pull for shore.

Pick one hook after another, seven feet apart, each on a three-foot-long gangion, 350 of them per tub, and seven tubs. As the ground-line comes in over the roller, reach out and grab each hook as it comes aboard, pick the bait off it, free up the gangion if it is wound around the ground-line and set the hook in the tub at the outer edge of the coil of ground-line as it curls down. Some fishers are known for "getting their gear back in good shape" and those are the ones who baiters want to work for, while other fishers just "run the gear into the tub," which makes it tedious and slow for the baiter to be always digging around for the next hook in the coil.

When the fish comes in over the rail, it is possible to unhook it and throw it into the slatting pen and keep the gear coming without shutting off the hauler. It is called a slatting pen because that is where the fish go when they first come aboard. It is possible to use the three feet of gangion to swing the fish up and slat it into the pen by using the weight of the fish to rip the hook out of its mouth, but this straightens a lot of hooks and you can lose fish at the rail. The more cautious thing to do is to keep a good lookout over the side for fish coming up and to stop the hauler and either gaff the fish or lift it up by the hook in its mouth and unhook it and drop it in the pen. This is especially true for larger fish, or for cusk, that tend to swallow the hook. This requires stopping the hauler because it is not an easy project to retrieve the hook from its gullet. Haddock are soft-mouthed and can drop off the hook as they break the surface of the water at the side of the boat. It is better to stop the hauler with them floating on top of the water and gaff them in the head and land them that way. On the other hand, stopping and starting the hauler all the time can cause other fish to drop off the hooks on the way up. But as the old fella says, "There is no point in being one of those guys who brags about how fast they hauled a tub of trawl. All they have done is lost themselves some fish in the process. Take her easy, get the gear back in good shape, and save as many fish as you can."

"*Whitewave II, Karl and Jackie.* Over. How's it looking, Mert?"

"Not good, Art. Not good. I got about 150 pounds on two tubs. Baits coming back just the same as I set them. So the gear was on good bottom. Just no fish, that's all. Over."

"It's the same here, Mert. I was down in the mud for a while accordin' to the baits. I did pick up a small halibut, which helps. I have a tub and a half back and I might have a hundred pounds, take it all. Over."

"It's a sin the pounding those draggers put on any fish that school up. All we get are the scraps after they've done with 'em. Over."

"I guess so, Mert. I guess so. Dale probably is catching 'em all, Mert. Over."

"Yes, he's the old dog, Art. He's out there in that deep water laying on. A steaker as big as a man on every hook. Over."

"Now don't talk. No, there's not much going on here, Mert. Sometimes in the deep water, you do pick up a few. There is a sign of some shack, but you need a boatload of them to make up a day's work. Over."

"That's right, Dale. Not much going on. Anyway, I better get back at it. We'll hear you later if the skip doesn't get too bad. Over and clear."

"You never know, Mert, there may be a few bite on just now. At least it's brightened up. Make it a little better steaming back on. Over and clear for now."

After a while it feels like I am hauling downhill. The sun begins to break through, and, with the riding sail up, the sou'west wind makes for a nice haul, with the gear running onshore on the starboard side. I put the boat in gear for ten seconds or so with the wheel hard right, and it stays up on the trawl the finest kind. But no fish. A haddock here and there, and only small cod. Spend the morning picking baits. The bottom looked hummocky enough on the sounder during the set, but it seems very hard now, based on the good shape of the baits. Hooks are in one ocean, and the fish are in another.

"And what will you do, climbing your mountain of ashes?"

"Mojo Man. Mojo Man. I'm the Mojo Man. Come in and talk to the Mojo Man."   .

"The fine State of Georgia."

"Every morning he gets up before dawn and washes his Cadillac in cold, clear water."

"Yes, go through it all over again, but this time, this time, with you on the bottom and us on the top. Then you will know what it is to be righteous, what it is to be holy. Then will you learn humility."

"Talk to me now. Talk to me now. Talk to me now. The Mojo Man is here. Talk to me now."

"It may be hot, but I'm here in the shade with a cold glass of lemonade. The dog is panting, but I'm as cool as a cucumber. As cool as a cucumber."

"John 3:16. 'And God so loved the world . . .'"

"*Whitewave II, Karl and Jackie.* Over. How's it going now, Mert?"

"Nothing, Art. Just going through the motions picking the baits and getting the gear back. I've got three to go and I'll be on my way and glad of it. Over."

"Same here, Mert. No, nothing going on. I've got three and a half left to haul, I guess, and I don't have a hundred pounds to a tub. Over."

"I'll give you a call once I start back on, Art. But the skip has started and I don't want to listen to that racket, so I'm going to shut the set off. Over and clear."

"Good enough, Mert. Yeah, it's hard to talk over top of all that. I'm going to turn the set down some myself. Over and clear. *Kid Dynamite*. How are you makin' her, Dale? Over."

"Same old thing, Art. Same old thing. Nothing going on, getting the odd bit of shack here and there, and slime eels to boot. Over."

"Sounds like you're well down on the edge of the Hake Hole. Well, there's nothing on the hard bottom, that's for sure. So you may pick up some old steakers down in the dirt. I'll give you a shout when I get the gear back and start on Dale. Over and out."

"Good enough, Art."

A bare hook, and a bare hook and a bare hook, pick a bait, clear a gangion, hook. Put the boat in gear. Hook, small scrod cod. Stop the hauler. Unhook the fish and throw him back overboard. Take the boat out of gear. Start the hauler. Hook, hook, hook. Nice haddock coming. Stop the hauler when it reaches the surface, grab the gaff on the rail and stab the haddock in the head, unhook him and throw him in the pen. Start the hauler. Hook, hook, pick bait, pick bait. Ground-line going out in the water some. Put the boat in gear. Stop the hauler. Reach over and rev the engine a bit so the boat runs up on the trawl a ways. Take the boat out of gear. Start the hauler. Hook, hook, small snarl of five or six hooks. Stop the hauler. Grab the ground-line on the other side of the snarl, and put it on the hauler while I pull the baits off the hooks, unsnarl the line, and then coil it by hand back into the tub under the hauler. Start the hauler. Hook, hook, pick bait. Knot where the tubs are tied together and looped knot of middle buoy line. Stop hauler. Untie the knot. Pull the full tub from under the hauler and shift it to the offside of the boat. Grab an empty tub, put it under the hauler. Start the hauler and coil some ground-line into the tub. Put the boat in gear and run up on the trawl some so it is slack in the water. Take the buoy line, walk back in the stern, and start coiling the line by hand. When the keg comes aboard, tie the coil of line and throw it in a corner. "Stand up straight, arch your back and shake your arms." Look around. Andrew's and Milton's boats are inside, and to the east'ard. Further outside, I can see Merton and Arthur. Bud is to the west'ard, but I can't see Dale off to the south'ard in the deep water. The pump cuts in.

Walk back to the rail and re-enter a three-foot cone of existence. Start hauling the fifth tub. Hook, hook, bait, bait, bait. Market cod. Unhook it without stopping the hauler. Bait, hook, hook. Put the boat in gear. Stop the hauler when a huge monkfish comes up. Gaff the monkfish in the head and haul it aboard. Then grab the gangion, and pull a fully intact haddock out of the monkfish's stomach. It's fine except that the haddock's usual purple colour is a bit milky from the acids in the monkfish's stomach. "Two for one." Take the boat out of gear.

I pick up a few fish partway through the sixth tub. I turn on the sounder: thirty-eight to forty fathom. Just making the rise of the Fall-off. "I guess I steamed over top of 'em. Should have stopped twenty minutes earlier." There's 150 pounds on the last tub, and there is a fish on each of the last dozen hooks next to the anchor for the high flyer. As I coil in the buoy line, there is relief that I am no longer tethered to the ocean bottom. "I am in this world only." All the manoeuvring is over and the gear and fish are aboard. I look back into the slatting pen. I might have 650 pounds on seven tubs. And if it wasn't for the last tub, the trip would be a broker. I might make $75 after bait and fuel, and the $7 a tub I pay Stevie for baiting the trawl. But there's nothing for it now but to head for home, dressing the fish as I go.

I drop the riding sail, so the boat will jog along side-to in the sou'west wind. I turn the set back on to give Arthur a call.

"Breaker. Breaker. Who wants to talk to Hot'n'Heavy? Come in, come in, come in."

"*Karl and Jackie. Whitestreak.* Over."

"Did someone call me? Over."

"*Whitestreak* here, Art. Just wanted to let you know I've started back on. Over."

"Good enough, Ray. I had the set turned down. There's such a racket. I'm just hauling in the high flyer myself. I was going to give everyone a call. You pick up a few, did ya, Ray?"

"Didn't make a hundred pounds to a tub, Art. Over"

"Talk to me now. Talk to me. It's the Mojo Man. Talk to me."

"Same here, Ray, same here. Well, I might have a hundred pounds to a tub, take it all. Anyway, we'll see you in at the wharf. Over and clear."

"*Whitestreak.* Over and clear."

"And every dog shall have his day. And the lion shall lie down with the lamb."

"*Whitewave II.* I guess you are on your way, Mert. Over."

"I've been steaming on for about five minutes, Art. Just having a mug-up before I get to these few fish. My God, they won't take long to dress. Over."

"That's right, Mert. I thought I saw you starting to steam on. Well, she's cleared up some anyway. I'm just hauling the high flyer aboard, so we'll see you when we get in. Over and clear."

"It's a nice jog on, anyway. Over and out."

"*Miss Rebecca, Karl and Jackie.* Over."

"I read ya, Art. I've been steaming on for about fifteen minutes and dressing fish. I'll talk to you later. Over and out."

"Be sure your sin will find you out."

"Good enough, Bud. Just so long as everything is working okay. I won't bother you where you're busy. Over and out."

"*Kid Dynamite, Karl and Jackie.* Over."

"Gotcha, Art. I have about half a tub left to haul, and I'll be on my way. Over."

"Breaker. Breaker. Talk to me."

"I bet you're laying on out there in deep water. I'm just starting on here. I'll give you a call on the way in from the Can. Over and clear."

"There was no sign at all for a while, but I did pick up a few on this last tub. But it's too little too late, I'm afraid. Catch ya later. Over and clear."

"*Lydia B., Karl and Jackie.* How you makin' 'er, Milt? Over."

"My god, what a mess, Art. I couldn't believe it. Why the snarls, you. Took me forever to get the gear back. But a fella got a bit lucky anyways. Some of those snarls were where a few fish were biting on. But what a mess trying to get the gear sorted out and not lose too many fish at the same time. My, my, my. Why, that Danny, he'd screw up the Lord's Prayer."

"Sounds like you might have picked up a few in any case, Milt. Over."

"I might have a thousand pound, but my god the works, the works, you. I thought I would never see the end of it. By the Jesus, here comes another snarl. I'll catch ya later, Art. Over and out."

"Good enough, Milt. Well, it sounds like you made up a day's work, anyways. We'll see ya when we get in. Over and clear."

"*Diane Christine, Karl and Jackie.* Come in, Andrew. Over."

"I hear ya, Art. Man, I don't know where Milt is finding the fish. I'm right alongside of him, but I'm in a different ocean, I guess. I don't have a hundred pounds on a tub. Over."

"Same as the rest of us, Andrew. Same as the rest of us. I guess you're pretty well on your way, are ya? Over."

"That's right, Art. I'm on my way. I better get in before someone sees me and asks me what the hell I'm doing out here. Over."

"You got that right, Andrew, you got that right. We'll see ya when we get in. Over and clear."

"Good enough, Art. Over and out."

"*Bobby and Berty, Karl and Jackie.* How are you making out, Robert?"

"I hear ya, Arthur. I might have nine hundred pounds, take 'em all, Arthur. Over."

"You did all right then, Robert. Mostly haddock where you are I guess, Robert? Over."

"That's right, Arthur. I am just getting cleaned up and ready to steam on. Over."

"Good enough, Robert. We'll see you at the wharf. Over and clear."

I rev the boat up to 1500 rpm or so, and it jogs on side-to in the increasing sou'west slop. Sharpen up the ripper, and rinse the cotton gloves, greasy from the mackerel bait. Grab a codfish in my left hand, and with my index finger in the eye socket and my thumb at the base of the jaw, I cut the band between the two gills. Then I slice it the length of the belly. Shifting my left thumb to open up the cut along the stomach cavity, I tear out the organs and drop them into a bucket, and toss the fish into the pen in the centre of the deck. Every fifty pounds or so of dressed fish, I dump the guts over the side and rinse the bucket as the gulls dive on the entrails. I then dump a clean bucket of water over the fish I've dressed, washing the excrement and stomach contents into the bilge. The pump cuts in. Smell the offal as it pumps a dark slick alongside the boat. Dip my gloved hands into the water and squeeze the juice out of them. What with the wounds from the hooks and the acid from the guts, my hands are a welter of soreness. Haddock guts are especially rank, and yet this fish produces a tasty and tender fillet. One of nature's great mysteries.

The last fish I dress is the monkfish, which requires only that I saw through the last eight inches of the tail and throw the head and body overboard. Although it is probably the ugliest fish in the ocean, with a jaw the size of a barrel hoop, the meat of its tail is rich, and is marketed as rock lobster. When I finish dressing the fish and cleaning up the boat, I fillet a couple of haddock that I had set aside and put the fillets in the plastic bag in which I had brought my peanut butter sandwiches.

When I have steamed back on to within about ten minutes
of the Groaner, I re-enter the fog bank along the shore. I turn
the sounder back on: fifteen fathom. Because I have jogged
back on dressing fish, it is not as easy to judge how far I have
come in reversing the course from the night before. I therefore
slow the boat, take it out of gear, and listen. Nothing. Shut off
the engine. Listen again. *Clang. Clang. Clang.* My heart sinks.
That is Bantam Bell, not the Groaner. The wind had taken
me more to the east'ard than I thought it would. According
to the compass, the bell is due north of me. Just inside of it
are a series of breakers. "Thank God I stopped when I did." I
turn the boat due west and steam for five minutes. Eventually
I hear the *ooouf, ooouf* of the Groaner and look at the compass.
The sound is coming from the west-nor'west. I start the engine
again and steam west for another five minutes, before shutting
off the engine and listening. Now the Groaner seems to be to
the nor'west, not too far off. "I am where I am supposed to be."

I jog along for seven more minutes, until I see not only the
Groaner but also the *Lydia B* tied up to it. Milt's boat wanders
all over the ocean unless he stands at the wheel. If he tries to
dress fish while jogging on, he ends up going in circles. Rather
than aggravate himself, he steams back in and ties up to the
Groaner. I wave as I go by. A large flock of gulls flops and caws
as they dive for the fish guts alongside Milt's boat. He waves
back, knife in his hand, working his way through his fish.

Reversing the courses of the night before, I steam nor'west
for five minutes, as the sounder shoals up to six fathom.
Again, I don't see the Can buoy as I go by it in the fog. I now
steam west-nor'west for five more minutes, which I expect
will take me to the end of the wharf. After two minutes, the
sounder shoals up to a fathom as I cross Middle Ground—
at least I hope it's Middle Ground and not some rock pile in
back of the Marsh Bar. I slow down, and over the sound of the
idling engine I hear the sharp *eeooup* of the horn at the end
of the wharf. I idle along and finally in the fog the long dark

Figure 5   The *Whitestreak* returning from the fishing grounds. Photo by Laura Jane McLauchlan.

rectangle of armour rock and wharf comes into view, just where they should be. I turn in around the end of the wharf. The *Diane Christine* is unloading, so I pull in behind the *Karl and Jackie* and throw bowline to people on the wharf who offer their outstretched arms to catch it.

"Well, you made it back in one piece," someone calls.

"More or less," I reply. Because there were not many fish to dress, I have the boat all cleaned up and everything stowed away, and the trawl tubs are ready to be hoisted onto the wharf along with the fish. I climb the ladder and slide back into the metabolism of those on land: slack, noisy, and comfortable.

"Everything work good, did it?" asks Murray.

"Yes, everything worked fine. That spot in the tuck still opens up when I steam off on a sloppy night. But by the time I finished hauling the trawl, it was a lot better, and jogging on didn't seem to make it any worse."

"Well, the poor thing is twenty-two year old. I guess she's going to work some no matter what we do. Can't make it new."

"I think we did everything but—"

"I guess we did. On a fine day, lift up the hatches and let 'er dry out below decks enough that maybe we can see where it is seeping. Then we can put her on the half-way slip and pound a bit of oakum into the seam. I bet it is where the tuck is so sharp that we couldn't bend timbers around the curve of the planks. The hull timbers are end-nailed to the ones coming up from the keel. Those ends are getting a bit doughty and don't hold a nail as well as they should."

"We could put a partial bulkhead down from the deck beam, and the hull would probably work less when it's rough. The keel is still and the hull near the surface is working in the waves. Something has to give."

"Why, sonny, these days it's more taking than giving, the age she's at. She'll keep you going for another year or so maybe, but one of these days you are going to have to build a new boat if you are going to stay at it."

"And pay for it how?" I ask, pointing down to his catch.

"My God, man, five hundred feet of good lumber and a box of boat nails isn't very expensive, compared to what guys are paying for fibreglass boats these days. And it'll make you money. Well, not money, maybe, but it will make you a living—that is, if things don't get any worse than they already are. Pierce's will probably front you the money for the engine if you promise to sell them your lobsters. They did for me."

"The way things are going, I would be in hock to them forever trying to pay it off. I can't even get the money together to put a roof over my head. Every time I turn around there is something to fix."

"You might have to go out west for a while. I did. Why, half of Prince Rupert is from Lockeport."

"You want a haddock?" I ask, gesturing again to the fish pen.

"Not today. Merton has a few steakers and I want some tongues and cheeks for supper, so I better get back to the haul-up shed and get to work afore David has them all aboard Pierce's truck." Murray turns and ambles up the wharf, pulling a plastic bag and a knife out of his jacket pocket.

By the time I retie the boat, Murray is digging around in the ice to find a steaker from which to cut out the tongues and cheeks. Beyond him, the Pierce's sign on the bait shed is half lost in the fog, and below it sits a shiny new Department of Fisheries half-ton truck with two officers in it. The officers are eating their lunch, emerging from the truck only to take a leak in the armour rock before backing around and heading up over the hill.

I walk toward the sharp echoing sound of frozen mackerel and squid being chopped. Along a bench in the shed several young men are already baiting the tubs of gear that have come up from the boats. I confirm with Stevie that he can have seven tubs baited by tonight. "Looks like it is going to be fit to go again."

Arthur is unloading now, and Dale has tied up behind me. Milton is rounding the end of the wharf. "Better move the boat up, son, and make room for others," someone calls, and I hustle down the ladder after untying the bow-line.

A group has gathered above Dale's boat. "Why, you old dog, you. Seventeen hundred pound, you say. That's a good day, even if they are mostly cusk and hake. There must have been a few steakers amongst 'em, down there in that dirt. There was a time when the Hake Hole was the home of steakers, there and the Jim Young Ridge."

"Seemed like every time you came up on a bit of hard bottom and got clear of the slime eels, you picked up two or three nice steakers. Didn't take many of them to make up two hundred pounds on a tub."

After shifting the boat forward, I sit down on the lid of the fish pen. The gulls flutter and cry, whether over the frozen mackerel heads thrown out next to the shed or the last of the sweepings as Milton cleans up the deck of his boat. I am sheltered from the wind and and now feel some warmth from the sun through the fog. My skin becomes a little less porous, and I notice things at rest. Looking up, I see that my mast headlight is still on. "It can stay on for now." I fold my arms and lower my head. Feel the pain in my index finger against my ribs. Rub the smooth electrical tape with my thumb. It took quite a bit of digging to get the barb out, and the fish guts haven't made it any less tender.

My turn under the hoist comes and I pull the boat along by the wharf timbers. First hoist the tubs of gear up to the wharf. These will be delivered to Stevie in the shed by forklift. Then the grey wooden box is lowered. "You want a fork?" shouts David, Pierce's man.

"No, thanks. There's not enough of them to bother with it." I pitch the fish into the box by hand. Up goes the box when it is full. It is dumped into a pen from which David then forks the species I have most of into an elevated scale. After recording the weight, he opens the chute and the fish slide into an insulated box with ice. He climbs onto the forklift and switches boxes when it is time to weigh other species. When I finish unloading the fish, David hands the gas hose down and I fill up my side tank, since it was the only one I used last night, and then I climb up the ladder and get the slip for the fish and sign for the bait and gas I received.

Climb back down the ladder now, remembering to turn off the mast headlight, and I start the engine. Using the gaff, I give myself a push off the bow, and swing the boat around toward the mooring. I idle across the dock and swing into my berth. Gaff up the buoy that is connected to the chain and bow hook, then haul it up to the bow and drop the hook into the ring bolt attached to the stem. Put the boat in reverse and let it idle against the anchor chain while I gaff the buoy that is connected to the stern lines. I drop that hook into the ringbolt in the stern and take the boat out of gear and turn the engine off. "There, tethered to the land once again."

I gather up the glass water bottle, make sure the pocket watch is in my pocket, and then collect the bag with the fillets that will be my supper. After crawling across Arthur's and Andrew's boats to get to the wharf, I walk back to where the truck is parked on the gravel next to the baiting shed. I drop the bag of fillets into a plastic bucket tied to the wooden flatbed.

I sit in the cab of the truck for a long while, looking out at what is going on, the obvious things and the not-so-obvious things. I try to hold it all in my mind, so as not to forget it: the cries of the gulls, the sound of the surf over on the beach, the revs of the forklift engine, the irritating *eeoop* of the horn on the end of the wharf, all mixed in with the back and forth of the voices, softened by the fog and also by the refracted transparency of the windshield. I am again overwhelmed by the rusted wall of steel that bore down on me. And then the violence of the propeller chewing through the world. It goes to the very heart of me, as if it has searched me out and found me. If I choose to go away to find work, that rusted wall of steel will always be there alongside me. It is not a shift that would be measured in distance, it is a shift that would require entirely new marks in the landscape, not ones that would lead you to plenty, but rather marks that lead to misery and peril.

I head up the road and stop at a small white store set into Althea's and Mr. Ern's front yard. The large house behind the store was once the Spearwater Inn, where Althea would take in guests in the summertime. Now she just runs the store, while Mr. Ern, who used to fish and who later owned the gas pump at the wharf before Pierce's bought him out, pads around as a slippered ambassador for a disappearing world.

Althea rests on her chair behind the low counter just inside the door, while farther back down the centre aisle, several men either lean on the stove or sit on the chairs next to it. "Greetings," Althea nods as I make my way back to the stove.

"Well, you survived, I see," offers Frank.

"Got out and I got back. That's about all I can say."

"That's something, I guess."

I pick up a couple of cans of stew, some apple juice, and half a dozen pairs of cotton gloves from the back where the fishing supplies are kept.

"You figure it will be fit?"

"That's what they say." I pause by the stove and cast a glance at the jelly doughnuts in their cellophane wrappers.

"Got a hook in the finger, I see. I guess it don't hurt."

I look down at the toilet paper still sticking out from under the electrical tape. "It took some digging."

"They don't call them hooks for nothing."

"Most meat your gear had on it all day, I imagine."

"By far." I move along to the front of the store.

"Shall I just put that on your book?" Althea turns to the stack of white receipt books behind her as I set my items on the counter.

"Please, if you don't mind."

"Not a problem," she replies, as she finds my book. "Let me just make a note of what you have there."

"I'll be by next time I settle up in Lockeport."

"There we go now." She totals things up in her neat handwriting.

I gather the goods in my arms. "Thanks very much."

"You get some rest now."

Back down the hill and along the gravel. Just past Arnold's Hill, I stop outside a green house. Fillets in hand, I tap on the door and go in. Molly waves from her easy chair.

"Well, here he is."

"Brought you your dinner." I set the fillet in the sink and then sit on the chair just inside the door.

"Thank you very much. So how was it?"

"Same old thing. Not quite a hundred pounds to a tub."

"Other boats the same, I suppose?" Molly always pays close attention to the fishing. Her husband, Ronald, fished all his life and her son David is a fisheries officer over in Digby.

She was the only wife who baited trawl for her husband in Little Harbour.

"More or less. Dale had 1700, mostly shack."

"I suppose he cried poor all day long on the set too."

"Came up smelling like a rose, he told me."

"Likely story. It is always a shock to me when the old days feel like the good times. It sure never felt like the good times then. You pushed a pea around on your plate trying to wear yourself out so you could go to bed hungry." Molly laughs. "But I look at what is happening now, and I guess they were. We were never what you call well off, but there was usually enough, and if you ran short, a neighbour would help you if they could. Now the land is overrun with cat spruce and the ocean is a wasteland, and neighbours, well…"

"I hear Canada is trying to work with the UN on these Law of the Sea conferences. Maybe that will help."

"It might, but I doubt it. Not with who is running things. When I get up in the night," Molly gestures through the picture window toward the water, "I can see that foreign fleet going back and forth at the twelve-mile limit. 'Course I don't think our gang is much different. They want to expand the Canadian dragger fleet to compete with the foreigners. How's that gonna be any different? More devils on the deep blue sea. David just shakes his head when he sees some of the decisions that get made at the Department of Fisheries." Molly sighs. "It always seems like a bunch of idiots are in charge. World War III is on nature, I guess. Well, I'm old. It not going to change what I do, one way or the other. But a young fella like you. It doesn't look so good. Along with everything else, this place with no fishing. I can't see it."

"Maybe I'll have to go out west, to Rupert maybe, or work construction, if I am going to build a new boat or finish the house. Anyways, things to do. Probably going again tonight." I rise from the chair, and for the first time feel the grime and stink on me from the night on the water.

"Any word from Laura?"

"Nope."

"She's a good woman."

"I know that." I open the door and raise a hand that is half a wave and half a 'please stop.'"

"Well, I thank you. Come by again. I certainly hope you don't have to go away to live." Molly catches up to me on the step and hands me a jar of gooseberry jam.

"Thank you. I won't expect to live. I'll just expect to make some ready money."

"I'm glad it's you and not me," replies Molly with one hand on the door.

I continue along on the gravel, pausing to look north across the harbour to the wharf, just before the road bends south toward the head. Making the rise before turning into my laneway, I look out across the hazy view through the cat spruce and on out to Black Rock and Ram Island.

But for now, I can turn my back on the water. Head indoors where it is warm and dry. I unravel the tape from my left index finger and look at the ragged piece of white flesh that puckers near the base of it. It had long ago stopped bleeding. Run some water into a saucepan from the spigot of the five-gallon jug that stands beside the sink and dump some salt into it. Then swirl around the salt to dissolve it. The acidity of the fish guts leaches out as I flex my fingers in the water. While I am standing there soaking my finger, I take the Pierce's slips from my pocket and put them on the shelf with the others. Tacked to the wall is a list of jobs in order of priority that I continue to add to: "dig out the cellar drain, cut firewood, rebuild the window frames for the used windows I was given, get new sills milled out of the hackmatack I cut down on the edge of the bog, insulate the floor, dig a well line, fix the out-house door, go for a walk on the beach, cut the alders along the driveway, give it all up and join the circus." I add to the list, "build a new bulkhead in the boat." After a time, I dry my finger under my arm and dab Ozonol on it, and then wrap it in a Band-Aid.

Before long I am asleep on the cot. I wake later in the evening, just in time to make the trip around the beach to the wharf to take the tubs of gear out of the freezer.

Presence and Absence

The new grass on Hemeons Head has browned into magged-up twists spun by the wind. Ducks and geese make their daily shift between salt water and fresh. The rutted trails of the hunter's trucks testify to the close attention that is paid to these proceedings.

Down across what used to be fields where sheep grazed, there is the low rise and fall of a hill that may be a Mi'kmaq burial mound, still with a green crown. There is an indentation in the top of it where anthropologists were digging until band members arrived from Bear River to chase them off. Beyond the mound, the moss and grass crumble into loose stone on the shore inside of Alex's Rock, whose half-sunk rectangular shape is lined on top with the sawteeth of shags drying their wings.

To the east of Alex's Rock is an outcropping on the shore where oxen once dragged the foundation stones up to the home of Bythenia and Gideon Hemeon, which had stood out alone beyond my own home on the bare headland for generations. The foundation stones were squared before being set in place. The work had been made easy because of the eight-to-ten-inch-thick slabs that came from the fault lines in the rock that were already tumbled in heaps by the ocean. Once the loose ones were gathered up on the stoneboat and taken up to the foundation hole, the remaining stone had to be split out with a maul and wedges along the remaining fault lines of the ledge when the tide was low. Drive the oak wedges in and then leave them for a few tides, so that the swelling of the wood hurried along the ocean's slow dismantling.

When I think of the place now from so far away, it is the fall of the year and the November wind blows across the headland. Better to think of it on a cold and miserable day. I see myself standing next to the Hemeon cellar hole with a steel bar in my hand. The clunk of it is muffled by the wind as I bend, pry, and break the old foundation stones free of their mossy shoulders. Over rolls the blue-green stone onto the flattened grass as ants rush to retrieve the arrangements of white eggs, after the lid of their world is suddenly torn away.

My harvest of old foundation stones continues along what used to be the north wall of the house. There is an old collapsing cellar hole as well, with rocked-up walls and an outside stone staircase under what used to be the kitchen. The rest of the house was built on a perimeter made up of a single row of foundation stones. Easier to start with them, as I imagine each being placed in the new fireplace I intend to build with them.

My excavations were perhaps the final stage in the gradual disappearance of this dwelling. After the windows blew out in a storm in the 1960s, the Hemeon family's large "L"-shaped house disintegrated in stages. The wood frame went from a square and plumb rectitude to ship-like curves as it sagged and bent under a collapsing roof. The torn vestments of shingle and plaster fell away, gradually exposing the skeleton of rafters, as well as floor joists that were formalized on only one side with an adz, as if supporting humans were a part-time responsibility. Many of the vertical studs are entirely in the round, with only the bark taken off with a draw knife very soon after the trees were cut, so that the sap that still ran between bark and trunk made stripping the tree sticky and easy.

As time passed, the structure became a scattered collection of features that used to be a home, until mercy was shown and it burned bright on a still night with frost coming on in the fall. Volunteer firemen, smoking and talking next to their new truck, worried only that a grass fire might crawl back up the road toward a stand of cat spruce. Between periodic dousings with the hose, the sills of the house glowed red throughout the night, creating a rectangle of light sifting up through the smoke. Remnants of those burnt sills float in the foot of water in the cellar hole, the drain having finally become blocked with weeds and grass, so that it no longer flows out below the low hill to the southwest, beyond which a rocked-up well still lurks in the long grass.

The headlands are now landscapes of overgrown fields and abandoned cellar holes. Walk through the stands of forest, paw over moss-covered fallen trunks that collapse in a muffled crunch, and there will be stone walls that used to mark the edge of fields. See an old metal washtub in the undergrowth, ferns growing up through the rusted-out bottom, or the wagon-wheel hoop and hub, along with the remains of the oak spokes. Come upon an apple orchard still bearing fruit even after years of being overrun by the cat spruce, which is the only tree that can live here in any abundance, pleased as it is to take root in the rocky, acidic soil, and able to withstand blasts of salt air that come ashore in the three-day nor'easters in November. The odd maple or birch can survive for a time, if they are able to find a sheltered spot among the spruce, but otherwise bog, bayberry, fern, and spruce create a continuous assemblage in various stages of composition and decomposition.

The abandoned dwellings usually announce themselves with the presence of the bright green humps of Roman sailor that all but cover the original house foundation. Swath through it and see old bedsteads, wash basins, and cast-iron stoves that have sunk where they stood, held in place now by a tangle of purple branches, and farther down in the brackish undergrowth the stumpy ends of the rotting and rounded floor joists.

The Braille of former settlement begins to stand out: here's where the barn stood next to the road, with the house set back a ways, there the hill field surrounded by a stone wall, where there used to be sheep grazing as well as potatoes growing.

Farther along, there stood the house that also served as a post office and, directly across the road from it, another house, the two families not getting along although related.

Among these remnants, solitary monuments stand fast, at least for now: Donald McDonald's grave leans patiently toward the eroding shore beyond the desolated shell of the house that Robert tore down to build his shop, which now sits empty. He sold his boat and is working in a trailer park in Prince Edward Island, next to the Borden ferry. Others have left as well, gone here and there to make extra money to keep things going.

And across the road, my own home, finally capable of warmth after years of being a drafty shell, now sits cold and empty. A worn shovel is propped against the wall where I have left it, an act of hope. Slabs of stone for the new hearth are gradually disappearing in the lengthening grass. In a place where I have been so present for years, I am now absent, if only temporarily. All my thoughts are of this home, and the *Whitestreak* that is now across the road again, covered in a tarp, as well as the new boat I hope to build upon my return. It is a haunting of sorts from a distance, with plans for the future, as I lay now in a work camp in Western Canada surrounded by large machines that tear up the earth.

CHAPTER II

Lewis, Scottish Hebrides, Early Nineteenth Century

History from Above

Following the Battle of Culloden in the mid-eighteenth century, the victorious British engaged in a systematic eradication of the clan system in the Scottish Highlands and Islands, and along with it the dismantling of the communal runrig field allotment system. The traditionally close relationships between lairds and clan members became strained as well by the increasing com-mercialization of relations, which tended to impoverish clan leaders and led to the purchase of large tracts of land by absentee landlords. The intention of these new landlords was to increase profits by expanding sheep grazing so as to supply wool for the "satanic mills" of Manchester. This change required the dis-placement of the subsistence clan members.

The expansion of sheep farming was accompanied by the har-vesting of kelp, which had become another source of revenue in the Hebrides, along with the promise of an expanded fishery. Many of the clan folk were therefore forced to move out of the prime pas-ture in the glens so that sheep could gaze. By way of compensation they were given crofts in the bogland on the shore ("not a snipe could live there") so they could be employed in the harvesting of kelp as well as in pursuing the fishery. In broad terms, the com-mercial rent economy was replacing the more traditional family economy of Highland society (Hunter 33). The narratives set out

*here chronicle displacements to the bogs on the shore ("we have
slid down the hill like mud in the rain") as crofters struggle to
maintain their way of life. In the context of these dwindling prospects, "redundant populations" of crofters—many young men in
the clans, including Donald McDonald—were conscripted into
the British army and sent off to fight in colonial wars.*

History from Below

*I would say this, that they lived more substantially then,
and they live more extravagantly now.*
— Rev. John A. Macrae (1883)

Having lived to an advanced age on croft on the Isle of Lewis,
Malcolm McDonald begins feeling poorly. Despite his
wish to be left in peace, his daughter Millie seeks medical help
when Malcolm cannot rise from his bed. Several members of
the village push the boat out through the surf so as to fetch
the doctor from Carloway, returning with him two days later.
This is the first time a doctor has been to the townland in
twenty years and Malcolm has no interest in seeing him now.
"I have no faith in them," he says. "They can give you stuff
that will kill you in a minute." Following the failure of all
concerned to persuade Malcolm otherwise, the doctor, after
examining the children, climbs back aboard the boat for the
trip home.

Malcolm is visited by family and friends. His wife, Margaret, provides food for all who come by, at the same time telling many of the stories, while Malcolm dozes next to the fire.
"The bustle of the spring is a wonderful time. The animals
are roaming in search of new shoots of grass, accompanied
by their young. The weather turns fine and the land, which
for months had been little more than a quagmire, begins to

dry and firm up. Everyone is going about with a *cas-chrom* on their shoulder, as the soil is turned in the fields. The roofs are taken off the houses, and the thatch is dug into the potato ground. Then the winter's manure is forked out over the wall of each home and it too is spread on the land.

"But my favourite time of all is when the animals are taken up to the shielings after the crops are planted. This is a busy few weeks but there is the finer summer weather to look forward to and some ease in our days as the crops mature in the fields.

"Yes, it is a grand time. We women are all together up in the hills, and besides making butter and cheese, there is time to enjoy ourselves, knitting and singing, or just wandering the hills. Down below, the men dig peats from time to time, and stack them, or do some fishing. And then they travel up and down the glen to see how we are making out with the animals. In those times, we possessed little but enjoyed much.

"The day we move the animals is always exciting. Having finished the tilling in June, things are readied for the trip up the glen with the animals so they can enjoy the summer's grass. The people are up and in commotion like bees about to swarm. The different families bring their herds together and drive them up the hill. The sheep lead, the cattle go next, the younger preceding, and the horses follow. The men carry burdens of sticks, heather-ropes, spades, and other things needed to repair the summer huts. The women carry bedding, meal, dairy, and cooking utensils. Barefooted and bareheaded boys and girls flit hither and thither, keeping the herds together as best they can, every now and then having a race with some animal trying to run away home. There is much noise. Women knit their stockings, sing their songs, talk and walk as free and erect as if there were no burdens on their backs or in their hearts, nor sin nor sorrow in this world of ours, so far as we are concerned. Above this din rise the voices of the various animals being thus unwillingly driven from their homes. All who we meet on the way bless the 'Trial,' as this removing is called.

"When the grazing ground up in the hills has been reached and the burdens are laid down, the huts are repaired outwardly and inwardly. These huts are conical in shape and usually made of stone, although sometimes they can be made of turf. There are usually two of these bothys: one for the humans and one for the animals. The apex of the cone roof for the humans is finished with a flagstone with a hole in it, to allow smoke out and light in. There is a low doorway that is just big enough for a person to crawl through with a removable door made of wicker or heather. In the walls of the hut are recesses for storing utensils, as well as a larger recess where people sleep.

"Then we all bring forth our stock, and every family's animals are separated out as they are being driven into the enclosure. The constable and another person at either side of the gateway see that only the proper *souming* has been brought to the grazing. This precaution over, the cattle are turned out to graze.

"Having seen to their cattle and sorted their shielings, the people repair to their removing feast, which is simple enough, the chief thing being a cheese that every family is careful to provide for the occasion from last year's produce. The cheese is shared among neighbours and friends, as they wish themselves and the cattle good luck and prosperity. Every head is uncovered, every knee is bowed, as they dedicate themselves and their flocks to the care of Israel's Shepherd and sing together:

Thou gentle Michael of the white steed,
Who subdued the Dragon of blood,
For love of God and the Son of Mary
Spread over us thy wing, shield us all!
Spread over us thy wing, shield us all!

Mary beloved! Mother of the White lamb,
Protect us, thou Virgin of nobleness,

Queen of Beauty! Shepherdess of the flocks!
Keep our cattle, surround us together,
Keep our cattle, surround us together.

Thou Columba, the friendly, the kind,
In the name of the Father, the Son, and the Spirit Holy,
Through the Three-in-One, through the Three,
Encompass us, guard our procession,
Encompass us, guard our procession.

Thou Father! Thou Son! Thou Spirit Holy!
Be the Three-One with us day and night,
On the machair plain, on the mountain ridge,
The Three-One is with us, with his arm around our head,
The Three-One is with us, with his arm around our head.

Thankfulness and ease fill our days up on the hills. The young animals grow strong on the rich grass, and one day flows into another as we make cheese and butter for the year ahead.

"Only when the crops are harvested in the fall do the men come up and help us in our return to the township. The animals are brought down again at this time, as the grass in the highland fields begins to brown and there is the stubble in the harvested fields to feed on. Then all winter long the cattle and sheep wander freely on the land in search of any blade of grass or left-over fodder. The long narrow fields that contained crops in summer are marked with a corner stone. The only other marks on the landscape between the high hills inland and the sweeping green that swings down to the tides of the Atlantic are the places in the heath where the peat has been dug and stacked to dry, as well as our long, low dwellings, poking up out of the landscape."

Malcolm and Margaret's home is about forty feet long and twelve feet wide, and rounded on either end with no gables. There are interior and exterior vertical dry stone walls that are four feet high. The space between these dual stone walls is packed with turf. The roof beams rest on the interior wall, creating a grassy walkway on top of the wall that is occupied by children, sheep, and goats. This walkway is made accessible by a series of longer stones that are inserted in the outer wall, creating rough steps up. The roof is covered with turf and thatch made from heather and oats; it is held down by heather ropes tied to rocks hanging off the lower edges of the roof. The rope and rocks protect the thatch from being blown away in storms. There is a wooden door at the lower end of the building, the top half of which is kept open to allow smoke to escape from the hearth, for there is no chimney, or any windows, only a hole made in the thatch to let the smoke out.

The entrance is next to the animals, where there is a large pile of turf mixed with manure that has accumulated inside the door. Given that it is early spring and there is a winter's accumulation, the floor of the cow's stall is raised to such a level that the animal has eaten a hole in the roof thatch, through which the smoke now passes, and it has given the cow a view of goings-on outdoors.

These houses are said to be occupied by Highland couples—the animals and the tenants going in at the same door. All live under the same roof. At the most, there is only an old sail between the animals and the fire. Chickens spend their time perched in the warmth of the roof rafters, giving their eggs a taste of peat. When walls were gradually erected to separate the rational and irrational members of the family in some areas, the banishment was felt keenly by the irrational inmates, especially the cows, and milk production often suffered.

<hr />

Malcolm is propped up on a tick mattress that rests on a raised shelf near the fire. He looks around the room as visitors come and go and his family busies itself with various domestic tasks. "It is wonderful to see you all, with your glasses of good cheer and the good food you have brought. I am happy we are all together, even in these hard times. I am so old and tired, and my body feels almost like the little wooden *tulachan* with a skin thrown over it." Nearby, the turf fire burns on a layer of small stones that are held in place by the rusted metal rim of an old cart wheel. Tea is passed around with the oatcakes.

"When we arrived here, it came by way of a proposal from the Factor that we take advantage of the opportunity presented by being moved to the seashore to prosecute the fishery. These lochs had not been fished extensively in the past, except by foreigners who arrived in large numbers when the herring were running. The proprietors of the island deemed the fishery a rich resource that he said could enhance his revenues from his island holdings, and then set about sending us to this place."

Malcolm falters, and waves his hand for Margaret to continue. "Originally, when the proprietor had decided to create a sheep farm on our lands, we were told that he would give us larger crofts of equal quality elsewhere, with the added advantage of being suitably situated to prosecute the fishery, as well as take part in the kelping. The access to the fishing and kelp was to replace our access to the hill pastures that we had traditionally used for the summer grazing of our animals. Fourteen families were moved down here ten years ago. When the people saw this place, they at first refused to go in.

"Yes, this was at one time an important township, and used to contain a large, prosperous, happy, and contented population. But the bulk of the people were expatriated through the agency of the Factor, who wished to form a sheep farm for his son. The Factor had expressed his determination to have us evicted, and said to us: 'Go you must, even though you should go to the bottom of the sea.' In the end, we were allowed this mere fringe of the township we have now, bordering on the rocky seashore. As I said to Malcolm when we first arrived here: 'We have been cast out on the bog.'"

Others among the visitors also tell their stories. "Not very long ago, these crofts we are in now were peat-moss and quagmire; but at the commencement of the sheep-farming mania, when people were regarded as a nuisance to be got rid of by driving us out of the country like noxious vermin, or by crowding us into barren promontories or boggy hollows which were useless for sheep, our township was then formed by locating families here who had been deprived of good land in other parts of the estate. We have for a long period borne poverty and hardship patiently, while we have seen strangers growing fat on our native land. Our patience is nearly exhausted.

"We are hemmed in on all sides to make room for sheep and our hovels are so close to the sea, and in such a low place, that the tides are coming into our houses; sometimes so that now and then we are almost drowned, and obliged to save ourselves on top of our beds. Our peats and potatoes are swept away by the tide.

"Shortly after we had settled on the shore and the Ground Officer had parcelled out the bog among us, more tenants were thrown in upon us, with no allocation of new land to support them. At first, there were fourteen crofts here. There are twenty-seven houses now. Many of these were sent from the other townships that were cleared—poor people that could not go away to America. Because there was no other place for them, they were hurled in upon our headland.

"We who are without land are a burden upon those who have a little of it; and if it were not that they accommodate us out of their little, by giving us potato ground, we would have starved in a heap.... The end of it was that my family, when they grew up, scattered into all parts of the earth; and some of them are dead in a foreign land, and others I know not where they are, and I am alone.

"The Laird's Factor complained about us continually. He said that we are getting numerous, because we do not go away, and we intermarry among ourselves, and just grow on the places where we are. It is a terrible thing: just growing on the place where we are. He said that is what needs to be stopped above all.

"We crofters could not produce enough for our families on these new plots and had to work to earn food. I have been obliged to knock about, and serve here and there to earn food for my wife and family, which could not be grown upon our three acres of moss. So our home is here and gone. When I open my own door there is no place within the range of my sight except where the big sheep are, and as a result I am required to earn wages through the world."

Daily Life on the Edge of Existence
From the outside, Malcolm and Margaret's home looks like little more than a hovel, built as it was by the people themselves with the materials that were near at hand, except possibly for the roof rafters, which are sometimes bought from the Laird if useful driftwood could not be found on the shore. Along with the fourteen crofter families and a number of cottars who have been thrown in upon them with only a cow's grass and some potato ground, there are also several *scallags* who live at the end of the settlement near the beach, and who have nothing at all, living under a few sticks and an old sail, and shifting about where there is a little work.

The township is held to the shore and is not allowed to expand its holdings farther up the hill, for that would encroach on the new sheep farm. There is therefore a newly built earthen dyke that separates the crofters and their fields from the sheep farm above them, and this division is strictly enforced by the Ground Officer. So the misery of the place is washed on one side by the cold waters of the loch, and on the other by the bleating of sheep, and the barks of the shepherd's dogs, who now occupy the lands, as well as the hills above, where the township used to be.

"When I look upon the hill and see our former homes under sheep, and so many from the township blown here and there, I would like very well if those who are wallowing in wealth would go away instead; go where no crofters would obstruct their wishes. At present, we are blasted with permanent poverty, and that takes away from our courage. We are pulled down under debt and poverty in many ways, which those who are at ease cannot understand.

"So above us now are rough hills that have been our home, the land now almost all rock and heather, closed in on all sides, leaving in the valley a gentle declivity of arable land, dotted over by cairns of stone, as signs of our ancestors. It is from this home with a right of pasturage on the hills, to this place here called Newland that we were sent, where, if it were not a fact that sheep do live, you would not credit that they could live. It is such a place that the people say it is the last place that God created, and that He must have been in a hurry while He did so.

"And on the hill above us now, it is quiet with the sheep of others. Since we were moved down here, and our hill fields taken from us, where we each had ten or twelve sheep and four or five cattle and their followers, many now have no sheep and barely enough for a cow's grass. Milk and cheese are things of the past. It is hard now on the shore, as more and more of us are wandering about in the rain. Last week a preacher came, and he declaimed in the face of a storm and he said that end times were nigh, and that we must gather ourselves for the Lord cometh. We have been indolent and sinful in the eyes of God. We have not followed his instructions. The Lord has spoiled us by giving us gifts. We have not been worthy of them and so they have been taken away. The struggle for us now is to learn to be worthy of God's gifts. In these times, how can we prepare for facing our Lord? Here among the hills and lochs, we must transform ourselves. In the past we were born soldiers. Now it seems we are born to starve or flee. Misery, danger and want fill our days.

"If I were able to go up on the hill, if I were able to rise, I would see that the farmer's sheep have again come down across the dyke and into our fields. There is little we can do, except stand out all night to protect our crops. We asked the proprietor to fix the dyke, and he said go ahead and fix it if you like. But we have neither the money nor the material to do so. I then decided to get a dog to help keep the sheep out, but the Ground Officer said I had to do away with it because it might hurt the farmer's sheep or the Laird's game. I said that I needed the dog to keep our cattle from his fields. I then made my stockyard where it could be seen from the window, and I got a puppy, and then the Forester and the Gamekeeper and the Ground Officer came to me and insisted that I should put out the dog that they might kill it. I hid the dog in a barrel. The Ground Officer told me that if I did not put it out I would be ordered to quit the land. I told them I did not care should they put my family on Black Rock, that they should not get the dog. They left then, but came back when I was not there and killed the dog and left it at my door. So mornings again the sheep are in the corn. And if we protest, it will only be the gallows succeeding the fever.

"An official came around last year, gathering information about the township. I am not sure why. He was with a number of others and he came to me where I was cutting peats up on the heath. He was disgusted about trekking across the bog and he spent a long time in wonderment and complaint to me about the lack of roads.

"'Why do I want roads?' I said. 'There is no where I want to go and there is nothing the road could bring me that I need.'

"Then he asked, 'What rent do you pay?'

"'I have no land.'

"'What do you pay for your house?'

"'Nothing; I have no house but one built between sea water and land, which is habitable only six months of the year. It is dry when the weather is good.'

"'Do the other cottars live in like manner?'

"'They must needs do so.'

"'Where do you get milk if you get any?'

"'I know no such thing as milk.'

"'Then of course you are obliged to take tea, sugar, treacle, and such things, instead of milk?'

"'We are obliged to take gruel.' And he left complaining of his wet boots."

Malcolm has rallied some and is sitting up. "I am old so I want to be as near the truth as I can. We are hemmed in on all sides now, not just by the sheep and the loch, but also by our own poverty. It was bad justice we got when we were sent to this place. It was only for a year we were meant to be here, and they promised to bring us out of it afterward. And when we went to make the Factor keep his promise, he said, 'It was a good thing I did not promise you much.' This world I can no longer understand. Sheep and a purse full of money are the whole go. Years ago, things were not like this. We had enough food and we did not stand in each other's shadows. And the women did not have to work so hard. Now I see women pulling the plough because we cannot feed a horse, and they are waist deep in the waves cutting kelp in the winter wind.

"I was the father of a family myself before I could distinguish between tea and coffee. We always had milk, cheese and butter to eat. The children now can distinguish between the two articles before they are four years of age. They are not at all so innocent in that respect as I was. Yes, my father was forty years of age before he saw ready money. And I remember fifty years ago, that we were clothed with the wool and home-made cloth of our district, whereas today they have senseless rags that they buy here and there in other places. Spending on the godless fashions of France has ruined us all."

Malcolm rests again. Margaret stirs the peat, shaking her head. "We have no clothes of our own in Lewis anymore, although the sheep's wool is everywhere on the hill. It used to be that even the poorest cottar had a few sheep and the family made all their own clothes and bedding and they were warm and dry. All winter long the women and children would be engaged in dying, carding or weaving articles for the family. Enter a home and there would be a whole wall of ells around on which the yarn was wound, maybe dipped in the black oil from fish livers to make it more workable. Then the dying with the grey moss that grows on bare rock to make a rich brown colour, or the soot from the iron pot that makes a nice maroon, or the root of the water lily for black, or heather for a yellow, and dulse for blue. The cloth was then woven at home, or by a neighbour on their loom, and everyone was well-dressed and warm and no one had to leave home to do it. Yes, the places I knew in my young days where the grass could be cut with the scythe are now bare with the proprietor's sheep. I could not tell the history of it. It would take the apostle Paul himself to tell it."

"There are times I wonder, if we should not have gone with my brother Donald," said Malcolm. "I would not have followed him into the King's Army, but when he came home for a time after one of the wars, he said that there was land elsewhere and that we should come, and I wonder now that we should not have all gone with him then. That is twenty-five years ago, and I do not know what happened to him. All I know is he was given land in Nova Scotia after the American War. That is what he told us when he came home the last time. But that was long ago, and it is too late for me now to be thinking of it except that I miss him and I am vexed by our misery here.

"When we were young, the Factor came around—sent by Seaforth himself—and he said that all families must give one son for the regiment he is raising for the King. I was the oldest and already working my own plot and with a family as well. Donald was younger and did not have a family. He also had some difficulties with the Ground Officer over hunting for game, and so the Ground Officer would not give Donald a plot for himself. He was living with our mother and father, which the Ground Officer did not like either. So it was decided that Donald would be the one to go into the army. It was very sad when he left. He was gone for years at a time and whenever he came home he would tell us stories of foreign wars, his times in India, or in the Caribbean, or the Mediterranean Sea. He could see that things were only getting worse in the glen. So when the British Army offered him land after the war in America, he took it. We only knew this when another Lewis man came home after the war and told us. This man had been given land as well, but it was poor land, no better than what he had here, so he came home.

"We heard nothing else of him until years later when Donald arrived home. He had cleared the land he had been given and built a house and had saved enough money to come for a time. Mother and Father were not well so he stayed on to help. And it was over a year before he left again. And then he was lost to us. While he was here, Donald was none too polite in letting those in authority know his thoughts. I believe that if he had stayed, he would have been taken off to Stornoway on one charge or another. They called him a bad neighbour, but he was only speaking his mind. They also told Donald he was no better than the American rabble who had defeated the King. He did not like that much either and he told them: 'It is sad to see that the people whom God created for His own glory should be crowded in together upon each other to make room for big sheep. The landlord says that the land is his, while the Scripture sayth that the earth is the Lord's, and the fullness thereof.' The Factor shook his stick at him for that and threatened to put him and his parents out on the bog, 'so they could be closer to their God.'"

Someone shouts that a boat is returning with the minister from Carloway. Villagers go down to the shore to help pull the boat up the beach. They carry the minister ashore and escort him up to Malcolm's house. He is a new minister and has been to the township only once before to bring his initial greetings.

There had been some commotion among the people and at one point the new minister was accused of being a murderer of souls in his own church. "You aid the devil in damning the all." He retreated quickly and had not been back since. In the meantime, members of the township held their own services on the hillside that they led themselves, or on occasion, by wandering brethren who would appear in the community from time to time.

As the minister approaches Malcolm and Margaret's home, the people who had been inside file out and create an impromptu greeting party as they line the path between the hovels. The minister greets each person before he finally reaches Malcolm's open door, at which point the cow that had come along with the crowd sticks its head out through the roof thatch and lows loudly, as if announcing his arrival.

Malcolm is left alone with the minister except for Margaret, who had made special tea and scones, with butter no less. The minister is thankful for the repast. Having given a blessing, he asks Malcolm if there is any other thing he needs. Malcolm asks him to please hear the peoples' concerns and carry them back to the proprietor. "You are a literate man and you have his ear, I am sure. Except for a few of the young scholars who are at school just now, none of us can do aught but mark an 'X.' Please speak to him and let him know that we are ill-used by his officers. I am sure he is a good man and cares for us, and if he knew our suffering he would come himself and make things right again, as they were in times past."

The minister excuses himself with a prayer and another blessing, and enters the home next to Malcolm and Margaret's where the people of the township gathered. As the minister enters past the animals, the intensity in the peoples' voices moderates, so that by the time he reaches the fire there is an uneasy quiet.

"It is Malcolm's wish that I come and listen to your concerns, that I might communicate them to the proprietor.

Although I have met Lord Seaforth on only two occasions, I would be pleased to hear your concerns, make note of them and pass them on to him, when he returns to Lewis this summer from London."

There is another pause while the members of the township look to one another. Murdo McLeod rises with some solemnity, as if the mention of Lord Seaforth's name and the promise of passing on their concerns has turned this exchange into a more formal proceeding.

"With regard to our land, it is dear, it is bad, and there is little of it. Our ground is peat and bog altogether." Murdo pauses, before starting again. "There was one year everything was blown into the sea. The remains of our crops were delaying the passing of vessels." Murdo's thoughts seem to circumnavigate a broad expanse of past events before they come to rest on the gaunt faces that beseech him through the peat reek. He pauses, swallows, and begins.

"The land above this loch, which nature seemed to mean for man, with all its arable lands, hill pasture, and bays of the sea, offering grand opportunities of comfort, as a reward to human industry, was quite unprecedentedly relieved of the inhabitant population. To the perpetrators of such deeds, the discontentment and bitter feelings of the fugitive inhabitants appear as nothing at all compared to the peculiar pleasure they enjoyed from the fact that now the sheep could graze on the meadows and on heaths so impiously depopulated. Some of these families were evicted to America, others scattered here and there at home, on small patches of land in the less-thought-of districts. There is a man whom the sheep began to chase to three or more different places in Uig, then drove him over to Carloway, and he had no sooner been there than the land was considered too good for him and his family, and so to make room for sheep, his family was turned out again, and they had to make another painful flitting to here as poor scallags at the end of the beach.

"Not only were we removed from our homes to here, our places were crowded first when the neighbouring township was cleared. Six families of that township were thrown in among us; the rest were hounded away to other kingdoms; some to America, some to Australia, and other places they could think of. I hear the cry of the children till this day.

"This is a thing which causes great vexation of spirit among the people: that we see the land which our ancestors brought under cultivation by the sweat of their brows is put under tacksmen, or, as they should more properly be called, desolators of the land, and ourselves heaped upon one another on small patches of the very worst portions of land, and many without any land at all."

After a pause following the first speaker, an older woman rises from the other side of the fire. "I myself was born in Rodel. I saw my mother with her youngest child taken out of the house in a blanket and laid down by the side of a dyke, and her place pulled down. My mother was in child-bed at the time. The child was only born the previous night, and my father asked the Proprietor whether he would not allow them to remain in the house for a few days, but permission was not given. Only when he later came to the dyke-side where she lay, and asked what this was, did he then ask my father to lift her up and remove her to an empty barn, and it was there she was put."

The minister asks, "What has become of the people who were put out by the present proprietor?"

"As we have been telling you," answered the older women with some impatience, "they were removed down to narrow and small places by the shore; some of them have a cow's grass, and some of them are simply cottars. For the last fourteen or fifteen years, I did not put a shoe on my foot, a shirt on my back, or a bonnet on my head, with any profit we derived from the new croft given to us by the proprietor. It was only through selling our labour here and there that we survive at all."

"I know that in times gone by it was easier for people to come through than today," responds the minister as he raises the palm of his hand.

"Those were our times," a hand points out toward the hill, "and we should go back to the old order of things under improved conditions. This is what I think. Unloosen the cords, and allow the people to fill the land again. Let them expand by filling up the central rungs of the land ladder, all of which are absent, rendering it impossible for a crofter, however industrious, to rise higher than he is. To my thinking it is impolitic, as well as unjust, to hem the people into a corner, thereby impoverishing the many to enrich the few. The people of the Outer Hebrides are admirable workers by sea and land, and if they are less persevering than they might be, it is the fault of circumstances."

A man next to the animals steps forward. "Eight or ten years ago the Factor was charging us with being thriftless and worthless; and threatened us with the wholesale importation of Morayside farmers, and the first symptom of that threat being real was the appearance in our midst of a poor Morayside crofter, with all his goods and chattels. It was on the evening of a beautiful Sabbath in summer that this distinguished individual happened to come. He took a good look at his new home, and little time was needed to convince him that he had been miserably duped. So he about-ships, and took his departure across the Ord, a sadder but wiser man. We heard no more of the Speyside crofters."

"I have been told that these changes were made in the name of improvement of conditions and increased efficiency. Has there been no benefit at all?" asks the minister.

"Quite the contrary. We have been dealt with as a herd of sheep driven by dogs into a fank," replies a young man as he rises up and stands above the minister, who remains seated, looking off into a low dark corner. "If any of us would have opened our mouths in protest, we would be sure to have our teeth drawn." The young man leans over him. This final bitterness brings proceedings to an end as the minister rises abruptly, almost butting heads with the final speaker.

"I have noted your concerns and I assure you that I will pass them along when the proprietor returns for his summer visit. You will have to excuse me, but this is all new information. I will also consult my brethren who have been here longer than I and have more experience with these issues."

"Don't listen to them too much. They have not been of any use in the past."

"I am sure there are good intentions on all sides, and common sense will prevail." The minister looks round at the gaunt faces that hover in the peat reek, and smells the manure of the animals as they shuffle in their stalls. He looks down at the iron pot of gruel that hangs above the fire, and the barefoot raggedy presence of the children next to him. The minister looks for a way out. As he passes the animals and leans under the low door frame, the minister almost loses his balance before staggering up into a lope down the hill toward the beach. Members of the township who are to take him back to the glebe hurry after him, out of politeness, although the frightened backward glance of the minister might have created a different impression.

Other members of the township follow along down to the shore. The minister is in the boat when the rest arrive to shove it off into the water. With him in the boat already, and the tide having dropped, the push to the water's edge is much harder, but no one asks the minister to get out. After wading back and forth through the surf for some time carrying ballast aboard, four townsfolk row out through the waves before setting sail to take the minister home.

Cutting Kelp in the Tide

Millie carries a load of kelp up the beach to the three fires that are burning along its length. She feels the heat rising from the glow of the rocked-up trough in the sand. "To be warm and dry, if only for a time." Pick up the pole and stir the liquid chunks. Acrid smoke from the molten kelp burns her eyes. Stand aside while Morag and Mary dump a creel of tangle into the flames, damping the fire temporarily. Millie uses the pole to spread the tangle around in the kiln. Then the vapour turns to smoke, and in a minute flames lick up through the broad green-brown leaves as the heat rises again, and there are hisses and whistles and pops followed by the intense crackle of full flaming.

The tide continues to drop throughout the afternoon, meaning the women will be back down here after midnight as the tide drops again, to roll up their skirts and wade out with a sickle to cut a new swath three feet underwater. Walking on the sand in the dark is easy enough, but the tangle grows on the rocks, and so they are faced with stumbling among the boulders and the surf to cut and gather what they can. Before, when the township used the seaware as fertilizer for their crops, they could wait for a storm to do the harvesting for them, and then they would have to carry it up to the plots only from the wave row at the top of the beach. But now the proprietor wants all the kelp gathered in the spring and early summer so the burned clumps of ash can be collected at one time and shipped to market, where it is used in the making of iodine, glass, and soap.

The women are waist deep in the surf, filling the creel countless times and carrying it up above the tide line to spread the tangle on the beach rocks. Each time, they pause by the fire a while to stir it and warm themselves. Even when they are dripping wet, the home-spuns they wear help keep them warm. Stand by the fire and wring out the long skirt. The tips of it steam in the heat, despite the cold wind. Then it is back you go, yes, back you go. This is what will pay the rent on the croft. The Ground Officer has been trying to take our land away. "It's only a pitiful piece of bog and moss anyway that has never seen a spade until we were put here ten years ago. Has he not the decency at least to leave us be?"

When the township had been evicted from their homes farther up the glen, it was with the promise that Millie and her husband Duncan would get a full plot, whereas now they have only a cow's grass and some potato ground that Malcolm and Margaret have given to them. They live now at all only because of the kelp and Duncan going to the herring fishing in Wick.

As a child, Millie could not remember privation like this. If the family fell short of something in the spring before the new crops came in, there were always neighbours who would share whatever provisions they had. Now Duncan spends a good part of the year away, and Millie spends the spring of the year cutting kelp and tending fires on the beach. Whatever could be grown on the sorry piece of ground could be tended by their two younger children, Donald and Maggie, who could also be trusted to keep an eye on their three sheep and the cow. They have not the land to support themselves, and they have not the money to buy the things they need as a result.

A lot of the best places for seaware are inaccessible to a horse, so the women from the township crawl down the steep cliffs and over the rocks to more distant beaches if there is not a boat nearby to take them. And to the accompaniment of the gulls, they stay there until all the kelp is cut and burned. Then the Factor's boat comes and picks up the ash.

"When we were moved to this patch by the shore, the proprietor made all the kelp his own, and decreed that it would be burned, and the ash exported. None for our crops, none for the sheep to pick through after they returned from the hills. Food from our mouths, that's what it is. And instead we have the privilege to pay him his price for bolls of meal when all our stocks run out. There are days when the cow eats before we do. And with the hill fields taken from us, we no longer have a horse. That is where all their schemes end up, with me pulling the plough in the field, me out at low tide in the surf in the middle of the night, bent at the waist cutting tangle underwater, me pulling the boats up out of the tide, and cleaning and splitting the fish, and spreading the guts on the land. It is no wonder the pipes are not heard in the evenings anymore. Instead, we hear the orders from the Ground Officer, the gripes from the families, and the fears of the shallow thoughtless, the scoffs of the severely wise.

"The kelping is hard enough, but this terrible toil comes at a time when we should be tending to our crops, and it also comes at a time when the fruits of last year's crop have run out, and we are half-starved and in a weakened state. So those of us who are not going to the ebb to cut seaware, are going there to gather whelks or oysters off the rocks so that we will have something to eat. It will be this way until the new crops come in the fall, unless there are some fish in the loch, as there are wont to be now and again. And there are those who say that since we started cutting the kelp, the herring have stayed away.

"So we work night and day now, here and there and every other known place where seaware might grow. And if the Ground Officer, upon inspection, finds unharvested seaware in our area, he deducts his estimate of that amount from our total weight, chiding us for robbing the proprietor of his rightful profits: 'The pretended losses of the cruel men.' So by tomorrow we will finish with gathering the tangle here, and move over the ridge and out toward the open water, where we will stay until all the seaware along that shore has been gathered and burned.

"We would take food with us, except we have none. So some of us will travel over the ridge and along the cliff, climbing down the narrow saddle in the rocks to the beach below. At the same time, others will travel there in the skiff, bringing the sickles, the creels, the stirring poles and an old sail to sleep under. We do this now instead of going to the shielings. We are here now in the cold and wet, instead of up in the hills with the animals.

"The next morning we rise from our beds before light, and pack some of our heavier belongings in the skiff. We stop to say our goodbyes to mother, and to father who waves to us through the smoke. Donald is coming as well, along with Torquil and his sons, Adam and Angus. Leaving the dyke at the edge of our fields, we travel alongside the farmer's sheep, quiet and billowy in the morning light. There is a silence that deepens as we continue to climb, eventually coming to the outlines that mark the foundations of our former township. Donald runs over to the submerged rectangle that used to be our home, and standing in the chewed grass that now covers our hearth, raises his arms in triumph, as he has done at other times when we had permission to come up this way. He left this township when he was three years old, so his rejoicing may be remembering to remember from the stories he has heard, rather than his own remembering.

"Farther on up the hill, we stop to rest at a standing stone where our sheep used to graze. From here we can look down on our new homes below, and the smoke that is still rising from the remains of the fires on the beach. Across the shoulder of the hill, we can also look down to where we are going today, or at least we can see where we will be wading at low tide. The cove itself is below a steep cliff and is out of sight, although we can now hear the surf, as the wind has picked up from that direction. The children run and laugh while Torquil and I sit in silence. It begins to rain. Up until now it has been easy walking, but as we start the descent through the cleft to the beach, the sharp rocks will cut our feet.

"When we finally arrive at the cove, the boat has come and gone, leaving the poles, the sickles, creels, and the old sail for shelter. Donald and the others begin to dig trenches in the small patch of sand among the rocks. After that is done, they carry stones to line the trenches for the fires. There is no sign of the ones we made last year. It is raining harder now, and the wind has picked up. The tide is dropping and there is nothing for it but to pick up the sickle and begin. The salt water and the grit sting the fresh cuts in our feet, but the cold of it is almost a relief. As we cut the tangle from the rocks that are exposed in the falling tide, we slide it into the loop of a heather rope, which, when it is full, we will float ashore as the tide begins to rise again. At the high tide, it will be pulled up on the rocks. Then the creels are filled as we carry the tangle above the tide to be spread and dried. And if not dried, at least the rain will wash out some of the salt so the smoke won't hurt our eyes so much.

"We sleep when dark comes, and then we rise in the middle of the night as the tide begins to fall again. The rain has stopped but the wind has picked up, and the sea makes up into an undertow that throws us around and forces us to carry each armful of tangle ashore, as it will not lie tied in the loop of the rope.

"During low tide the next afternoon, we stop for a time so we can go to the ebb and pick some whelks from the rocks, as we are very hungry. It is hard work when our spirits are low. The bolls of meal are gone, the stores of potatoes and parsnips eaten, and we are forced to live on whelks and nettle soup. If there is a boat nearby, there might be the chance of some fish. Kelping is a tyranny beyond all others.

"As the tide begins to rise again, we take turns tending the fire, while others sleep under the flapping sail. The fire requires constant attention—especially in this wind—as the kelp has to be fed slowly into the fire and care taken that the fire not burn too hot.

"Once the ash has achieved the consistency of moist clay, the kiln is covered with kelp leaves—or turf divots if we are near to home—to protect it from the weather, and it is allowed to cool. The ash is then cut into chunks and set aside in preparation for loading onto the Ground Officer's boat.

"We burn here for three more days until the ash is all prepared. We wait two more days after that for the Ground Officer to come and make sure we have cut all the kelp that is available. He then supervises the loading, castigating us now and again for the poor quality of our work. The ash is weighed aboard the vessel, counting 2200 pounds as a ton, to allow for impurities such as sand and pebbles. Before beginning the work, we had to swear to the Ground Officer that we would not adulterate the kelp with rocks, so as to artificially increase its weight. We are paid 30 shillings cwt. Shortly after that, the boat from the township comes to pick up our tools, and also takes the children back with them, since the wind has died down. Torquil and I climb back up through the cleft in the cliff, and make our way across the hill, silently passing our former homes once again.

"That is how our lives have changed. There is no regard for the seasons. There used to be some ease in our lives, when you could walk on the hill. Fine days to sit in the sun and warm our souls a bit. Now it is drudgery and poverty, as we are hemmed in on all sides. The creel is on our backs continually. Knit and carry, knit and carry. We never see the women now without their creel and their knitting, walking along the path and bent over under the load of divots or tangle, with their needles flying on a pair of socks. Things are dark and hard by land and sea these years."

Gone to the Fishing

"We have slid down the hill like mud in the rain. We have gone from the pasture to the shore and now out into the surf. We have moved the door of our home that had, in the past, faced the animals grazing on the hill, to now face the weather and the water. When we had planting ground and animals, our livelihood seemed near at hand. The animals were in among us sharing our home. But under the circumstances, that life is now far away, and we are left hungry on the shore. Fishing seems farther away, but we are told a livelihood from it is nearer at hand. There are ling, cod, haddock, herring, and lobster if you turn the surface of the loch with a hook or a net or a trap. But how will we ever know them, for they are in the deeps and they will never be living among us. We will never see them in their lives.

"They say the waters along this coast can teem with fish. Go down to the shore. Turn your face away from the land and toward the wet. Not the wet of the horizon, but the wet whose waves you can see now breaking in toward the shore. Turn your hand to the net and not the spade or the herd. It may not be what you want. It may not be what you know. So we move from the desolation on the hills to trafficking the waters in a chase for creatures we will never know and who flee from us in the dark depths. We are strangers on the land and now on the water. We are driven to the edge of our existence.

"For in the past when we were hungry, we could go to our neighbor or to our animals, or if we were all hungry, we would go to the ebb for whelks. But the Proprietor says that the whelks are his. So now we take the sheep skin and instead of making clothing, we sew them into sacks and blow them up to make buoys for our nets or for our hooks. There is nothing for it but to look to the end of the needle that mends our nets, or to the point of a hook. That is our life now, although we have never taken kindly to the sea, given that our forefathers had been engaged in agricultural pursuits for so long. I don't know whether it is to be accounted for by heredity, or otherwise, but it is a fact that we are not in the habit of becoming fishers and sailors entirely.

"For we are accustomed to quiet firths. The petty heavings of the sea were noted only in passing among our fields. We knew nothing of the gigantic workings of the northern sea, which can arise suddenly without apparent cause into mountainous billows, and when the north winds prevail its appearance becomes terrific beyond description. To this raging element, however, we poor people are now compelled to look for our subsistence.

"It is hard to extinguish the love of the land we had in past times, and yet we struggle to accommodate ourselves to this new and appalling circumstance of pursuing the finny race. Nothing could seem more helpless than the attempt to draw subsistence from such a boisterous sea with such poor means as we possess and with the most complete ignorance of seafaring matters. The boats we use are those that regular fishermen had cast off as unserviceable or unsafe, and we poor creatures are obliged to go to sea in them, at the peril of our lives.

"For when we were first moved to the shore, the only way we could get a reduction in rent from the Proprietor—for we had got ourselves into arrears from a number of poor harvests—was if we signed a paper stating we would fish for him. After that, we were forced to fish on the half-catch system, and we had no choice but to sell our fish to the Proprietor, and he paid us any price he liked. He supplied the boat and nets, and for that he kept half the catch. He also kept stores in the place and we were always on the book for our expenses. We had little ready money throughout the year, and when there were fish, all our earning went to pay off our debts. If we had ready money, perhaps we could have gone elsewhere, but we did not. We were completely in the thrall of the truck system, and we felt it very much, because we had no power over our fishing. We had to fish for the tacksman, and never know the price of the fish until we come to settle, and the tacksman could give us just what he pleased. We felt very much aggrieved, and had several meetings among ourselves to see what plan or principle we might honestly and legally decide upon to keep ourselves clear and free, like Englishmen, for they have the boast of liberty. We could boast of none, although we are in Britain. We are in bondage and slavery.

"Although there are fish in the waters off Lewis, there are still no fishing stations or quays to moor a boat. The Proprietor says the fish curers should build their own facilities, while the fish curers say it is the Proprietor's job, since they must pay him a bounty for using his shore for the salting and curing. So, because we have nothing, we can only fish from small boats that can be hauled up on the shore at the end of every day. That makes it dangerous work because of the storms, and very hard work as we have to push the boats out through the surf at daylight. We are then wet as we work the whole day long, and wet again when we come home at night, as we carry our catch ashore. The women are a great help in this, splitting and curing them, but we are much aggrieved by the hardness of the toil, and the danger.

"That is why I went to Wick to the fishing, and after a number of good years, some of us went together and bought a boat there. We all had a share in it, the boat and the nets among the four of us, and Jack was as good as his master. That way is much better. But the fishing at Wick went back and got worse, and so we found ourselves unable to follow the fishing with profit in our own boat. We were losing all the proceeds of the fishing. So a number of us now are hands, working for a share.

"But it is still better in Wick, where the boats are bigger and there are proper mooring facilities. Many of us go for the summer, and return only when it is time to harvest the crops, if the weather has not blasted them, or the farmer's sheep or the proprietor's deer have not eaten them. With the profit from kelp less now, fishing at Wick is the only way many of us keep from slipping into poverty entirely. For in Wick we are not so much on the book, but rather deal in cash. That makes it easier to come and go, and debts do not follow us around so much.

"Night and sleep become strangers when we arrive in Wick. In fishing, it is night and work. The wind dies out, and hopefully the fish come up. We are lying asleep in a row under the forward deck, as we have been at this time over the past two months. If the boats are thrashing on their lines and it is hard to sleep, then we get to sleep. If the boats sway quietly back and forth and nudge each other like sheep in the fold, then we rise and climb to the fires that have been lit on the wharf and have some tea and gruel, before we lower the nets aboard and row out free of the others before raising the sails to make our way further offshore. There are six of us aboard the boat. Two men from Thurso own the boat and are fish curers there. A man from Wick is the skipper, two of the crew are local—a tailor and a shoemaker—who come down from their shops on the fine nights, and the rest of us are from the Western Isles.

"We have fifteen nets aboard, each twelve yards long and ten yards deep. When we reach the grounds there is a fresh wind from the sou'west. We drop the sail so as to lay side to it, and begin to drift the nets out. Along the top line we tie sheepskin buoys that we have blown up and plugged. Along the bottom of the net, we tie rocks on here and there to make it sink, so the net will hang like a curtain in the water, with the buoys glistening in the moonlight. The tide has only just turned to the nor'east, and so it takes us a goodly time to drift the full length of the net out. When the last of them go over the side, we tie the net end to the bowline of the boat, and as it comes tight the boat swings around with the bow up in the wind. There is nothing for it now but to let it drift and keep an eye out for other boats, so as not to get tangled up. We are drifting offshore and are in twenty fathom of water, so there is no worry about shoals. At times there can be more of the herring in close to shore, but then it is easier to get yourself in a fix, caught between other boats and the rocks, especially if there is any sea on at all.

"Our skipper likes the open water and to get away from the others, and I am with him there. We are not the top boat, not anywhere near, but we are in one piece, and are doing well enough, and have lived to tell about it. After we have drifted for an hour, we begin to haul the net back. There is only a handful of fish to pick out of the mesh, and most of them are near the bottom of the net. So as we set the nets back, we add five-fathom pieces of rope between the buoys and the top of the net as it goes back overboard. This way the net will set lower in the water, as there is hope there are more fish farther down. 'They do not want to come to us, so we must go to them,' says the skipper, flicking the last buoy over the side.

"This we leave for a good while more, and begin to haul it back only when we hear a boat to the west of us calling out and making the noises one would associate with fish. When we haul back, there are a goodly number of fish and we begin shaking the net as it comes aboard, reaching over here and there to push the gilled herring back through the mash to the deck. 'So this is where thee are, and this is how I know thee.'

"We set the net back as quickly as we can, and this time we let it drift off the bow for only half the time. And when we haul it back, we have the same number of fish again. And so on through the night, until the herring are above our knees on the deck and the wind picks up as daylight begins in the east. We stow the nets ahead of the forward bulkhead and raise the sails for land. We are the last boat in but for one, and the one that is most heavy-laden. The rest of the fleet stayed closer to shore, and since there was nothing in the shoals, they had come in earlier in the night. Yes, the fish are leaving, then. If we are the outside boat, and have fish and no one else does, then the season is over, unless you want to follow the schools moving south. The curer wants us to go, but we said no. So someone else is coming up here from Banff to take the boat. It is now mid-September and most of the herring boats have already left for Fraserburgh and Peterhead that morning. For those like me, it is now time to return home to the Long Island to work on the harvest. Later in the day, we will be paid for our share of the catch. It should be enough to balance the rent-roll with the Proprietor and also to buy supplies for the winter. There is nothing for it but to find a way to make the journey home."

Sailing for Cape Wrath

Men from Barra have their own boat and have offered me passage back to Lewis. In return, there is a stack of flagstone now piled on the quay that needs to be delivered to Seaforth Lodge in

Stornaway. After we unload the cargo there, I will make my way home on foot, if I cannot find a local boat going to the township. A number of other boats will be similarly laden and will be leaving in company for Stornaway, as has been arranged by an agent of the Lord's. It is good for all, because the boats would have to ship ballast in any case, if they are to sail for home through the rough waters of Pentland Firth and around Cape Wrath.

Along with the horse-drawn carts that are unloading the flagstone, fish-curing crews are still hard at work. A long row of women are splitting, gutting, and packing the last of the catch into wooden barrels, while a line of men set the lids and pound the metal rings into place, while another group of men with barrows wheel them away to be stacked and stored for shipping to Germany. These crews of men and women will be moving south along the coast with the curers in the days ahead, finishing up in the north of England later in the fall.

At daylight the next morning many of the herring boats leave for the south, and there is now room to tie up along the quay below the heaps of flagstone. As we are waiting for the tide, we lift the floorboards of the deck and clean out the bilge. Herring scales float like mica in the water as it is bucketed over the side. The slabs of stone are lowered carefully aboard using a block and tackle and are distributed around on the timbers. The boat is twenty-four feet long, with a beam of ten feet, so a thousand pounds of stone set her down quite well in the water, leaving only about sixteen inches of freeboard. The boat is only partially decked over, which means it will be necessary to keep it headed up into the wind. This will be difficult if the wind is in our faces, since there is just the one sail for tacking back and forth.

By eleven o'clock, we are loaded and laying outside of the breakwater waiting for the last of the boats to take on their cargo. When we have all rowed beyond the line of rocks that would be our last shelter for the next five or six days, we step our masts and jog north in a light sou'west wind.

As dark comes on, we pass John o' Groats and the island of Stroma and haul to the west'ard until we are beyond Dunnet Head. The sou'west wind freshens when we are no longer in the lee of the land. The fleet sacrifices headway by tacking close to the wind and remaining near to shore, rather than setting out across Pentland Firth, where the hills of Hoy are just visible as the sun goes down.

Throughout the night the wind checks in to the south and increases to gale force, driving us farther out into open water, despite our efforts. All we are able to do is keep the boat headed up into the wind and take turns bailing water out of a space midships that we have left purposely between the stones and timbers. One man at the tiller, one man bailing, four men under the foredeck, all taking their turn.

By daylight, we are exhausted, wet and cold. The cliffs of Hoy are now clearly visible in the slanting rays of the morning light. The wind takes away our breath and it has begun to rain. By noon, the township of Rackwick can be seen to the nor-west, set in a low break in the cliffs along the coast of Hoy. If the wind had not been so strong, we could have tacked to the east'ard of Hoy earlier and sailed into the calm waters of Scapa Flow. But that is not possible now.

For the rest of the day, all attention is focused on surviving the next wave breaking over us. Being dashed on the cliffs seems like a far-off eventuality compared with bailing and steering, as the boat keeps wanting to turn side-to-it, despite our sea anchor. The water in the bilge surges fore and aft between the flagstones and timber frames, as the boat pitches down into a trough, and then rises up again like the palm of a hand holding back the surge of the next wave.

We have long ago given up trying to make headway and are struggling now just to stay afloat, hoping there might be enough sea room to carry us beyond the cliffs. But there is a strong current coming in from the Atlantic and we seem doomed to make land.

The anchor is readied as we get nearer to Hoy, and we throw it as a last attempt to keep from going ashore. As the next wave rises up the anchor line comes tight, and then pops loose again as the anchor not so much drags as springs from the bottom. On the next rise, the anchor catches and the line comes tight with a crack, tearing out the top half of the bow stem.

Amid the roar of the wind and waves, there is now the deep continuous thunder of the breakers on the cliffs. The sun is setting again and for a time we can see the faint lights of Rackwick, before they disappear behind a promontory of rock. All of the boats are in the embrace of the cliffs, except for the one that had left the quay last and had been trailing the fleet before the wind checked in and drove them to open water. This last boat is well enough to the east'ard that it is blown into the sheltered water between Hoy and Flotta.

For the rest, they are carried one last time to a great height atop a wave. At that moment, the force of the wave turns the boats so that they are pointed toward the cliff rather than out to sea. All those aboard hold their places as the boat descends into a following trough and is then thrown against the cliffs by the next wave. The crew and cargo are strewn among the boulders, a collection now of shards in the tangle and the swirl.

Ceremonies for the Dead

Malcolm's coffin is made of wood gathered from the beach. It is tied to two oars that aid in the carrying of it from the dwelling to the shore. Mourners follow between the rows of stone and thatch. Meandering to avoid the stacks of peat piled next to each home, the group of crofters descends the steep bank. There is rough going across the rocks, and when they reach the narrow strip of sand at the edge of the water, they gather for a minute before moving into the surf where the skiffs are being steadied out beyond the breaking waves by several women, their heavy woollen garments tucked up above their knees.

The coffin is raised unnecessarily high above the waves before the weight of it comes to rest across the gunwales of one of the skiffs. Several men jump up into the skiff, and the coffin is then shifted into the bottom of the boat. Led by Margaret and Millie, the skiffs fill with mourners, moving out gradually into deeper water so as not to ground out in the troughs of the swells.

Only a short time before, Malcolm fished from one of the skiffs that is now carrying him across the loch. A breeze comes up and the mast is stepped and the sail is set. They make good time in reaching the small island in the loch. Because there is no good place to land, several men and women jump into the water to steady the skiffs in the surf so that one end of the set of oars supporting the coffin can be shifted to those in the water while the other end rests on the gunwales. Others then jump into the water and take up the other end of the oars, and the procession moves up through the surf to the steep bank. The rest of the mourners climb down into the sea as they fall in behind those carrying the coffin. The skiffs are then pulled up on the rocks. In a world without roads, the preferred transportation of the dead is by water, whenever possible. If not by water, then it is the rough going of carrying the coffin over the uneven ground of the moor, and later, with burning peats held high, making their way back home.

No fence, no church, no names on the stones; just rough shards at the head and foot pushing up through the moss and bracken. Once up among the graves, there is a discussion about the appropriate place to bury Malcolm. Central to the conversation is a recitation of those who already lay below the turf. The mourners move from stone to stone as ancestors are recounted. Eventually, the place for the grave is agreed upon, and spades are passed around. Beginning with his oldest daughter Millie, Malcolm's family breaks out the turf that has taken root in the rocks and sand. The turf is set aside, and in succession others take turns at the digging.

There are nods around as the group surveys the grave that is now about four feet deep. Malcolm's coffin is brought over and set down on the clods of turf. The heather ropes that had lashed the oars to the coffin are untied. The oars are shifted out from under it. The ropes are now used to swing the coffin over the hole. As it is lowered down, the mourners silently gather. Millie steps forward and crosses herself and recites a prayer:

Blessèd is thee and blessèd are we
For thee is commended
Unto thy hands
Forever.

There are several loud cries of grief from those assembled. Malcolm is keened into the grave and on to the next life, the depth of feeling being the element on which the spirit is carried away. Then the spades are again passed round and the grave is filled in. Turfs and ash that have been brought from home are placed on top along with the fresh earth. Stone markers, recently retrieved from the beach, are set at the head and foot. Margaret and Millie remain by the grave while others wander among the stones pointing down and speaking in low voices to each other. Some spread pieces of peat from home on the other graves.

Gradually a group of mourners gather down by the boats beneath a ledge of rock. They pass around a bottle of aqua vitae and a tin of biscuits. In discussing Malcolm's passing, the crofters also call up stories of the township of which Malcolm had been so much a part.

"He was the best and truest man in the glen."

"Malcolm has seen very difficult times, all of us have, but we are people with whom the fates will have to bargain before we are annihilated."

"You say so, Adam, but as a consequence of the hardship we have endured in these times, we are unable to do more for ourselves. Our fires were quenched, and many of our hearts are broken. Our children have left, and many of us have not done much afterward. And now we are paupers."

"Last spring we began to wake up stones to erect a new house, but our son said he was going to America, which put a stop to our proceedings."

"And for aught we know if we go away, fortune might so far befriend us, but death might come upon us also."

"Yes, our fires were quenched. Had you seen it, you could scarcely bear the sight. Our houses were broken down and our fires were extinguished."

"And when we were sent to the bog on the seashore to make room for sheep, we had no idea what to do and we were tumbling on the ground and greeting and tearing the grass with our hands. Any soft-minded person would have pitied us."

"For the land our forefathers lived upon so happy and prosperous is now under sheep, while we are huddled together in this small township on the seashore, exposed to all the fury of the wild breezes, which generally carry away the little corn we have. Every good piece of land was taken from us and we were planted on every spot for which no other use could be found."

"It is like penal servitude for people to cultivate such a place. It was a bleak spot before we got there, but it is a far bleaker spot now that we are here. It is a place where hardly a snipe could live."

"My brother, who is buried up behind us, lost his reason because of all the changes. At the last, he said, 'I am lost and want nothing at all. I want nothing but raiment and daily bread, if the Lord provides that for me.' He died out there on the hill, wandering."

"God bless him."

"And our only reward in this life is that we are allowed to gaze with admiration on the retreating wheels of the proprietor's carriage when he is going away."

Some go down to tend the boats on the shore, others gather up the spades. The prayer said over the grave when they all gathered to lower the coffin is the only ceremony performed, along with the prayers that had been said over it before it was removed from the dwelling. Slowly, the mourners—the whole township, really, or what is left of it—begin to make their way back down the hill through the heather to the skiffs that are once again out in the water, awaiting the procession. Beyond them the gulls bob, hoping the assembled skiffs mean that herring are being dried up in nets on the shore.

After the mourners climb into the skiffs, much effort is called upon to row out through the breakers and into the chop. The trip back across the loch is against the wind so the sails are stowed for the hard row ahead. Although it is June, the water chills the wind that blows across it.

Standing on the beach near the still-smoldering kiln of kelp and looking across at the approaching boats, a twelve-year-old boy is gathering whelks with the younger children. He looks out now and again as the skiffs make their slow progress into the wind, each alternately disappearing in the troughs of the swells. As they reach the lee of the land, the tops no longer break off the chop, and easier progress is made. There is much commotion as the skiffs finally land on the beach and are pulled up out of the tide.

"That is enough for today, Donald," says Millie. "Gather the other children and come up to the house for some cakes. I only wish Duncan had returned from Wick in time for the funeral."

Remittances Home

Chapter III
Hudson Bay, Seventeenth to Nineteenth Centuries

Chapter IV
Long Spruce Rapids, Nelson River, 1976

These two migrant narratives of crofters and fishers are situated in outposts near the shores of Hudson Bay. The Scottish crofters from Orkney and Lewis, who came to the Nor' Wast to work for the Hudson's Bay Company, were some of the first migrant labourers in Modernity. With regard to the fishers, one of the dominant migrations in the latter part of the twentieth century in Canada has been made up of people moving from the faltering economies of the Atlantic Provinces to the resource-rich Canadian West.

In the case of the crofters, they came to the New World to supplement a threatened way of life in communities back in the Highlands and Islands by signing on for a term as "wintering servants" in the fur trade. As Philip Goldring states: "Enlisting with the Company was a way to avoid emigrating: it solved a short-term cash problem at home without uprooting a person for good from their friends and native place.... They went not to build a new society but to sustain, from a distance, their old one." Even if it was considered at the time to be only temporary, the transition from subsistence relations to migrant working-class relations—although depicted as a "natural" next step in the "culture of improvement"—retains in the narrative presented here all the dislocation and alienation these subsistence groups experience when entering the wage economy.

This same dislocation and alienation is central to the experience of Atlantic Canadian migrant workers who went "out west" in the 1970s to work on mega-projects such as the building of a hydroelectric dam on the Nelson River near Hudson Bay. This section presents the stories of wintering servants and construction workers who came to Hudson Bay to endure a harsh existence in order to earn ready money in aid of life back home.

The reality of workers sending money as remittances to support their families permeates large areas of the Global South, and is an increasingly noteworthy aspect of a globalizing economy, in some cases outstripping foreign aid that supports communities struggling to survive. Currently, large numbers of Atlantic Canadians are working in the tar sands in northern Alberta so as to support families back in coastal communities. In the mid-1970s, I worked for six months on the Manitoba Hydro dam on the Nelson River at the Long Spruce rapids. There were many Atlantic Canadians there as well, and each had a story to tell about the social and economic constraints that brought them to this place.

The unique geological features of the land just west of Hudson Bay brought the fur traders, and later the Hydro engineers, who would make use of the rivers that linked the central continent with salt water. The Churchill, the Hayes, and the Nelson are the only rivers that flow across the Canadian Shield from inland North America and reach the salt water of Hudson Bay. Otherwise, the Shield is an erosion-resistant divide where rivers inside the ring of rock flow across the Hudson Bay Lowlands to salt water; while rivers outside the ring, such as the Mackenzie and the St. Lawrence, flow around it as they are fed by smaller rivers that flow away from the Shield. Because this geological feature links a huge navigable continental watershed with the saltwater ports like York Factory and Fort Churchill, it became an important route in the expansion of the fur trade from the seventeenth to the nineteenth centuries. The drops in elevation of these same rivers as they crossed the Shield and descended into the Hudson Bay Lowlands, when combined with the large volume of water in this system, later became central reasons why the Province of Manitoba embarked on a series of ambitious hydroelectric projects in the 1960s.

This territory therefore created outposts of progress that drew crofters in the eighteenth and nineteenth centuries to work in the fur trade, and fishers in the mid-twentieth century to work on hydro-dam construction. Whether it is the crofter in the frost-bitten hovels of the trading post with the Hudson's Bay Company, or the uprooted fisher plunked down in the antiseptic alienation of the hydroelectric dam work-camp on the Nelson River, these extreme environments engendered a world from which it is hard to return to one's community unchanged. These sojourners exist in an ill-begotten world, neither home nor away.

As extreme as these environments were for the migrants, they are, of course, home to the Swampy Cree, whose spiritual views and day-to-day life were deeply rooted in the places that the migrants found so difficult. The historical record is full of references to the many calamities the ill-suited migrants experienced, and the unfolding disasters witnessed by the First Nation groups who passed by on their seasonal rounds, helping where they could with whatever food they had to share, before shifting along to their next campsite. So the Cree become themselves a "cloud of living witnesses to the destruction of their homes" as they suffered the incursions of the fur trade, the settlers, and finally the hydro engineers.

CHAPTER III

Hudson Bay, Seventeenth to Nineteenth Centuries

History from Above

The harbours of Stromness in Orkney and, later, Stornoway in Lewis were ports of call for Hudson's Bay Company ships that departed each spring for the Nor' Wast. Along with stowing supplies and taking on water, the ships would sign on crew members who were engaged by the company to work in the posts on the bay, as well as to transport goods and to venture inland to set up forts on the rivers.

The initial trans-Atlantic departures from Stromness were largely made up of adventurers in search of a Northwest Passage that would lead them to the riches of the Far East. As these dreams of instant wealth met with one disaster after another, the more pedestrian goals of securing fur trade routes and building posts inland became a more attainable and lucrative enterprise in the Nor' Wast. The infrastructure put in place by the fur trade served later as a conduit for settlers, such as the dispossessed Kildonan crofters, who were transported across the Atlantic aboard Hudson's Bay Company ships, and then travelled inland in company York boats to Red River to establish an English presence in what became Manitoba.

History from Below

LOGIN'S WELL

THERE WATERED HERE
THE HUDSON BAY COY'S Ships
1670–1891
CAPT COOK'S VESSELS
RESOLUTION AND DISCOVERY
1780
Sir JOHN FRANKLIN'S Ships
EREBUS AND TERROR
On Arctic Exploration
1845
Also the Merchant Vessels of Former Days
Well Sealed Up 1931

Login's Well is adjacent to a cobbled street next to the harbour in Stromness, Orkney. With the town rising above it on a steep hill, the harbour faces east toward Bring Deeps and on to Scapa Flow, with the island of Mainland to the north, and Graemsay to the east. Hoy is to the south across a narrow ten-knot tideway leading to the Atlantic Ocean. All the islands of Orkney are rolling, treeless, and pastoral except for Hoy, where Ward Hill rises like a sentinel, ever watchful over the changeable weather.

Water from Login's Well was bucketed into wooden barrels that then were sealed for their long sea voyage. They were rolled up planks into ox carts that then clattered along the narrow streets of Stromness to the wharves where vessels lay at high tide. The barrels were lashed along the rails or were lowered into the hold. Once all the supplies were taken care of by local hands, the ship's captains and the chandlers would come down from their quarters to make sure all was in order for the voyage ahead.

Those first voyageurs who drank the water from Login's well ventured out across the North Atlantic in search of a route to the riches of the Far East, where it was believed that spices and jewels lay on top of the ground for all to take. The captains and crews on these ventures had come from many different ports of call before arriving in Stromness and had received their charters from authorities across Europe.

This search in North Atlantic waters consigned these crews to the ice-jammed channels at the top of the new continent to the west. Henry Hudson was one such adventurer who sailed into a bay in 1610 with this dream of riches, and he and his son, along with seven crew members, lived out a nightmare of mutiny, as the *Discovery* sailed home without them. Thomas Button arrived in the same bay two years later and was trapped in the fast-forming ice, forcing him and his crew to spend the winter on what became known as Hudson Bay. Button too witnessed the perils that awaited the many explorers who followed him and his crew in their own searches for the East:

"This morning was calme but the night before was full of Strange Harbours, as they call them, which is a streame in the Element like the flame that cometh forth the mouth of a hot oven, which upon this coast how faire so ever the weather be, when you see them, yet it is an infallible signe of a storme to follow…"

After surviving the winter in the mouth of the Nelson River, where one of his ships was crushed in the ice, Button spent the following summer searching unsuccessfully for the Northwest Passage in the blind rivers and ice-chocked channels of these waters before returning to England.

Seven years after Button, Jens Munck, a Dane, became trapped in the ice of Hudson Bay while searching for a passage to the Orient. As the cold of winter deepened, his crew of sixty-four began to die. Although he was too weak to leave his bunk during that winter, Munck kept a diary, much of it written while his cabin boy lay dead on the floor beside him:

"Jan. 25—I had the body of Hans Brock buried and ordered two small cannon to be discharged, which was the last honour I could show him. But the trunnions burst off both falconets and the man who fired them very nearly lost both his legs, so brittle had the iron become on account of the sharp and severe frost." When spring finally came, Munck and the two remaining crew members managed to crawl ashore and grub for roots and grasses. After regaining some of their strength, they set off in the smaller of the two ships and with great difficulty managed to sail back to Europe.

After a very difficult crossing of the ocean in which he was besieged by storms and pack-ice, Thomas James and his crew reached the waters of the bay in July of 1631. He had with him in the pocket of his vestments a letter from the King of England that he was to present to the Emperor of Japan. Their search for the passage yielded no route to the East and they spent a very difficult winter trapped in the ice at the head of what became known as James Bay. The following summer, they refloated their vessel and sailed north, replenished by flocks of migrating geese. At one point they spotted a herd of caribou onshore and sent several men off in the ship's boat, along with the two greyhounds they had brought along on the voyage for hunting purposes. But "the deere ran clear away from them at pleasure. We tired the dogs and wearied ourselves, but to no purpose." Since the dogs proved to be of no use, this "caused them to be left ashore" when the boat and crew returned to the vessel. Four months later, James limped into Bristol harbour with a discouraging tale about "so unknown a place."

Near the end of the seventeenth century, winter residences were established on the bay. In 1708, John Oldmixon wrote in his journal: "We were loath to let our history open with the Description of so miserable a Wilderness and so wretched a colony. For rich as the trade to these Parts have been or may be, the way of Living is such that we cannot reckon any Man happy whose lot is cast upon the Bay...for that country is so prodigiously cold that Nature is never impregnated by the Sun; or rather her barren Womb produces nothing for the subsistence of Man." Life at outposts on the bay such as Fort Prince of Wales, which was built to resist French incursions, was very difficult. James Isham writes: "The walls of our houses we here live in are 2 foot thick of Stone—the windows small with 3 inch wooden shudders, which is Close Shut 18 hours Every Day, in the winter, four large fires are made in Large Brick Stoves (Built for that purpose). Everyday, which as soon as the wood is burn't down to a coal, the top of the chimney is close stop't with an iron cover, this keeps the wood within the houses, tho' at the same time, the smoo'k makes our heads ac'h, and very offensive and unloesome—Notstanding of which 4 or 5 hours after the fire is out and the chimney still close stop't the inside of the wall of our houses are 6 or 8 inches thick of Ice, which is Every Day cutt away with Hatchetts—three or four times a Day we make iron shot of 24 lb. weight hott in the fire and hang up at the windows of our apartments, yet will not hinder a 2 gallon Bottle of water freezing by the fire side as already observed."

Farther south, at York Factory, clerk Joseph Robson records different challenges: "Fort York, at the mouth of the Nelson was built of logs of white fir eight or nine inches square, which are laid one upon the other. In the summer, the water beats between the logs, keeping the timber continually damp; and in the winter the white frost gets through, which being thawed by the heat of the stoves, has the same effect; so that with the water and the damp below, the timber both of the foundation and the superstructure rotts so fast, that in twenty-five or thirty years the whole fort must be rebuilt with fresh timber." Robson had a similar view of the stone fort at the mouth of the Churchill River, on which he had worked: "Instead of a defensible fort capable of resisting the force of an enemy, it had in many places yielded to its own weakness and the attacks of wind and weather and was not only unworthy of the name by which it was distinguished, but even of the persons at whose cost it was built."

James Knight wrote home in 1714: "My own Place I have to live in this Winter is not half as Good as our Cowhouse at the Bottom of the Bay back home. Since I have been without a Candle it is so black and Dark Cold and Wett with all nothing to make it better but heaping up Earth About it to make it warm." By the end of his time in the Nor' Wast, Knight may have yearned to be back in such a place. He and his crew set out in 1719 from York Factory to find the rumoured riches of the East. They were not heard from again.

Landing at Marble Island many years later, Samuel Hearne reported on a possible explanation for the disappearance of Knight and his crew: "They found guns, anchors, cables, bricks, a smith's anvil, and many other articles, which the hand of time had not defaced, and which being of no use to the natives, or too heavy to be removed by them, had not been taken from the place in which they were originally laid. The remains of the house, although pulled to pieces by the Esquimaux for the wood and iron, are as yet very plain to be seen, as also the hulls, or more properly speaking, the bottoms of the ship and sloop, which lie sunk in about five fathoms of water, toward the head of the harbour. The figurehead of the ship, and also the guns, were sent home to the company, and are certain proof that Messrs. Knight and Barlow had been lost on this inhospitable island, where neither stick nor stump was to be seen, and which lies near sixteen miles from the mainland."

Hearne continued: "In the summer of 1769, while we were prospecting the fishery, we saw several Esquimaux at this new harbour; and perceiving that one or two of them were greatly advanced in years, our curiosity was excited to ask them some questions concerning the above ship and sloop, which we were better able to do by the assistance of an Esquimaux, who was then in the company's service as a linguist and annually sailed in one of their vessels in that character. The account which we received from them was full, clear and unreserved, and the sum of it was to the following purport:

"'When the vessels arrived at this place (Marble Island) it was very late in the fall, and in getting them into the harbour, the largest received much damage, but on being fairly in, the English began to build the house, their number at the time seeming to be about fifty. As soon as the ice permitting in the following summer (1720), the Esquimaux paid them another visit, by which time the number of English was greatly reduced and those that were living seemed very unhealthy. According to the account given by the Esquimaux, they were then very busily employed, but about what they could not easily describe, probably in lengthening the long boat; for at a little distance from the house there is now lying a great quantity of oak chips, which have been most assuredly made by the carpenters.

"'Sickness and famine occasioned such havoc among the English, that by the setting in of the second winter their number was reduced to twenty. That winter (1720) some of the Esquimaux took up there, above on the opposite side of the harbour to that on which the English had built their houses, and frequently supplied them with such provisions as they had, which chiefly consisted of whales' blubber, and seals' flesh and train oil. When the spring advanced, the Esquimaux went to the continent, and on their visiting Marble Island again, in the summer of 1721, they found five of the English alive, and those were in such distress for provisions that they eagerly ate the seals' flesh and whales' blubber quite raw, as they purchased it from the natives. This disordered them so much, that three of them died in a few days, and the other two, though very weak made a shift to bury them. Those two survived many days after the rest, and frequently went to the top of an adjacent rock, and earnestly looked to the South and the East, as if in expectation of some vessels coming to their relief! After continuing there a considerable time together, and nothing appearing in sight, they sat down close together, and wept bitterly. At length one of the two died, and the other's strength was so far exhausted, that he fell down and died also, in attempting to dig a grave for his companion. The skulls and other large bones of these two men are now above ground close to the house. The longest liver was, according to the Esquimaux account, always employed in the working of iron into implements for them; probably he was the armourer or smith.'"

Such skills as could have been useful around the village forge were all but useless here in a land of skin and horn. Grand schemes and inappropriate skills confounded the strangers, although they became passably good at digging graves. This blindness to necessity was evident in Sir John Franklin's journey to the polar sea. He and his military crew arrived in Stromness to prepare for their first excursion to the west. Because of the abundance of herring in the Orkney islands that year, Franklin had a difficult time recruiting carriers and boatmen for his trip. The reluctance of Orkney men to sign on might also have had to do with the travails of the journey that were outlined to them. Rather than venture into the treacherous waters to the north of Hudson Bay, Franklin was to carry out an overland assignment given him by the British Admiralty. He was to search for the polar sea by first travelling along the rivers to the west of Hudson Bay and then head north to the Coppermine River, which was known to empty into the polar sea. On arriving at the mouth of the river, he was to travel east, mapping the coastline for five hundred miles.

As would have been well known among those who had returned to Orkney from the Nor' Wast, this route was full of toil and danger for those charged with the tasks of rowing the boats and portaging the large amounts of equipment and supplies that Franklin regarded as essential to his success. As Franklin stated at the time regarding the crofters, they had a "fearful apprehension either of great danger that would attend the service or that we should carry them further than they would agree to go" and that these crofters "looked narrowly into the plan of our route, and still more circumspectly at the prospect of return." These possible crew members were the first, but by no means the last, to express reservations about the viability of Franklin's project.

After crossing the Atlantic in a Hudson's Bay Company ship, Franklin's group gathered at York Factory before venturing along the Hayes River. It was already clear that there would be troubles ahead. His party took over a month to reach Lake Winnipeg, even after shedding large amounts of equipment that other groups were supposed to deliver to him after they arrived at Cumberland House on the Saskatchewan River. Conditions deteriorated quickly as winter set in. There was already a shortage of food, and the supports Franklin was promised by the Hudson's Bay Company and the North West Company did not materialize. As they set out northward across land in search of Great Slave Lake, the voyageurs who accompanied him were carrying hundred-pound loads and the work dogs struggled in the deep snow. Although Franklin did eventually arrive at the mouth of the Coppermine River, little mapping was done as members of the group starved and froze to death during the two years they were gone. Among the half of the group that did eventually return to York Factory, there was talk of murder and cannibalism.

For explorers such as Franklin, the land was an inhospitable barrier for which he had little feeling and which he struggled to overcome. Even those Indigenous bands and voyageurs, well adapted as they were to the place, and who showed him every kindness, and who bent a knee in his service, suffered greatly at the hands of these grand designs. Later hailed as a hero of Victorian culture, Franklin was the cause of a cascading storm of suffering for all who came across him.

Life in the Nor' Wast

As other routes to the Far East were found in the Southern Ocean, the grandiose dreams of a Northwest Passage gave way to more proximate opportunities for ships heading out across the Atlantic from Stromness. This was especially true after the British charter for Rupert's Land was granted in 1670, which gave company merchants control of the drainage basin surrounding Hudson Bay, along with the watershed of the Nelson River, stretching all the way to the Rocky Mountains. This commercial-minded group drank the waters of Login's Well as a matter of course as they travelled back and forth to the posts that were established on the bay.

Rather than finding a passage through the land to the riches of the East, the Hudson's Bay Company ships returned each fall with the animal skins they had bartered from those who were native to the place. The land was no longer a barrier to the fulfilment of dreams; it instead became a repository of goods that were in demand in the centres of culture. Over the next hundred years, voyages back and forth across the Atlantic, as well as the routes inland from Hudson Bay, became well established, as did trading relationships with those who made this territory their home.

During the long days of summer in Stromness over three centuries, Hudson's Bay Company ships came and went, the cannon at the mouth of the harbour announcing arrivals. Sailing up from London, the ships took on supplies from the warehouses that line the harbour. Repairs were done. The stink of pitch rose from the steel drums as ropes were coated and ships' timbers swabbed in preparation for the long trip ahead.

But the main purpose of the stop in Stromness was to take on "wintering servants" who had signed contracts to work in the fur trade posts in the Nor' Wast. The ships would depart in the spring or early summer of the year, laden with the wares of civilization: rifles, blankets, animal traps, knives and pots, along with the newly conscripted crofters. In the fall, the ships would leave the fast-forming ice in Hudson Bay and return to Scotland with 80,000 to 100,000 beaver pelts, along with the servants who chose to return home after their contracts had been honoured.

> Wanted for the Hon. Hudson's Bay Company's Service.
> Several Stout, Active YOUNG MEN as LABOURERS,
> And a Few BOATBUILDERS and BLACKSMITHS
> Parties intending to engage will require to lose
> no time in coming forward, the time for engage-
> ments in Orkney being limited.
> Certificates as to moral character, age, and fitness
> For the service will be required as usual, and, to
> Save time, should be brought at once.
> > Apply to
> > Edward Clouston
> > Agent for the Company
> > Stromness

At the beginning of the Hudson's Bay Company tenure in Rupert's Land, the great majority of the recruits who worked for the Company in its forts came from Orkney. In the nineteenth century, the balance shifted to the Isle of Lewis, with Stornoway becoming a major port of call for those who signed on to be "slaves in a savage land." The shift from Orkney to Lewis reflected the levels of misery that had risen more sharply in Lewis than they had in Orkney. As a result of the displacement and poverty in the early nineteenth century, more Lewis crofters were willing to leave their homes on the promise of work—no matter how severe the privations—and to do so at lower wages. The competition to sign up workers for the fur trade became so intense that in Stornoway in 1811, at a reception held by Lord Seaforth, a fight broke out between recruiters of the Hudson's Bay Company and those from the North West Company.

One of the main tasks of the "winter servants" was to work as crew on the York boats that carried supplies to the inland posts and, on the return journey, transported the fur pelts to York Factory for shipment back to Britain. This opportunity was one of the few offered to crofters to supplement their failing prospects—the other was enlistment in the British military—as they were caught between rising rents in the Highlands and Islands, and the meagre funds they could raise while working their small plots of land. The company continued to depend on Orkney and Lewis crofters because they would work for less than the Métis in North America, who had other options near at hand and were well able to live off the land, being not so tightly thrown in together as the crofters were.

The conditions in Lewis became increasingly dire throughout the nineteenth century, and so there was a steady increase in workers from Lewis signing up for five-year terms, leading the Hudson's Bay Company to assign a resident agent to Stornoway. Indeed, the Factor on Lewis helped the recruiting agents to meet their quota by identifying those crofters who were in arrears on the rent for their croft, so that pressure could be exerted on them to sign up. Becoming a wintering servant for the Hudson's Bay Company therefore was a way to avoid looming expulsion and possible emigration. So rather than being a stepping stone to the building of a settler society in a "new" land, going to the Nor' Wast was predicated on the opposite: it aimed to inject much-needed money into the crofter accounts so as to enable them to remain in their place.

Although the goal of the migrant workers was to preserve life at home, upon their return from abroad these temporary exiles, according to Reverend Liddell of Orphir in Orkney, "bring home with them all the vices, without any of the virtues of savages: indolence, dissipation, irreligion, and at the same time, that having earned a little money, they are enabled to overbid the honest, industrious farmer, who is encumbered with a number of small children, and who perhaps may have fallen into a temporary arrear, upon whom the unfeeling landlord has no compassion." So the survival of the community was not only an economic matter of paying off debts, the selling of one's labour in the Nor' Wast could undermine the crofter townships from within by introducing the coarsened behaviour of former employees and the commercial relations of which they had been a part.

In the transporting of goods and furs for the Hudson's Bay Company, these workers followed the Hayes River because it ran along a friendlier path between Hudson Bay and Lake Winnipeg than did the Nelson River. Therefore the four-hundred-mile route along the Hayes River, as it passed through the Hudson Bay Lowlands and then crossed the Shield before arriving at Norway House on the northern edge of Lake Winnipeg, was the main commercial route that supported the activities of the Hudson's Bay Company between 1670 and 1870.

The watercraft that was commonly used on this route was a York boat, an adapted version of an Orkadian fishing vessel, with a flat bottom and raked sides as well as raked bow and stern. Most York boats measured thirty feet along the keel, with an overall length of forty-two feet. They were nine feet wide and three feet deep and could carry up to five thousand pounds of cargo. They were steered by means of an oar that passed through an iron ring in the sternpost. Each boat had about eight crew, with one steering, one with a bow oar for manoeuvring in the many rapids, and with five or six crew working the oars, along with a provisional sail for crossing lakes in a favouring wind.

After the ice went out and spring floods subsided, the boats would leave York Factory, which is situated in the mouth of the Hayes River. Sailing inland on a favouring wind and carried by the flooding tide through the collapsing white mud banks and toppled trees, a York boat might travel five miles before running aground in the shallows at the head of the estuary. For the next one hundred miles, it was necessary to pole along through the mud flats of the Hudson Bay Lowlands or pull the boat by a line on rough towpaths on the river-bank. Many times, it was a combination of the two, with crew members wading in the freezing water to free the boats from shoals. Tracking along a tow line was rough work, given the vagaries of the landscape, and so turns were taken on the slow ascent. At the many portages along the way, this work became more difficult as the rocks of the Shield began to appear in the landscape.

Upon entering the Shield, the crew were faced with many more portages, over which the boat as well as the cargo had to be dragged or carried. There was also a succession of lakes that, if it was windy, would either cause delays or, if the weather was fair, provide some respite from rowing as the sail was raised. This forty-mile section of the river in the Shield can be very beautiful, and of course there was always excellent fishing and game to add to the pemmican and ship biscuit diet.

The landscape changed again in the upper reaches of the Hayes. After rowing through a narrow lake, crews came to the Echimamish River. It was a small river that flowed due west through marshland and bulrushes that were flooded every so often by beaver dams, which did the favour of raising water levels and making travel easier. When the crew had pushed the boat through the top of these dams, they rebuilt them so as to maintain the higher water levels. Having now left the Hayes River, the Echimamish carried the crew west to the much larger Nelson River, which in its southwest track would take them to Norway House. Partway along this low and swampy stretch of the Echimamish—which means "river that flows in opposite directions" in Cree—there was a short portage called the Painted Stone Passage. It afforded great advantage to those who crossed this land, and for this, thanks was given.

The diary of David Thompson (1786) records one such voyage on the Hayes River: "It was now thought proper to make a trading house higher up the River...to be under the charge of Mr. Mitchell Oman.... I was appointed to be his clerk and embarked with him [from York Factory]...the natural route to the inland country would be by the big river [the Nelson], but its immense volume of water, heavy falls and waves make it dangerous for small canoes, and the route by the Hayes River is preferred as being more safe.... On the evening of the seventh day we came to the first (rapids).... The river now formed lakes and small streams with several carrying places over which we passed to a low winding ridge of land which separates the waters that flow eastward into Hudson Bay, and those that run westward into Lake Winnipeg. On the short carrying place by which we crossed this ridge the Indians time out of mind had placed a Manitou stone in-shape like a cobbler's lap stone but three times its size to which they make some trifling offerings; but the stone and offerings were all kicked about by our tolerant people..."

Crossing the portage thirty-three years later, Sir John Casey stopped at the same carrying place: "On the third day...after leaving our encampment at the White Falls we passed through several small lakes connected with each other by narrow deep grassy streams, and at noon arrived at the Painted Stone...

"The Painted Stone is a low rock ten or twelve yards across, remarkable for its marshy streams which arise on either side of it, taking different courses. On the one side, the water-course which we have navigated from York Factory commences. This spot may therefore be considered as one of the smaller sources of the Hayes River. On the other side of the stone the Echimamish arises, and taking a westerly direction, falls into the Nelson River."

As this route came to be more firmly in the grip of the commercial interests of the Hudson's Bay Company, the stopping place was no longer called Painted Stone Passage, and was subsequently referred to as "The Gates." Passing this way on his journey to the polar sea and the beginnings of his search for the Northwest Passage, Sir John Franklin recorded: "It is said there was formerly a stone placed near the centre of this portage on which figures were annually traced, and offerings deposited, by the Indians; but the stone has been removed for many years and the spot has ceased to be held in veneration."

During one such portage by the Hudson's Bay crews, there happened to be a group of Cree who were making their way to Shamattawa and who were crossing the portage in the other direction. They pulled their canoes off to the side and went up into the bush to wait for the York boats to be on their way. They watched the many machinations of the York boat crew members from a low hill to the north as those workers trudged across the rocks heavy-laden with the wares of civilization. An elder of the group spoke to those sitting around the fire:

"If I knew how to speak English I would tell these people a few things. The Great Creator is the one who provided everything on this earth—everything that we use in order to survive—which is why we give thanks. Today we see that the white man wants to stamp out God's laws and make his own. He thinks his laws are higher and more important than the Creator's. After God completed his work, it is written that creatures can be used by humans when they needed them to live. This is what was promised to us. The white man was also promised this. To have gardens and eat what the bear eats, to live off them. To live off the gardens. Humans were also promised other things that lived and grew in their areas. Now the white man has gone above these laws the Creator made. He wants to control everything. Even our hunting. So I often think someday the white man will see the wrong they have done, their mistakes. This is not right, to go against the Creator.

"The white man thinks he can take from the earth. He thinks he can teach it his lessons. He does not know that he has it backwards. The earth teaches us. We have to pay attention and learn. The lessons are there, but the white man is not listening. He is making too much noise to listen. He is dumb to the land and he will parish as a result."

When all was quiet again at the portage, the Cree returned to the river, gave thanks as they had time out of mind, and continued downriver to the portages that lay ahead.

Crofter Migrants

Making use of the routes established by the fur trade, a third group made their way from the port of Stromness. They were not searching for the riches of the East. They were not signing on as wintering servants in the fur trade. This third group were organized around export rather than import, as this group was composed of redundant populations that had been displaced from their homelands in the Highlands and Islands and were being dispersed upon the far-flung colonial shores of the British Empire.

Over the course of three centuries, the goods that travelled through Stromness became less and less refined. The main cargo was not the riches of the East, nor the tanned and dried skins of animals brought back from North America. It was now the unwanted crofters who were being shipped out to the contested colonial lands of North America. The direction of the goods reverses itself here. Commercial interests at the centre of European culture overtake the mercantile interest at the edge of empire. The mercantile capture of highly prized animal skins and the shipping of them to the colonial centre was replaced by industrial interests at the centre shipping out the most poorly thought-of members of that society who stood in the way of improvement and progress. Industry at the centre of society and colonialism at its edge combined in an arrangement for resettling these groups who were impeding industrial expansion, and located them in the "empty" lands of the empire, all of it presented in self-congratulatory terms by the desolators of the land: "In cultivating the barren land [of home], the crofters strive against nature to force a miserable pittance from the earth, while another element [far away] is presenting its treasures to enrich them."

In early June of 1813, Sutherland crofters gathered in Thurso on the north coast of Scotland, with the promise from Lord Selkirk that they would be compensated for the devastations they experienced in being cleared from their lands in Kildonan with new plots of land at Red River in the heart of North America. They were to board the *Waterwitch* for the choppy voyage across the Pentland Firth, skirting the cliffs of Hoy, to Stromness, where they would await the arrival of ships coming up from Gravesend, near London.

Lord Selkirk himself was there to meet them as they stepped onto the wharf. He assured them that they had the support of the Hudson's Bay Company ships that would carry them across the North Atlantic, as well as the provision of inland transport by its York boats into the heart of the continent. In return, the crofters were to serve as a British presence in lands that were becoming increasingly contested between British and French claims as well as by those native to the place.

The departing fleet was to be made up of the *Eddystone*, the *Prince of Wales*—which would carry the crofters to York Factory—and the military escort *Brazen*. These same two ships— the *Prince of Wales* and the *Eddystone*—had carried crofters from Stornoway in Lewis the year before, and six years later they would carry Sir John Franklin and his crew to York Factory.

After provisioning the vessels, including stowing water from Login's Well, the ships remained anchored in Stromness harbour, as they were becalmed by several weeks of "light air." There were a great many soldiers in the port during this time, so the crofters were billeted in less favoured quarters that were rife with lice and fleas. By the time the ships headed out into the Atlantic, several of the group aboard the *Prince of Wales* were exhibiting symptoms of typhus: high fever, mental confusion, along with coughing, nausea, and vomiting.

The living conditions "between decks" proved a fertile ground for the spread of the illness. The first passenger to die was the doctor who had been contracted to care for the crofters. Conditions aboard the *Prince of Wales* became dire. Almost daily, passengers and seamen succumbed to typhus. The situation was made worse by the slowness of the crossing. In early August, the ships became trapped in pack ice in Hudson Strait and the hull of the *Prince of Wales* was breached by a grappling berg—a breach possibly helped by the fact that the carpenter had cut a number of holes in the hull's planking in an attempt to alleviate the conditions of the crofters, who were discouraged from coming up on deck for fear of infecting more of the crew. When the ships finally entered the open waters of Hudson Bay, the *Prince of Wales* had four feet of water in the hold and only a skeleton crew remaining.

Rather than push on to York Factory, *The Prince of Wales*'s captain decided to make land at Fort Churchill, 120 miles to the north. The featureless shore of Hudson Bay in this area was an unimpressive sight, bog and swamp presenting a thin line broken only by the scrubbiest kinds of stunted spruce, situated as it was on the northern edge of the treeline.

Eventually, then, the *Prince of Wales* dropped anchor not in York Factory—which was well supplied with food provisions and the implements needed for the crofters' future life, as well as York boats ready to transport them south to Red River—but at Sloop's Cove, below the Hudson's Bay Company fort in the mouth of the Churchill River. When those at the fort heard of the distressing state of the passengers, tents were pitched for them on the shore so as to keep contact with them to a minimum. So rather than setting out well supplied for their new homes, the crofters were delivered of a number of coffins so they could bury their dead in the stony ground above their encampment. One of those buried on the frost was John Sutherland, who had been a tradition-bearer of the community, as well as a leader of the crofter protests against the banishment from their traditional homes in Kildonan.

Many of those working at the fort were either British or Lowland Scots and so were already biased against the "savages" from the Scottish Highlands, whom they scorned as lazy and barbaric, and in no way up to the task of making a new life for themselves. All this was made more unappealing by the difficulty of the Highlanders' unyielding dispositions and refractory spirits.

The Captain of the *Prince of Wales* wanted to abandon the crofters and make his way back to the Atlantic rather than be caught in the ice, and the Factor at the fort wished to have the troublesome and ill crofters delivered to York Factory. After the Captain agreed to return the crofters to the ship, he promptly ran aground and everyone had to disembark. After more uncertainty, the crofters were finally transported fifteen miles up the Churchill River so that they could begin to prepare for the winter ahead. With the help of local guides, they built four small log dwellings in which to shield themselves from the elements. Provisioning for the winter was made more difficult because the head of the fort confiscated the flintlocks from their rifles, making it impossible for the crofters to hunt ptarmigan, which were deemed to be the property of the Hudson's Bay Company. Many crofters died in the cold and dark over the following six months and more were weakened by the privations they suffered throughout an Arctic winter. They moved about the camp as the northern lights spread above them and crackled in the still night air, while during the day distant plumes like grey smokestacks rose from seams in the pack ice.

When spring finally came, the crofters decided they could not wait for the ice to leave the rivers and the bay. They set out to walk across the still-frozen muskeg to York Factory, hoping to make an early start on the trip to their new homes in Red River. Leaving behind the elderly and the infirm, who would follow when the ice broke up, twenty women and thirty-one men pulled the sleighs they had built over the winter, now heavily laden. They travelled along Hudson Bay in the direction of York Factory, trying to stay in sight of the shore in order not to get lost. Each evening they moved inland to find shelter and firewood among the scrub spruce. Snow-blind and crippled with leg cramps, they arrived two weeks later at Fort Nelson on the northern edge of the estuary of the Nelson and Hayes Rivers. They were able to walk across the ice to York Factory, except for a stretch of open water, which they traversed in small boats borrowed from the fort.

Once at York Factory, the crofters took time to recover as they waited for the ice to go out of the rivers. This happened on 20 May, and by 23 May the Sutherland crofters were on their way up the Hayes in two York boats. Although this mode of travel was a new experience for the crofters, as was the portaging around rapids and waiting for ice to break up in inland lakes, the adverse weather and snow were not, nor was the strenuous work. On 11 June they arrived at the post at Jack River, near the shores of Lake Winnipeg. To their surprise, they met Highlanders there whom they knew from Sutherland and who were now in the employ of the Hudson's Bay Company. There was dancing and good cheer that night, but on the following day the crofters encountered snow as they rowed out onto Lake Winnipeg. Ten days later they reached the mouth of the Red River at the southern end of the lake, and shortly after that they disembarked near the forks of the Red and Assiniboine Rivers.

The older and infirm crofters arrived by boat at York Factory in the weeks that followed. They brought with them the bales of clothes and utensils that those who walked overland had left behind at Fort Churchill. The new arrivals were described thus: "Their condition was as miserable and distressing as it could possibly be." In their sixties now, Donald and Janet Gunn, who had once been substantial farmers in Borrobol, "were in the most destitute state imaginable." Their habitation consisted of a "few poles on which was stretched a piece of what had been in its better day a boat sail, but was now so tattered and torn that it was pervious to every blast of wind that blew and every drop of rain that fell." Two of the Gunns' children had died the previous winter at Churchill. When asked about the trip ahead up the Hayes River, Janet Gunn replied, "We are tormented by exile and misery. They say our new life is near at hand, but it feels very far away. All the things that we held dear are flitting in the wind or buried in the clay, and the promises that have been made to us have all been broken."

When they finally arrived in Red River that summer, they found that crofters' claims to new homes were caught up in the ongoing struggles for furs between the North West Company and the Hudson's Bay Company, as well as the growing resentments of the Plains Cree, Saulteaux, and Métis, whose traditional lands were being annexed. They were not granted their choice of land, contrary to assurances they had been given, and their belongings were not shipped south to them and instead rotted in the weeds at York Factory.

Because they were unable to plant their crops as expected, the crofters could not become self-sufficient in food by the fall, nor would they have their own roofs over their heads. They were thus dependent on handouts from the powers that be for foodstuffs such as pemmican, which was, in any case, in short supply. The privations they suffered during their second winter were hardly less grievous than those of the first, at Fort Churchill. The crofters continued to feel resentment from all sides, and they were in no way embraced as newcomers. The crofters were by now "wearied and disgusted" by their many trials and "heartedly wished themselves away from Red River."

There was much discussion and disagreement over that second winter about the fate that had greeted them, as they felt pushed and pulled between the competing forces at Red River. Because they felt aggrieved over what had happened to them and did not see their prospects improving, a great many of the Sutherland crofters cleaved eastward, if not to return to Scotland, then at least to leave this far-flung outpost and travel down the Winnipeg River and back through the Great Lakes to Upper Canada, where they hoped they would be more secure within the established colonial realities that existed there. Those who remained behind in Red River had to retreat to Jack River on the north shore of Lake Winnipeg in order to escape the strife that followed.

Far from being an "empty" land, Red River was a hive of conflicting interests, all of it underwritten by the gradual dispossession of those who were native to the place. The ones who came later forced the land into new moulds as they did the bidding of those from far away. These marks remain on the land even now, along with the visions of the landscape that drew these interferers to this place in the heart of North America: the land as desolate barrier to the riches of the East, the land as repository of wealth in the fur trade, the land as empty and without community and therefore suitable for redundant populations from elsewhere who stood in the way of progress. Within these residual realities lurks a history of Canada that we are reluctant to face in ourselves or show to the world.

This tale began by highlighting the mismatch from above of those whose dream it was to "discover" the Northwest Passage en route to the riches of the East. These explorers had the dream but not the survival skills to carry out their grand schemes. As a result, there was much suffering and loss among those who made the attempt.

The story ends with a mismatch from below. The crofters had only subsistence skills and therefore found no place in the modernization schemes of the Industrial Revolution. As a result, the crofters were driven from their homes and experienced much suffering and loss.

And the greatest suffering of all was on the part of those who were made strangers in their own home. Those from far away caused great suffering near at hand. This suffering hides behind the grim visage of the proud immigrant taming the land, whose "brave countenance" not only erases their own grief-stricken passage, but also the history of those they displaced.

So it was for those who drank the waters of Login's Well. This water travelled with all those who ventured out from Stromness. It touched the lips of those who dreamed of glory. It touched the lips of those who grieved for home. It touched the lips of those who became stuck in the ice. It touched the lips of the crews as they rose in mutiny. The water from Login's Well touched the lips of those who watched their homeland drop below the horizon, and as they witnessed their families die of typhus, and months later they drank its last drops as they sighted the desolate shores of Hudson Bay.

CHAPTER IV

Long Spruce Rapids, Nelson River, 1976

History from Above

As well as displacing Indigenous groups and altering landscapes, the hydroelectric dams built by Manitoba Hydro imported a megaproject approach to industrial construction carried out by large consortia, where migrant labourers worked twelve hours a day, seven days a week. As with the crofters who sign on as "wintering servants" for the Hudson's Bay Company, many of the people doing this construction work came from small rural communities, and so these forms of alienation were keenly felt. Work-related fatalities were a regular occurrence. One such event is recounted in the following narrative. Each of these deaths was followed by a twenty-four-hour strike, which is central to the story I relate here from my own experience, as the camp moves from excessive regulation and control to an almost complete breakdown of authority, and in doing so it evokes the constrained and conflicted lived experience of contract workers who leave home in order to subsidize their families and communities. Currently, the tar sands in Alberta are populated by migrant Atlantic Canadians, an example of a staples economy "solving" one ecological crisis (the collapse of the fishery) by generating another (climate change).

History from Below

*We are all Brave and Hearty at present (except the Surgeon
troubled with the Gout, and One Young Man Raving Mad).*
    — *Letter from Ferdinand Jacobs to James Isham*
            York Factory, Hudson Bay, 1754

Arranged on a north–south grid on level ground that is
covered in crushed stone, the smooth gleam of the camp
buildings appears orderly, deserted, and antiseptic in the
afternoon brightness. The long rows of white metal trailers
resting on wooden posts are surrounded by bulldozed heaps
of scrawny tree roots. Each trailer unit is made up of a pair
of two-hundred-foot-long rows of room units set three feet
apart, with a floor and roof added between them to create
a long hallway. Halfway along, a bathroom/shower unit is
inserted into the row. Among the grid of trailers are two large
square modular buildings. One is a dining hall, the other is a
pub—the largest in Manitoba.

In one of the rooms in Trailer H, four men sit around a
cardboard box marked "Lysol." A half-empty bottle of whisky
is on the floor next to it. The room is small and square. A
white aluminum-covered door is in the middle of one wall.
On either side of it are two small closets at the foot of the
two beds in the room. Above each bed are a small shelf and a
reading light and between the beds are a desk and chair. On
the back of the door is a declaration in a black frame. It reads:

Manitoba Hydro is the owner of these trailers and
reserves the right to evict anyone without notice if they
are in violation of the rules stated below:

1. no alcohol is allowed in the rooms
2. no gambling is allowed in the rooms
3. no women are allowed in the rooms

4. no excessive noise is allowed at any time

5. proper regard must be shown to the room and its contents

6. the camp badge is to be worn at all times and shown to camp police upon request.

Long Spruce Rapids Camp,
Nelson River

By order of the
Chairman of Northern Generation Projects,
Manitoba Hydro

"A dollar he bids," scoffs Alfred Ronnie, his elbows resting on the back of the desk chair as he looks at his cards. "You'd think you could do better than that on payday."

"For God's sake, Ronnie, I have to have a few bucks left over to buy lottery tickets," replies Don, the young man sitting on one of the beds.

"I gotta get into the lottery business, that's all there is to it," says Ronnie. "It would fit right in." His musing turns into a wide toothless grin.

"Why don't you get into the women business while you're at it?" asks Waz, the stocky man sitting on the other bed. "That's where the real money is."

"No way," protests Ronnie. "Too much trouble. Booze and gambling are simple. Women!" Ronnie shakes his head. "'Course, maybe I could talk to some of the Crawley dollies in the kitchen. See if they want to make a little money on the side, on their backs." Alfred Ronnie is a short man with a gut that makes him waddle when he walks, and long red hair greased back off his freckled face. "Speaking of money, hurry up, will ya. It's your bid, you bloody Newfie. 'Course I forgot, it's always a half hour later in Newfoundland." Without his teeth, Ronnie's words come out soft-edged, despite the vigorous working of his lips.

The fourth man sits on a stool with his back to the door. "When are you going to learn some geography, Ronnie. I'm from Nova Scotia. How many times have I got to tell you?"

"You're all bloody Newfies as far as I'm concerned. Cape Bretoners are just Newfies with their heads kicked in."

"I'm not from Cape Breton either. My. Oh. My. Look at this hand."

"By the way, you hear the one about the Newfie bank robber? He goes in to the bank and hands the teller a note that says, 'Don't stick around, this is a fuck-up.' That should be the motto of this place. So you gonna bid or not, you lousy Bluenoser? There, you feel better now?"

"I fold."

"Nothing. I fold, too." Waz drops his cards on the box and picks up the bottle. He takes a long drink. "That clears away some of the dust." He purses his lips and runs his hand through his brush cut. He passes the bottle to Ronnie, who tips it up quickly, his Adam's apple bobbing as he drinks.

"I'm over cashing my cheque." Don pauses to take a drink. "Everyone's waitin' in line for the bank to show up, when this guy shoves his way through, cursing away. I think he works in the diesel garage."

"Tall skinny guy with bloodshot eyes?" says Ronnie.

"That's him."

"Jigs—one of my best customers," replies Ronnie, proudly.

"Anyways," continues Don, "he goes over to the weights and picks up a set and pumps them over his head half a dozen times and then drops them. He digs around and finds a heavier set and he grunts and groans until he finally gets those ones over his head. The whole time it's 'Screw this' and 'Screw that' and 'Those bastards.' Next he goes over to the bench press and picks the big suckers off the rack. By this time his face is red, I mean beet red. I couldn't believe it but the bugger managed to get the weights up to his shoulders. Anyway, he gives it the big push and gets them as far as his forehead. I mean, here's this guy staring up at this bar that's about two inches above his eyeballs. His arms start shakin' and his back arches until he jerks them over his head and they crash down on top of the other weights. Then the bugger stumbles out of the place, still cursin'! You wouldn't have believed it."

"Why's that?" says Waz. "There's nothing wrong with trying to stay in shape."

"Poor old Jigsy," says Ronnie. "He musta lost another cut. For the last three months, Jigs has bet his cheque on a cut of the deck. Half a dozen guys go together and match his cheque and they cut. Jigs has lost all but one."

"Just the thought makes me want to puke," replies Don. "Anyway, no sooner does Jigs stumble out than some Portuguese guys start eyeing each other, and before you know it they're all lined up in front of the weights. Each of 'em gives it a try and only one guy manages to get them over his head. After strutting around in front of his pals, he goes over and digs out the big set Jigs had heaved into the pile." Don laughs. "Never got it past his knees."

"Those geese," says Ronnie. "Always showing off. I wish more of them played cards. There's a thousand of them here, with all that money saved up, and I don't make a nickel off them. Instead I'm stuck with losers—I mean players—like you guys. I'll raise you a fin. How about it?"

"No fucking way," replies Don, dropping his cards on the box.

"What a bunch of chickenshits," says Ronnie, "losing to a guy with a pair of deuces. Well, that calls for a smoke." Ronnie reaches into his shirt pocket. "Have you guys seen a picture of my wife?" Ronnie holds up a photograph.

"Hey, not bad," says Don.

"Young and firm," winks Ronnie.

"How did she get mixed up with an asshole like you?" asks Waz, studying the picture closely. A slim girl in a white dress with a wide red ribbon around her waist is standing in front of a fake fireplace.

"I knocked her up," replies Ronnie.

"What the hell are you doing up here with something like that at home?" asks Waz.

"Complications," replies Ronnie.

"Like she dumped you?"

"No, complications like I jackknifed a brand-new semi-trailer after I'd had a few drinks. It belonged to her old man. Nothing serious, but I figured I better disappear for a while. Besides, I'm not much of a family man. Gets in the way of my drinking and bootlegging."

"Not me," says Waz. "When things were going good with the wife, there was nothing better than coming home from work and spending the evening with her and the kids. The boss could yell at me all day and it didn't matter, 'cause when I came home, I was king."

"Christ, Waz, you're gonna make me cry," says Don.

"Don't shed a tear for that bitch," Waz shakes his head. "She took off with a guy from the nightshift. Turns out she was banging him all along."

"Wake me up when you get the deck shuffled, will ya, Captain Haddock," says Ronnie. He leans forward and calls through the half-open door. "Hey, gramps!"

"What do you want?" Casey turns reluctantly in the hall.

"Come join us and tell us about your holiday. We need more suckers—I mean players—for a friendly game of cards."

"I got better things to do with my money." Casey unlocks his door.

"Come on, gramps. You must have thousands tucked away by now. It's time the rest of us had a shot at it."

"You're crazy if you think I'll play cards with you," replies Casey as he enters his room.

"Casey," shouts Ronnie. "Hey, Casey."

Casey opens his door. "What?"

"Write me, Casey. Every day."

Casey shakes his head and closes the door. "Idiots."

"What are you doing now? Counting the damn things?" asks Ronnie. "You better not. I got a couple up my sleeve—just kidding. By the way, are any of you interested in joining the Alfred Ronnie Body Beautiful Fan Club? One thin ten-dollar bill gives you the opportunity to sit with me at supper, buy me cigarettes, and sign your paycheques over to me. Whatdya say?"

"Now what the hell have you done to deserve a fan club?" asks Waz.

"It's not what I've done," says Ronnie. "It's who I am and what I represent. Just look at this face." Ronnie pats his cheek. "Soft as a baby's bum."

"I agree it looks like a bum," replies Waz.

"Listen to the guy." Ronnie stands up and smooths his hair and pulls his pants up over his belly. "Who do I look like? I mean, what movie star?"

"Get serious," replies Waz.

"Now come on. Guess." Ronnie turns his head in profile.

"The Flying Nun," replies Waz.

"We give up," says Don. "Who?"

"Lloyd Bridges, you fools. You know, from *Sea Hunt*." Ronnie forms the oval of a diver's mask with his thumbs and forefingers and made gurgling noises.

"Jesus, he does look like him," says Don, falling back on the bed laughing.

"Now that I've broken your concentration, let's get back to the game." Ronnie picks up his cards and smiles broadly. "Right on, Saigon. The hand of heaven hath anointed me."

"Christ, Ronnie, are you ever full of shit," says Waz. "We'll have to get Casey over here to give us one of his 'shovelling for Hitler' lessons if you don't shut up."

"Wasn't that funny the time Ralphie threw that dirt on Gene?" says Don.

"Yeah, Ronnie," continued Waz. "Your pal Casey was giving Ralphie one of his shovelling lessons." Waz imitates

Casey's accent. "'Yes, son, when you shovel for Hitler and are starving in one of his camps, you do it right or you die. Stage one: You stand with your back to where you want to throw dirt. Stage two: Lay the shovel handle across your thighs, gripping with both hands. Stage three: Push shovel forward into the earth using your whole body, not just your arms. Stage four: Straighten up and arch your back. Stage five: Throw dirt behind you by swinging your arms. This way you save energy and you might live.' Ralphie followed along with Casey and when it came time to heave the dirt, he let it go without looking. Gene was walking up when Ralphie did it and the dirt landed right on him."

"Was Gene ever pissed off," laughs Don. "I thought he was going to fire him right on the spot. He can be a real prick sometimes."

Casey swings open his door. "Don't you make fun." He steps out into the hall, as if to challenge them. "You guys have no clue what suffering is. You are fools, all of you." Casey is shaking with rage, his fists clenched.

"Too bad you didn't get laid on your vacation, Casey," says Waz. "It would have fixed you right up."

"We meant nothin' by it, Casey," adds Don, as Casey turned and slammed his door. "It's just a funny story."

"Come on, you guys. Bet," goads Ronnie. "I got to clean up Ralphie's room while he's still in hospital. I was supposed to clean it this morning, but I didn't feel too good. I took one look at the mess in there and figured I'll need a couple of drinks before I tackle it. If there is one thing I've learned in my time up here, it's that you can do housework drunk. Come on, ante up." Ronnie peeks at his cards. "The main thing is we get a shot at everyone's money. Not like Casey. Got thousands stashed away, and the government will get it all." Ronnie leans toward the door and shouts, "A real tragedy. The pain of it all."

"You hear those Hitler stories about the camps Casey tells. Makes you wonder why he's in a place like this. I asked him

Figure 6   Long Spruce Construction Camp. Photo by Ray Rogers.

that once, and he looked at me like I was crazy. "'Oh, no,' he said. 'They treat me good here.'"

"Casey is here because he wants to be my friend," shouts Ronnie out the door. "Because he wants to be President of the Alfred Ronnie Body Beautiful Fan Club." There was a thud on the inside of Casey's door.

"Ralphie, the poor bugger. A hundred and twenty-five pounds soaking wet," says Waz. "Nice enough fella, but just couldn't cut it. It takes a certain kind of person to stand around doing nothing all day in the cold. It's a real skill to piss your life away kissing Ford Lady's ass. Not everyone makes it."

"I came here to make money," says Don, "not to work. As my Chatfield buddy always says back home: 'In every situation, there's a fucker and a fuckee. Somebody's always getting fucked.' The fuck-*er* and the fuck-*ee*. The fuck-*er* and the fuck-*ee*."

They all sing in unison. "The fuck-*er* and the fuck-*ee!* The fuck-*er* and the fuck-*ee!*"

Casey's door swings open. "That's it. I'm calling camp security." Casey starts down the long hall. "They'll fix you guys up good, once and for all."

The four card players follow Casey, goose-stepping as they go. "The fuck-*er* and the fuck-*ee!* The fuck-*er* and the fuck-*ee!*" Casey screams as he pushes through the outside door and falls down the wooden steps onto the gravel. He is still laying there shaking when the four men burst into the evening light of a northern summer, their shouts swallowed instantly by the calm of the air, and the roar of the rapids a mile to the north of them as the Nelson River tumbles off the Canadian Shield into the Hudson Bay Lowlands.

Working on the Dam

The field offices of Long Spruce Contractors are situated on the upriver side of the partially built dam. Amid the scattered array of construction equipment and piles of gravel, the smooth undulating ledges of the old riverbed are now visible, as if the worksite had been spread out on a giant grey blanket laid across a stubble field. The river itself is relegated to a narrow channel along the north bank by a horseshoe-shaped cofferdam constructed to expose the riverbed.

Ford Lady leans against the company truck parked next to the field offices. Surrounded by his crew of foremen, Ford's casual manner conveys a sense of control that appears effortless. "Yes sir, I've worked on a lot of big ones—the Murray River in Australia, Churchill Falls. It's my life. It's what I do." And with a flick of a hand, huge machines grind their blades into the earth, rock faces crumble in a blast of dynamite. What he likes best is pouring concrete. "You take the rock, the sand, the water, the lime and gypsum—nature's elements— and you mix 'em and they come out hard and smooth, and just the shape you want." Whenever Ford finishes a large pour of concrete—a thousand cubic yards in a night, say—he gets on the two-way radio and in his lazy drawl announces, "Well,

I guess it's time for a hot roll and a coffee." That is the signal to his crew that the job is done. Over the years, Ford has gathered together a group of men who follow him from project to project. "When a company hires Ford Lady, it also hires the best goddam crew anywhere. 'Lady's Men.'"

Resting his forearms on the truck box, Ford goes over the day's plans: the wait for the part for the crusher that still has not arrived; the moving of more forms over to the spillway; the setting in place of circular forms of the draft tube in Bay One; and the search for a way to raise the temperature of the river water used at the batch plant in the making of the concrete. "And if we can get all that done," says Ford, by way of encouragement, "Pete and I are going to take Sunday and do a little hunting. The chopper is going to fly us up north for a couple of days. Got all the gear right here." Ford pats the side of his truck. "Gonna take a little target practice on the way home. That's the one thing I regret about this kind of work. You're in some of the finest hunting territory in the world and you never get a chance to fire a shot." Ford shrugs his shoulders and grins, "Christ, when I was young, my brother Lon and I would go hunting for weeks at a stretch. We had some times."

"Tell the boys about the cat in the sack, Ford," said Pete, looking around at the other men.

"Oh, that one…Jesus." Ford pauses for a minute and looks up at the sky. "One fall, Lonnie and I had been out for about a week. Hadn't seen a thing, not a thing! Well, if it doesn't start to rain. Man, did it rain. Lon got real disgusted—he was hotheaded at the best of times—and he wanted to start for home. Of course, the fact that we had finished off the last of the Jim Beam had nothin' to do with it. So we decided to break camp. First thing Lonnie does is empty his rifle up into the trees overhead. Well, by God, if a wildcat doesn't drop right at his feet. We near pissed ourselves laughin'. That was until it moved. 'Lon,' I says to him, 'there ain't no blood. You only scared him half to death.' So Lonnie, the crazy bugger, grabs the canvas tent bag and stuffs the cat in it ass first, and ties it up. 'Won't the boys at the pool hall get a kick out of this,' he says, and we get to laughin' again. Well, we finally get all the gear in the back of the station wagon, then Lonnie picks up the tent bag and throws it in the back seat. That near finished us for ten more minutes. 'Okay,' I say, finally, 'you drive and I'll ride shotgun.'

"About halfway home, we start to sober up a little and about the same time the cat starts moving around in the bag. Lonnie looks over at me. 'Jesus, Ford,' he says, 'we got a live wildcat in the back seat.' He pulls over on the shoulder, jumps out, and drags the tent bag out of the car and rolls it down into the ditch. 'Hold on, brother,' I say as he jumps back in. 'We can't leave him tied in that bag. Turn around and I'll untie it. You just keep the gun handy.' Finally I convince Lonnie to make a U-turn and go back. Just as we get there, we see two black fellas drag the bag up out of the ditch and throw it into the back seat of their Caddy. We start yelling at them and they just take off. About a half mile up the road that Caddy screeches to a halt, all four doors fly open and those boys are going in every direction. Then the cat jumps out, shakes his-self off, and saunters off into the woods." A ripple of laughter and guffaws pass through the assembled foremen. "Lon ain't been half as much fun since he became a preacher. Anyway, that's enough of my bullshit," says Ford, looking out over the dam site. "God, it's good to finally be getting above ground. Now if we can only keep this gear working, we might make some headway this summer."

"I called about the part for the crusher," says Guy. "It's sup-posed to be on the plane today."

"That's what he said yesterday," Ford pushes his hardhat back off his forehead. "We only got two, maybe three days of three-and-a-half-inch aggregate left and there are some big pours coming up."

"He promised," Guy shrugs.

"Hydro is complaining that the temperature of the concrete is too low," says Gene.

"What the hell do they want? The river water was snow a week ago, for Chrissake," replies Ford.

"They're talking about making us heat the water on the way into the batch plant."

"By the time we got the parts for that—and I have no idea where we'd find them—the water temperature of the river will have climbed into the forties."

"Maybe we can delay a couple of the big pours. That might satisfy them."

"Just when we were making some bloody headway. This is our big summer. This is when we have to separate the men from the boys and get this thing in shape. Otherwise we'll have those German turbines rusting on the bank this fall, and we will be paying big penalties to Hydro. Anyway, let's get at it."

~~~~~~~~

The rapids on the Nelson River that had discouraged the Cree and the fur traders have encouraged the bulldozer, the earth-movers, and the gantry cranes hired by Manitoba Hydro to build a series of dams at the steps and cataracts along its route. This large continental watershed, combined with the abrupt drops in the Nelson as it crossed the Shield, made the area ideal for hydroelectricity, for which Lake Winnipeg was a natural reservoir for the waters of western North America.

Up until the 1960s, the electrical demands of Manitoba were supplied by a series of small dams on the Winnipeg River, as it flowed from Lake of the Woods to Lake Winnipeg. The Pinawa Dam was the first one built, in 1907, and McArthur Dam was the last, in 1954. But with the anticipated skyrocketing demand for electricity through the latter part of the twentieth century, as well as export potential, Hydro engineers began to look north.

The Kelsey Dam was the first one built on the Nelson in 1961. Its goal was to provide power for the nickel mine in nearby Thompson. The Grand Rapids Dam at the mouth of the Saskatchewan River at Lake Winnipeg was built in 1965. This was followed by the plans for the Lower Nelson River, beginning with the Kettle Rapids Generating Station, completed in 1973. Work began on Long Spruce Rapids shortly after that.

Because the Churchill and the Nelson run parallel to each other, the beginnings of the Rat River tributary of the Churchill and the Burntwood River tributary of the Nelson are very close together and on the same elevation. In order to increase the volume of water passing through the Nelson, engineers proposed diverting the last three hundred miles of the Churchill into the Nelson by digging a diversion channel between the Rat and the Burntwood tributaries. This would be achieved by building a control dam at Missi Falls at the eastern end of Southern Indian Lake, which was part of the Churchill, so that the water would be forced up the Rat, and then through the diversion channel to the Burntwood and into the Nelson. This in turn reduced the Churchill to a trickle in its lower reaches, and at the same time expanded the watershed of the Nelson by over a hundred thousand square miles.

~~~~~~~~~~

"They are drilling exploratory holes in the bedrock," says Don, pointing through the dust-filled air on the upriver side of the dam. The yellow school bus rolls down the steep incline of what had been the south bank of the river and out onto the road built on the exposed bedrock. He is talking to Johnny Shingoose, who has just been hired for the third time by the contractor, but this is his first job on the actual dam site. "Any voids that are found in the substrata need to be pumped full of grout, sealing what will become the bottom of the large reservoir held back by the dam. That way water will not leak through the bedrock and percolate out below the dam. Those there are the four gantry cranes that travel back and forth between the spillway and the powerhouse on railway tracks. Each of them is over two hundred feet high. They transport material and concrete along the worksite on the upriver and downriver sides of the dam."

Johnny looks around. "Man, this was just a hole in the ground the last time I was here." In the centre of what was the old riverbed, the spillway has begun to rise above the bedrock. When the spillway is finished, a second horseshoe-shaped cofferdam will be built adjacent to the northern bank, and the river will flow through the open gates of the spillway, which will also act as a bridge connecting the north and south construction sites.

"The powerhouse will be built inside the southern coffer-dam, which is where the focus of the construction will be. Within the northern cofferdam, a combination of rock and concrete will extend the dam from the spillway to the north-ern bank and then bend west for four miles as it turns into the northern wall of the reservoir, carrying the elevation of the dam back upriver until it peters out into the rising Shield." Don was turned in his seat so he could point back upriver.

"Man, you love this shit, don't you?" laughs Johnny.

"Sure do. I want to be a grader operator someday. Just not in a place like this. Maybe for the Department of Highways near my hometown. I'm a Chatfield, Man. man," sings Don.

The bus moves along the riverbed past the powerhouse and down a steep hill to the downstream side of the dam. Don turns to Johnny. "Do you know why the Kettle Dam and the Long Spruce Dam are nine miles apart?" asks Don with apparent seriousness.

"Not this one again," moans Waz, sitting behind them.

"Now come on, Johnny. Gene is going to ask you and you better have the answer."

"Shit, I don't know. Because of drops in elevation?" replies Johnny.

"It's because the river needs time to build up the electrical charge that the Kettle dam takes out of it. That's why."

"Really?" Johnny pauses and looks around as the others start laughing.

"You guys are sounding like Ralphie now. Never listen to these guys if you want to survive here," confides Casey as he gathers up his lunch bag and rises to wait. "Every minute there is danger."

The bus stops next to the large temporary hoarding that shelters what will someday be the powerhouse. Don motions to Johnny as they move toward the worksite. "Come on inside. This is the really great part." A diffused light sifts through large plastic sheets in the upper walls. Because the bedrock has been blasted away on the lower side of the dam, the gradual descent of the rapids has been transformed into a single abrupt drop at the powerhouse. "There will be ten turbines. Each bay in the rock face will house one of the draft tubes and turbines. In order to maximize the efficiency of the turbines, it is important to use the weight of the water falling through them. The draft tubes deliver the water from the reservoir, going down through the turbines and out into the lower part of the river. See those circular wooden forms that look like the hull of a giant ship? Those are the concrete forms for the draft tubes. They have to be exact within a sixteenth of an inch because the turbines fit inside them. Aren't those forms beauties? Great workmanship."

Several panels of the roof of the hoarding had been removed. Down through the opening comes a large steel bin connected to the cable of a gantry crane. Workers coming on shift filter away to their various jobs, passing those who are coming off night shift and moving toward the buses. A crew of labourers gathers at the foot of the draft tube forms near Unit Two. Plans on blueprint are rolled out on a pile of plywood, and fingers are pointed here and there, voices rising and falling until there is a crackle of two-way radios and all attention turns to the bin that drops from above and comes to rest near a pallet full of ten-by-sixteen-foot concrete forms made of steel.

Leaving the other white hard hats and climbing down a long wooden staircase to where the pouring of the concrete perimeter of the powerhouse had begun, Gene motions for the crew to come over to the pile of forms. "Okay, guys. You know the routine. You are going to fill the bin with whatever isn't stuck down. The crane will take these forms out of here. And no dropping them on your foot like your buddy Ralphie did, all right? Then you guys are going to clear all the loose rock, gravel, and debris off the face of the stone to get it ready for the concrete pour tomorrow. When you get as much off as you can, use the hose to wash the last of it into low places that you can shovel." Gene looked over at Johnny Shingoose. "You're the new guy, again?"

"I guess." Johnny extends his hand.

Momentarily disconcerted by this act of decorum, Gene pauses and then pulls off his glove to shake Johnny's hand. "Get a shovel from the shed with the rest of them." Gene turns and moves to the concrete forms that are stacked on a large steel platform. "Don, first thing, let's get these forms out of here so you have some room to work. Jump up there and hook up the cables from the platform when the hook comes down." Gene pulls out his radio as Don jumps onto the pile of concrete forms and lifts the steel cables that are attached to the corners of the platform. "1404 to 1402. Kenny, we've unhooked the bin. Now you are going to take up a load of perimeter forms and place them outside with the others. Down and to the north about ten feet. More...more...good." Don slides the eyes of the cables into the crane hook and jumps down off the pile. "Take her away, Kenny." The crew members stand with their arms out as the platform shimmies before slowly rising from the old riverbed and ascending through the noisy air as the day shift kicks into gear.

Over the next twelve hours, the crew fills three bins, as they move across the bedrock of Unit Two. The final drilling going on near the rock face makes conversation difficult, especially when the crew has to clear away the smaller pieces of rubble that split off the face. By the time the shift is over, the noise has exhausted them all. The three Portuguese workers on the crew know very little English, so any jokes are wasted on them. Tony has been on the job for a year and has learned enough English to translate Gene's commands for Alfonso and Miguel, although most of the time the jobs are so obvious that a few waves of the hand and pointing are all that is required.

Casey seems to have an endless string of stories about life under Hitler, which he tells in an animated way, but otherwise is humourless, except when it comes to pointing out other people's failings and possible dangers. "In my part of Bohemia, a lot of German was spoken, although I also learned Czech as a kid. I was in a camp with a big Czech fellow. He was a masseur and he was big and strong with hands that could break you in half. He had just come from another camp, where he had managed to fall in love with a German girl, although they couldn't understand each other's language. You know young people. One day this boy takes me aside and says he has a letter from this girl, but he can't read it. Turns out he had been carrying it around for weeks, so pleased to have it, but can't read it. He heard me speak German to one of the guards that day. He takes out this letter, now so rumpled and creased, and he hands it to me with great tenderness. I unfold it and start to read it to him. First it tells about life in the camp and who had died or been transferred. He is walking back and forth, the poor fellow, so embarrassed to have the letter read aloud. Near the end, she gets more personal and says she misses him. He is now pacing behind me, so he doesn't have to look at me. I come to the last lines where she says she loves him and just as I am saying these words I feel those big powerful hands gently cover my ears."

"Christ, Casey. You're going to make me cry," says Waz. "Next thing you know, I'm going to be mooning around under some Crawley dolly's window."

"Don't waste your time. They are all tramps."

"Oh, come on, Casey. One of them must remind you of your mother."

Casey raised his shovel. "Don't you talk about my mother."

"I don't know about the rest of you, but I came here looking for love."

Crew members come and go every day. Waz has quit and come back a number of times. After a tearful phone call one night with his children, Waz agreed to take their mother back. "Jesus, she put my son on the roof of the garage, just so she could keep track of him. I know he's hyper, but Christ…" The next day he was gone. Three months later he was back, with a restraining order against him in his suitcase.

Because Long Spruce Contractors is required to give Indigenous people and northerners priority in their hiring, locals come and go regularly. After riding back and forth from Gillam to work during his other stints, Johnny has decided to live in the camp this time around, so as to avoid the distractions of his extended family in town. Because he's a good worker when he is here, he always gets a job. Several times, Johnny brought his cousins along as well, but they would last only a short time, announcing as they departed, "Everyone here is crazy."

Johnny's father Walter has lived in Gillam for seven years. He has a trapline there. Before moving to Gillam he lived for ten years in Split Lake and worked as a guide for Manitoba Hydro engineers and geologists, having learned English during his time as a boy in the residential schools down south. He had paddled the canoes and carried the instruments when sightings were made and seismic tests were done for the dams at Wuskwatim and at Manasan, at First Rapids and Upper Gull, at Kettle Rapids, at Long Spruce Rapids, at Upper Limestone and Lower Limestone, and at Gillam Island. Walter was with the engineers when they planned the Missi Falls Dam on the eastern end of Southern Indian Lake. He paddled the Rat/Burntwood tributaries between the Churchill River and the Nelson River during the planning of the diversion of the Churchill. Back in the 1950s, Walter had worked with his father on the dam at Kelsey, and he has heard the stories his father, Alex, told about cutting brush for the Hudson Bay Railroad early in the century, mixed in with Alex's other stories of life on the land.

Everyone who comes here has their own story about why Long Spruce seemed like a solution to their problems. No one can claim they are here to have a normal life, except maybe Casey. You come for the money and you can leave with your life torn open. And as for me, I came here to save money so I can finish my house and build myself a new boat. There are a goodly number of Maritimers and Newfoundlanders here. Ralphie is the only one that I knew from back home. Not so much knew him as knew some of the same people and places he did. He had gone on the offshore boats mainly and we commiserate from time to time about life here and how it compares with life back home.

For the most part, I try to keep to myself, do my job, save my money, and count the days until I can take up my hammer again and work on my house and begin to build a new boat. But that is not the case for everyone there. Long Spruce can knock you sideways and change you in ways that seem irrevocable. If you survive, you are a different person on the other side. This is what worries me above all else. I want to be able to take up a life again that had seemed to have only just begun.

Itinerant Ease in the Land of Toil

It is a fine summer evening as the day shift files off the buses and makes its way into the dining hall for supper. Some hustle up the stairs so they can get to the front of the line, showing more enthusiasm now than they did on their shift down at the dam. Others loiter outside, smoking a cigarette and enjoying the quiet. Inside the dining hall, a long line of workers is cordoned off by a rail around the outside of the rows of tables covered in white plastic sheets. The cafeteria-style kitchen is on the other side of the room, and as the workers move up in line, they are required to show their camp badge and their number is recorded. There are four meals a day (morning, noon, supper, and midnight) and workers are entitled to three of them. After giving their number, they pick up a tray and make their way along the serving line, where the women working for Crawley–McCracken Catering dole out the food. The women live in trailer units directly across from the kitchen, where there is a chaperone who tends the door to their rooms. Men are allowed to enter these units, if invited, but are permitted only to sit in a small living room and visit.

A common survival strategy for the women working in the kitchen is to attach themselves to one of the bigger, tougher men in the camp, so as to lessen the continual harassment from the other twelve hundred men, preferring to fight off the attentions of one big lug rather than deal with an endless string of propositions and comments. This situation leads to fights, as these *beaux* have to remind other suitors to watch their manners.

On this evening, steaks and eggs are being served, raising the hum of conversation a little higher than usual, as well as the clatter of knives and forks. Over the course of the meal, noise and hunger gradually turn to weariness over a last cup of coffee.

"By the liftin' Jesus, leave the plate where it is."

"You look like you're finished eating."

"I may be finished eating, but you'd think a fella could set for a few minutes with a toothpick in his mouth and have a little peace as he rests after a meal, rather than being reminded that he should push off so another can take his place. Is that too much to ask?"

"Is there a problem here?" A supervisor comes over, responding to the raising of voices.

"I was just trying to gather up the dishes, as I am supposed to."

"All I want to do is sit here for a couple of godforsaken moments with the remains of my supper in front of me and finish a cup of coffee in peace."

"Others are just trying to do their jobs."

"Jobs. Jobs. Jobs. For just a few bloody minutes, I'd like to sit and try to forget about jobs."

"I don't like your language, and if you keep it up, I'll call camp security. If you want quiet, go back to your room."

"My room. My room. My bloody roommate is drunk by now, I'm sure, and Christ knows what is taking place." He stands, disgusted. "Take your fucking plate."

Outside, there is the faint sound of music, which gradually grows louder as an accordion player turns the corner of a trailer unit, followed by a group of Portuguese men who have already changed out of their work clothes and are talking and laughing as they hobble along on the rough stone, swatting mosquitoes and waving away the blackflies. As the group makes its way between the trailers, an ambulance rolls up behind them, as if making a parade of it.

"All we need now is a couple of fire trucks. Back home, they would come for miles," offers Ralphie as he slowly gets out of the ambulance. With the help of an attendant who passes him his crutches, Ralphie steadies himself on the gravel before he hobbles to the stairs.

"You makin' 'er okay?" asks the attendant as he fetches Ralphie's overnight bag from the vehicle.

"I got 'er, pard'. These jeezly crutches and this cast—man, I tell ya." With a couple of hitches, Ralphie makes it to the top of the stairs and enters the hallway. "The cast is some awkward. Plus those codeine painkillers got me higher than a kite. It's okay if you are laying abed, but if you are up and around you get right dizzy."

He fumbles with his key until eventually it slides into the lock. "There we go. Finally." The door swings open and the smell of Lysol hits his nostrils. "What the heck?"

"Looks pretty good to me." The attendant peers in over Ralphie's shoulder. "Why don't you just set yourself—"

"Where the hell is my stuff? I don't believe it." He opens the closet to see a couple of work shirts hanging there.

"Listen, Ralphie, I got to go. There's a guy with a broken hand waiting in the medic's office."

"You go down the hall right now to that prick bull-cook's room next to the shitter and you drag his sorry drunken ass back here. I want an explanation for this."

"Okay, okay. Just a sec." The attendant sets the crutches and bag on the bed.

A minute later Ronnie sticks his head in the door. "So what is your problem now? You want your other foot broken?"

"Where's my stuff? All my books and magazines?" Ralphie is pleading by now.

"Head of camp operations came over and condemned the place. He gave me royal shit for not keeping it clean and he almost fired me. I told him you wouldn't let me touch any of your things. He said to burn the works of it. You are no longer an employee of Long Spruce Contracting. You are merely a guest here, recuperating for a number of days, and waiting for your separation slip and compensation papers to be filled out so they can send you on your way. Sorry, pal. I hated to do it, but I had no choice."

Ralphie sinks down onto the bed. "Jesus, all my papers. You'd think they'd leave a fella something." The room has the anonymity of the hospital room he has just left.

"When you get back south, you better find yourself a woman who will do your housework for you. Keep you on the straight and narrow." Ronnie winks at him.

"Been there, got the tattoo." Ralphie reaches down with both hands and shifts the cast. Ronnie pulls a pint of Black

Velvet from inside his shirt and hands it to Ralphie. "Thanks." Ralphie takes a drink and hands it back.

"Keep it. You're gonna need it," says Ronnie as he leaves. Taped over the framed list of camp regulations on the back of the door is a cover from *Popular Mechanics* magazine showing a cross-section of the moon, from the solidified magma seas on the moon's surface, down through the middle mantle to the orange of the molten core.

〰〰〰〰〰〰

"How ya makin' 'er, Ralphie?" I tap on the door and partially open it. Ralphie is lying on top of the covers with his arms across his chest.

"Hey, Ray. Just trying to settle a little." Ralphie raises himself off the bed, as if from a drugged sleep. He looks down at the cast on his foot. "So much to deal with."

"How's the pain of it?"

Ralphie gives a faint wave of the hand and looks off into the middle distance. "What's a fella gonna do?"

"Guess you can't head home to heal?"

"I can't change 'jurisdictions,'" replies Ralphie, adding emphasis to the last word, as if quoting something he had been told earlier that day about his new situation. "Anyway, wouldn't I be the sight showing up back home like this. 'Oh, didn't you make good?' I can hear it now. 'You were going to get the big job and send money home. That's what you said when we lent you the money to go. Instead, it's you coming home to be taken care of.'"

"I know you didn't leave on the best of terms, but you have certainly made up for it by now."

"Oh, yeah. There'd be a freight train of love coming my way if I went back now. They have their own problems. I should never have left, I guess. That way we'd all be in the same boat, at least." Ralphie sighed as he shifted his cast. "I am heartbroken all the time. Day and night. I can't get over it.

It haunts me. My heart flops around in my chest like it can't go one more beat. Takes the starch right out of you. It's good I am getting out of here before I go completely off my nut. You seem to be able to handle this place all right."

"Just keep my head down and think about what I'll do when I get out of here. I am still trying to pay off Revenue Canada before they really come after me. But yeah, this is a very hard go. I lie in bed and design my new boat, or think about the things I have left to do on the house. That is about all that keeps me going. I hear there are jobs in Alberta. You don't make as much money, maybe, but you have a bit more of a life. Not like here."

"I thought anything would be better than getting seasick every time I stepped on the wharf. Just the thought of climbing down aboard the boat made me queasy. It turns out there are worse things. Anyway. They lined me up with this place in Winnipeg. Some kind of bedsit near the doctor. Wheelchair accessible." Ralphie wags his head back and forth as he makes a fist.

"You don't want to go down that road again."

"I know. I know. Get off in the ditch so far you can't find the road again. But it just seems so wrong, that's all. Imagine if my grandfather saw this place. A structure designed to hold the water back rather than work with it. There's nothing in a boat that is straight or flat. It is shaped by the waves and by the wind. It makes sense. But this here is the future, I guess. Fishing boats are the past. I know you have big plans to build a new boat and all, but from what I can see on the draggers, there is no hope for the fishery. They won't be satisfied until they catch the last one. So we just got here ahead of the crowd, that's all."

There is a tap at the door. Casey's large gnarled hand reaches around the cheap laminate of the door, holding a piece of cake in plastic wrap. "I thought you might want a bit of dessert." I pull the door open and the old man stands there with his offering.

"Thanks, Casey. I sorta lost track of time. Appreciate it." Ralphie reaches out and takes the cake.

"Wow, your room is clean now," Casey almost shouts.

"Well, it's not my room anymore. I am just a guest of Long Spruce Contractors until the paperwork is done and I fly out of here." More head-wagging and pinched pronouncements, and then he sighs. "Ronnie threw my stuff out, all my blueprints and drawings, my magazines. I can't believe it."

"At least you can see the floor. Well, time for sleep." Casey waves and is gone.

"Man, if I had his money," Ralphie sighs.

"But then you would have to be him."

"All this shit out in front of us, and nothing much behind us. It's like a nightmare."

I pick up the pint of Black Velvet from the bed. "Have a sip and get some rest. Worry about all this tomorrow. You'll be just as dumb then."

Ralphie manages a grimace. He unscrews the cap and takes a sip. "I started out as an asshole and ended up in a shithole." He hands the bottle to me.

"The only question is 'What took you so long?'"

"I know, eh? I'd mess up the Lord's Prayer. I guess I would." He looks up at the image of the moon taped to the back of the door. "How the hell did we ever end up high and dry in a place like this?" I hand the bottle back and Ralphie takes another cut through the imaginary dust lodged in his throat. He shivers as the drink goes down.

"The land of plenty. What?"

Ralphie shifts back on the mattress and props up his pillows before lying down. The bed appears to float on a narrow cushion of darkness in the otherwise shadowless solidity of the room.

"It's all a fella can do just to keep it together."

Casey, Don, Waz, Mac, and Johnny are grouped together with three Portuguese workers behind a pile of steel forms on a blasted shelf of bedrock between the powerhouse and the spillway, not far from the contractor offices.

"Man, that's a cold wind," says Don, shoving his hands deeper into his red-checked jacket. "Freeze the nuts right off ya. I thought it was supposed to be summer."

"Let's sell the place back to the Indians," says Waz. "Whatdya say, Johnny? Can we make a deal?"

"Bum me a smoke and I'll think about it," replies Johnny, reaching out a shaking brown hand.

"At least you have a warm bed at night, not like the camps I was in at your age."

"Which camp is that?" asks Johnny.

Casey looks at him, hesitating momentarily. "Hitler's camp in Czechoslovakia. You know, World War II."

"Oh," replies Johnny.

"I almost froze to death there. Rags tied around my feet and no coat. The other men had to carry me back to camp. That night six Hungarians huddled around me in the bunk to warm me up. They stunk, but—"

"There's Ralphie going in to pick up his separation slip. He must finally be heading south today." Don points to where Ralphie is being dropped off by the camp van outside the field offices.

"He was bitching because they made him come to the offices to sign the papers rather than bringing them to his room. Can you believe it?"

"Now he can head south and sit on his ass drawing compensation for the next three months."

"Gene's coming out of the office," Don announces. "Look out." They watch their foreman come down the stairs and stop to talk to Ralphie.

Across the way, Ralphie grabs hold of the stair railing to steady himself.

"Glad to see it has all worked out for you," quips Gene.

"What do you mean by that?" challenges Ralphie.

"Well, you got what you wanted. An all-expenses-paid three-month vacation."

"You bugger. What a thing to say to a man who just broke his foot working for you."

"Fucking the dog for me, was more like it."

"Why you..." Ralphie takes a swing at Gene with his crutch and catches him on the side of the head. Gene falls back on the steps and Ralphie gives him another poke as he lies there. A loud cheer goes up from the workers who have been watching from the jobsite. They begin banging their hammers on the steel forms. Frightened, then desperate, Ralphie turns to see what the shouts are about. He blinks up at the other workers spread out across the site. Realizing they are cheering for him, he raises the crutch in victory and shakes it. The veneration is more than he could ever imagine, and he is grateful as the banging on metal grows louder.

Gene props himself up on one elbow and pounds on the office door with his fist. Ralphie considers hitting him again, but then looks left and right and hobbles as fast as he can to Ford Lady's truck parked next to the offices. Its tires fling rocks at the walls and windows of the office as it speeds away across the old riverbed. Ford and the other foremen come out of the door to find Gene on the steps and Ford's truck heading up the riverbank.

"What in tarnation, Gene? Are you okay?"

Gene touches the blood on his cheek with his fingertips.

"Who the hell took my truck?" Ford watches it climb the bank.

"It's that Ralphie I told you about."

"That idiot who came to me with his Indian-approved energy plan? You should know better than get into an argument with someone like that in front of the other men." Ford watches his truck disappear over the hill. "My .303 is behind the seat. Geez, Gene. This is not good. This is not good at all. My ass will be in a sling." Ford turns in exasperation, and looks at the foremen who are assembled on the steps, and then beyond them to the workers who whistle and jeer. "Well, he can't go far. Someone call the Mounties. And call first aid for Gene, too."

The gantry crane cable swings down out of the sky as the men load the last of the forms on a row of pallets. "Maybe we should wait until Gene comes back," says Casey. They watch as the first-aid truck pulls up to the field offices. Gene is sitting on the steps holding a bandage to his cheek.

"He's already pissed off enough," replies Waz. "We may not see him for a while, by the look of it. He said he wanted this cleaned up. Besides, if we get rid of these forms, we can get out of this fucking wind."

"I'm all for that," says Johnny, climbing up on the forms and waiting for the other men to flip the pallet cables up to him. He motions with his hand for the crane operator to lower the hook. He snaps the cables into the hook and jumps down.

"Stand back," says Casey, motioning for the operator to take it away. As the pallet rises above their heads, its shadow passing over them, there is a snap as a corner of the pallet catches the edge of the pile of forms next to it. The pallet tips up and the forms slide off like cards from a spilled deck, raising stone dust and burying Johnny and Luigi.

"Oh, Christ. No." The wind whistles in the cables as Luigi starts to scream. Waz and Don lift the forms off Luigi, who stares down at his mangled legs, whining as he touches his bloodied thighs. When they lift the forms off Johnny, he lies there wide-eyed with blood soaking through the front of his jacket. His jaw is out of place.

"I'll go for help," Don runs toward the offices. Waz takes off his coat and lays it over Johnny's crushed chest. Faint gurgling sounds emerge from his mouth, followed by an ooze of red bubbles.

"He's gone," says Casey, touching Johnny's cheek. "I've seen it before."

When Don reaches the field office, Gene is climbing into the first-aid van, still holding the bandage to his cheek. "Two men are hurt, come fast."

"What happened?" asks Gene.

"Forms slid off the pallet. Luigi and Johnny were under it."

"Back over there," says Gene, turning to the medic.

Casey comes forward as men approach with stretchers. "Take him first," he says, pointing to Luigi, who has just vomited. "This one's a goner."

Setting the stretchers on the bedrock, they slide Luigi and then Johnny onto them and strap them in. The medic bends down and feels Johnny's throat. "He's still alive." By the time the van pulls away, other workers begin to gather around. Ford takes out his radio. "Kenny, what the hell happened?"

"How are they?" replies the muffled voice of the crane operator.

"One of 'em's hurt bad," replies Ford, signalling for the crane to lower the spilled pallet. With great deliberateness, he steps up onto the now empty pallet and unhooks the cables. "Well, shit." He stares at the cable in his hand and then throws it down in disgust.

"I couldn't see that well from here," says Kenny. "They gave me the signal to raise 'er up. Nobody had a radio."

"It's not your fault, Kenny."

"I told them to get back," says Casey, looking down at the blood-stained bedrock.

Workers gather into groups as word spreads that someone has been killed. Eventually they begin to move toward the buses parked near the field offices. When Ford sees the men moving, he takes out his radio. "1010 to all foremen. Fan out and persuade the men to stay on the job. The two men are only hurt. I repeat: neither of them is dead." He walks over to where some of the workers have begun to climb onto the buses. "Listen, no one feels worse than I do about what's happened," says Ford. "I hate to see my men hurt."

"You mean dead," replies one of the workers.

"Both men are alive," insists Ford. "So what does it help quitting for a day? We just get further behind and that makes life more difficult for all of us. If it's the man's family you're worried about, we'll pay them an extra $50,000 dollars if you just keep working." Turning their backs, the workers continue to file onto the buses. Ford curses and turns toward the field offices, where a Mountie stands waiting for him next to his cruiser.

※※※※※※

The yellow buses arrive back in camp at a horrid time of day, and instead of filing into the cafeteria as they usually do, the workers move down the road between the trailers toward the pub. There is no noisy boisterousness of a group looking forward to a few drinks with their mates. The group is surly and quiet. The cheap utility of the panelling, the carpet, the chairs and tables, and the acoustic ceiling tile seem to mock them. As word spreads, off-duty workers join those who have come up on the buses. Eyes are cast round the room. There are shouts and fists raised. Slights are remembered. Admonishments by camp security are delivered, badge numbers taken. Things calm down for a while. More beer is consumed. Voices are raised. A couple of Crawley dollies come in, greeted with hoots, until they sit down beside Igor and Big Al, whose eyes survey the room. "Just checking. I didn't think so. Not you. Not you. Not you."

Over at the jukebox, Gramps, one of the bull-cooks of long standing, has taken up his usual position on days when someone is killed. His chair is set right in front of the speakers, and he has his cane across his knees. The only song that can be played for the next twenty-four hours, or at least until Gramps passes out, is "Amazing Grace" by the Royal Scots Guardsmen. That is it. Try to play something else and you get a good whack with the cane. On his table there is a cup into which you can throw your quarters so Gramps can keep the machine churning out his anthem.

Then the beer bottles start to fly, and groups of men descend on particular tables and drag certain people outside and throw them down onto the gravel and kick them. More shouts and pointing. A man is walking alone along the road next to the pub and carrying a small brown paper bag.

"He's the one," shouts somebody in the group. "He's the one that threw the bottle that took the guy's eye out last time." A circle closes in on the solitary man, and he is jumped from behind. "Get him, Igor. Get him." The man falls to the ground, disappearing under boots and fists. The contents of the man's paper bag—a pack of cigarettes, a chocolate bar, a canned drink—spill onto the gravel as he is dragged and kicked and punched. When he is finally left as a lump on the road, someone picks up the chocolate bar and can of pop. "I think it's time for a Sweet Marie and a Pepsi," he drawls, and everyone laughs as they climb back up the stairs to the pub.

⎯⎯⎯⎯⎯⎯⎯

The static of the two-way radio chafes against the roar of the nearby rapids. Ralphie drags another spruce bough over to the truck, lifting it onto the hood and sliding it under a rope he has tied between the windshield wipers and the grill. Other boughs have been jammed behind the front bumper. A pup tent is haphazardly pitched in the truck box. Ralphie arranges and rearranges the spruce boughs and pulls at the tent ropes. Then he hobbles back to a nearby stunted spruce and hacks off more branches with a small hatchet and uses them to cover the sides of the tent. He opens the door of the cab, pops a couple of pills into his mouth, and takes a drink from the bottle of Jim Beam he found under the seat.

Ralphie then walks out onto a jut of bedrock that pushes against the swirling current of the river. He drops down on his hands and knees. "Fear the future. My life is a spark that pounds on a rock of unimaginable hardness. For a while today, the sun went backwards in the sky. Smell the broken chains."

"1010 to 1023," comes a voice over the radio in the truck. "1010 to 1023."

"1023 here. Go ahead, Ford."

"Yeah, Bert. Just send in a skeleton crew from town. There won't be any work tomorrow."

"I read you, Ford. That's what I figured. I got four men coming in. Over."

"Fine, Bert."

"Any word on your truck? Over."

"No. Nothing. I guess it's my fault for leaving the keys in it, but my Christ, man, you'd never expect anything like that to happen. It's been quite a day."

"That's for sure. It's terrible when a man dies. Over."

"Terrible...just terrible," replies Ford. "The union will give us hell, but where are they when their members walk off the job? Well, we'll let you go, Bert. I'll see you in half an hour or so."

"Right, Ford. Over and out."

"Over and out."

"Dead?" says Ralphie. "Dead?" His eyes are wide. "They may wish I was dead, but they haven't heard the last of me. Not by a long shot. They don't know who they are messing with. They will get more than they bargained for, I'll grant you that." Hobbling back to the truck, and throwing the hatchet onto the seat next to Ford's hunting rifle, Ralphie whispers into the compass that hangs on a string around his neck.

———————

The rotating lights of the RCMP cruiser reflect off the shiny white surfaces of the commissary, First Aid, and the chapel, which at this time of night normally serves as the TV room. The sound of bagpipes rises and falls as the door to the pub opens and closes. Then there is the rumble of a diesel engine as a front-end loader turns off the main road and emerges out of the dark. It idles down as it approaches the pub. Several boots can be seen dangling between the teeth of the bucket. The loader stops and lowers the bucket and four men clamber out of it. Then the loader moves slowly forward and the bucket slides under the rear of the RCMP cruiser and lifts it up. The swirling reflections from the lights on the roof begin to tip at odd angles, as if the constellations are shifting, until the vehicle rolls over onto its roof. The bucket is given a good shake, as if dumping a load of gravel. A cheer goes up as the loader backs off into the darkness and returns to the main road. Two Mounties bound down the stairs of the pub. One of the Mounties manages to yank the upturned door open, and crawls inside to reach the radio. This is met with more cheers and laughter.

〰〰〰〰〰

"Where's my son?" asks Walter Shingoose, walking up to the reception desk in the hospital in Gillam, followed by his father, Alex.

"I'm very sorry, Mr. Shingoose," says the nurse, coming out from behind the desk. "The doctor did all he could." She crosses the hall, and places her palm on a door without opening it.

Walter hesitates, then slowly eases the door open with a large trembling hand. Against the far wall is a stretcher covered in a light blue sheet. Alex begins to chant softly. Walter crosses the room and pulls back the top of the sheet. He looks down at Johnny's slack, ashen face. Peeling the sheet back farther, he can see the caved-in chest beneath the smock. He touches his son's face and then lays the sheet back over his head. Alex's chants become louder, breaking at times. Walter leans forward and slides one arm under Johnny's shoulders and the other beneath his knees. He lifts him as if he is a sleeping child. Alex holds the door and then follows Walter into the hall.

"Oh. Mr. Shingoose, are you sure?" pleads the nurse. She watches them walk into the shaft of light that shines through the glass doors.

Outside, they cross the parking lot and start back along Main Street. As they pass the shopping mall, there are loud shrieks as a woman drops her bags of groceries and runs over to them. She collapses on the road. Alex waves Walter on as he stops to comfort his wife.

The security guard makes his way to Trailer H. It is much quieter over here. He has a telegram in his hand, and reads the numbers on the doors as he walks down the hall.

"Hey, pal," comes a voice from a darkened room. "I need help." A pool of yellow vomit glistens on the floor. As the security officer's eyes adjust to the dark, he can see a short, fat man sitting on the side of the bed.

"What is it?"

"You got a drink to spare?"

"No, I don't."

"You sure? I'm real sick and I need a drink bad, real bad."

"You're Alfred Ronnie, aren't you? There's a telegram for you. Maybe you won a free bottle." He is about to hand it to the Ronnie and leave.

"Read it to me, will ya. I can't see so good."

The security guard opens the note and steps back into the light of the hall. "To Alfred Ronnie. Congratulations. Your wife has given birth to a six-pound three-ounce baby boy at Health Sciences Centre Winnipeg at 2:10 p.m. on June 10. Mother and son are both fine."

"How about that?" says Ronnie, his head in his hands. "Are you sure you haven't got a drink?"

As the officer turns to go, he notices a man lying under the urinals in the washroom across the hall. His pants are down around his knees. "Is your friend okay?"

"That's Jerry. He can't hold his liquor. He'll be okay. Hey, how about lending me ten bucks so I can get in on a friendly game of cards," entreats Ronnie. "I'll split my winnings with ya."

Dreams of a Golden Age

Ralphie struggles to build a fire next to the bank of the river. It flickers for a minute and then dies in the wind. "Man, it's cold. A storm is brewing. I can smell it on the wind." His whole body is trembling as he drops to his knees to protect the last of the embers before they are extinguished. He can barely keep his grip on the rifle, as his head jerks back and he stares up into the semi-darkness. "I am going to hide away in the moon's yellow blaze." And with that, he lies down slowly on the rock ledge and his eyes roll back in his head.

The swirl of reversal begins with the destruction of the hydroelectric dams on the Nelson River. The Cree god Wichikapache tricks the dams into thinking they are fishers' nets and the water tumbles through them. The concrete dis-aggregates into its former elements and they sift back into the landscape. The migrant workers sail home, flush with cash, as the tortured scrub spruce reclaim the bulldozed expanse of the camp. Transmission lines snap as their towers shimmy, creak, and collapse as if they have fourteen knees. The office towers of Winnipeg go dark and tip from the horizon. Cascading rivers swallow bridges, and prairie grass grows across highways as nature throws off the surveyed chain mail of the section survey. Cities shrink and towns disappear. Frightened farmers retreat from their land to the forts along the rivers, chased by the buffalo.

This reclamation accelerates when Riel and Dumont, in the name of infinite Manitou, execute Thomas Scott for trying to own the land. Terrified by this act of redemption and buffeted by privation, the settlers climb into the York boats and head down the Red River to Lake Winnipeg, crossing Traverse Bay and rowing up along the eastern shore of the lake avoiding as they go the large boulders that the winter ice shoves into the shallows. They hope to rest at Norway House but instead are harried along by spirits, and so they continue on over the many cataracts and portages of the Shield, to the boats that wait on the bay.

No longer able to possess the land, the remaining Europeans have to content themselves with being intermediaries in the purchase of furs at their forts on the inland waterways. Then the animal skins come alive among them and beavers chew through the remains of York Factory. European settlements finally sink into the permafrost and the barter economy collapses. The crofters from Lewis and Orkney leave the posts and, as they sail back across the ocean, their vessels are slowed by schools of fish, just as John Cabot was slowed five hundred years before. They return home to their families and there is plenty in the land. Everyone has milk and cheese from their own cows and warm home-spuns from their sheep. All the old songs are sung and there is happiness in the glens as the land that was previously under sheep is reclaimed. Everyone is going about with a cas-chrom on their shoulder and last year's thatch is dug into the potato ground, as preparations continue for the move up to the summer shieling.

The expeditions to the New World then become more crazed as lone adventurers arrive in the bay. They dream of finding a passage to the Far East, of becoming rich on the spices and jewels they find there, and of sailing home to be greeted by King and Queen. But instead they are harrowed into blind rivers jammed with ice, and barren shores that give no life to them.

Only the Swampy Cree survive the wrath of the elements. They do this by telling their stories. Even in difficult times, the stories help them remember. Thinking of remembering reminds them of one. It goes like this: "Things that wash up I live in. Old dead reeds wash up at the edge of the lake. I curl up in them. I live in them awhile. I can do this, I have no fear. The shells that wash up in the river—no snails in them, all cleaned out by the water tumbling. I live in them awhile. Anything. All things. Things that wash up I live in. So now I go walking with the sound of water in my ears. Little creek sound. Swift river sound. The sounds of waves on a lake. I walk toward them. Oh wash up new things for me to live in."

Outbreaks of Unrest

Chapter V
Scottish Highlands and Islands, Mid-Nineteenth Century

Chapter VI
Shelburne County, Nova Scotia, 1993

In much the same way as "Hemmed-In Communities" pairs fishers and crofters as embedded communities under threat, "Outbreaks of Unrest" links the narratives of strife and unrest that emerge in the midst of the enclosure of the commons. The mid-nineteenth-century expulsion of the crofters "to the four winds" and their resistance to and protest against the collapse of their way of life is juxtaposed with the blockade of a Russian ship in Shelburne, Nova Scotia, in 1993, which was the final protest by the inshore fleet as it faced shrinking fish quotas and ecological collapse, and the displacement that accompanied them. These two narratives mark the almost complete decimation of embedded social relations in the lives of crofters and fishers and the consequent devastation of the "rough and plenty" in these communities.

What links these two communities is that they are regions that were being absorbed into the industrial system. The enclosing forces favoured large corporations and consequently marginalized small artisanal participants. In the fishery, these enclosing measures included the creation of enterprise allocations and individual transferable quotas that privatized shares of fish quota among larger entities, and in the process eliminated the smaller players from the industry. For the crofters, there was a conviction among land managers at the time that crofters could not pay a rent sufficient to make the land profitable and that the fertile pastures "would be better cultivated and managed and pay better rates when let in large divisions" (Hunter 23). This belief favoured the large farmers and forced the small lot holders off the land. The social consequences of these new economic relations is recorded in the political strife that is presented in "Outbreaks of Unrest," as the crofters and fishers engage in collective resistance from below as they struggle against the forces that are destroying them.

Scottish Highlands and Islands, Mid-Nineteenth Century

History from Above

While the demand for sheep's wool continued to increase in the nineteenth century, the market for kelp collapsed in the 1820s and attempts to create a local fishery off the coasts of Scotland faltered because of a lack of investment in infrastructure. Having been displaced from their traditional homes in the glens, and with the alternatives of kelping and fishing having failed, the crofters were increasingly seen as an unprofitable burden on the ledgers of the large estates bent on "modernization." In this context, the crofters were viewed as insular, backward, and plagued by "inglorious self-content." With no inclination to be incorporated into the new ethos of "improvement," the only remedy for these "redundant populations" was to forcibly remove them from their traditional lands and send them off to a place where they could no longer hinder the new schemes of the managers.

These forced expulsions generated a series of protests and restiveness among the crofters, with many petitions being sent to Lairds and government officials in which the crofters made their case to stay in their homes. These protests were met with arrests and the criminalization of agitation that, in turn, provided those in charge with increased impetus to rid themselves of these "malcontents."

Within the larger frame of the links between colonialism and the industrial revolution, there was the simultaneous enclosing of Highland and Island land in Scotland so as to better serve industrial production in Britain, along with the concurrent opening up of large tracts of "empty land" in the colonies of the British Empire. This simultaneity afforded a "solution" for those in charge of the redundant crofters, as they furthered, at the same time, the political aims of land annexation in the colonies. The forces of capitalism and colonialism combined in sending the crofters off to North America, New Zealand, and Australia, transforming them in the process from being desolated wayfarers leaving their native shores—and if they survived the clapped-out and disease-ridden ghost ships—arriving in the colonies as agents of empire..

History from Below

> *About 300 cottar families were then said to have no regular means of subsistence; I was told they lived on the strong air.*
> —*Edward Charles Stanford (1883)*

We are eating an animal that just starved to death. It was our cow. I found her this morning breathing her last, collapsed against the stones of the knocked-down wall of what was the byre. It is our family's final meal here. Tomorrow it will be the roads, and the day after that, maybe the boats. Whatever happens, the dew will be on our heads.

The proprietor will be rid of us, and that is what he wants. The misery of the last years has finally come to this. We are strangers to the place that has been our home. Some of the crofters who were removed last spring were given allotments on the bogs next to the shore. And so, over the summer, famished people have blackened the beaches like the crew of some vessel wrecked on an inhospitable coast, that they might sustain life by the shellfish and seaweed laid bare by the ebb. Many of their allotments were barren in the extreme, unsheltered by bush or tree, and exposed to the sweeping sea winds and, in times of tempest, to the blighting spray. It was a matter of extreme difficulty to keep the few cattle they had retained from wandering, especially in the nighttime, into the better-sheltered and more fertile interior that they had known before. The poor animals were intelligent enough to understand the nature of the change effected. And because of the harshness of the shepherds to whom the care of the interior had now been entrusted, the cows added materially to the distress of their unhappy masters. For the animals were getting continually compounded; and vexatious fines, in the form of trespass money, came thus to be wrung from the already impoverished crofters. More and more often now, the animals will neigh from the shepherd's pens as they recognize their passing owners, who can no longer pay for their release.

Those who did not go to the bog or flee to a foreign land last year were allowed to plant their corn this spring. But soon after that, we were given the order to quit our homes as well. So although we had no roof over our heads, we were allowed—after much pleading with the Factor—to stay in the district to harvest our crops. Our hope was that after the summer our animals would have recovered from the poor winter and so their valuation would be higher, and that we would have food for the winter, wherever we would find ourselves. We are living outside all summer under an old sail, and are trying to save what we have planted. But when the Factor burned our houses after we left them, the fire destroyed many of the dykes as well. And the grass that could have been for our animals was burned with the houses.

Along with that, the new herdsmen and their dogs hunted us for watching our own corn, while their animals trample our crops. For the last month, we have been obliged to subsist upon broth made from nettles, thickened with a little oatmeal, along with our few remaining potatoes which we cook in the open air among the ruins of our former houses. So we have lost our homes and our land, and now our animals and our crops. We have lived to see ourselves wear out our lives. Meanwhile, more sheep farmers are seen daily traversing the country and viewing our lots, previous to bidding for them. These necessitous strangers appear to be in great fear of rough treatment from us whom they are about to supersede. But events proved they had no cause: we treated them with civility, and even with hospitality.

All of this turmoil began a number of years ago, when the Factor read aloud the new rules of the estate to those who had come to pay their rents on Martinmas. We were gathered by the road outside the public house where we annually pay our rents and are given our receipts. We were fingering the papers on which we had marked our "X" as we came round to hear what the Factor had to say. In a light mist he unfolded a long document, and before beginning to read it he stated that the proprietor wished everyone well and had set out new rules for the estate so as to insure peaceable relations, as well as to increase efficiency and promote an improved way of life for everyone as we look forward to the future. The Factor then began to read from the document that had to do with all manner of activities on the estate to be overseen by the Ground Officer and Factor, including things such as quantity of stock, use of kelp and driftwood, the building of houses, the cutting of peats, and the uses of our labour, along with the system of fines that would be imposed if we ran afoul of these restrictions.

After reading aloud the rules of the estate, the Factor then produced a paper that he asked each of us to sign, otherwise we would have to quit our places and leave the township. We did not know what to think, but one of us from the place stepped forward and said that we would like to study it more and could we please have a copy to take with us. The Factor did not like this idea, and said no, we could not have a copy, as it belonged to the proprietor. After talking with the Ground Officer, he did give us a week among ourselves to decide what we thought, and said that he would visit the township soon for our answer.

We were left to ourselves and after a time we came round to the idea that although we had heard a great many of these rules here and there, it was something new to hear them all together at one time. Everything set out was apparently on the assumption that the proprietor has to do with a whole population, every one of whom is so dead to self-interest that directions, restrictions, and written permissions must be given to keep them from running into all sorts of forbidden ways. Someone wondered if a set of rules for proprietors might be a better idea, since it would save them from committing all the cruelties that were about nowadays in the Highlands and Islands.

These are the kinds of thoughts that we worried about as we discussed the Factor's rules. It seems to us now, after all that has happened, that the grand plans of the Laird and his Factor are putting an end to us. The people of the township will be no more. We will be blown to the four winds. Where once we put out ploughs, briers and moss will now grow. The only way young people can live is for the men to sell their days ditching and clearing, and for the young women to go into service and have their morals destroyed. We have almost stopped being churchgoing people, so changed are we.

Along with these thoughts, we remembered those who are now lost to us. Over the past year, we attended the funerals of a good many of our neighbours who went to the poorhouse, and they got nothing but the funeral of an ass. Recently, an old couple arrived here. They had previously raised a large respectable family, but were now on the side of the road amid bits of their furniture. The man became distant in the mind and wandered off in the hills. We found him with his Bible under his arm. He was searching for his father, who had died thirty years before.

Among others who have suffered, Neil McDonald was, for no well-grounded reason, evicted from his home and farm by the Factor. He had no other home to go to, and was forbidden by the Factor to build a house in any part of the estate. The Factor also threatened with instant eviction any crofter or cottar who might, out of pity, afford him even one night's shelter from the cold. So his only place of refuge was an old boat turned upside down, with a hole in the centre for a chimney, and some straw laid round the openings to prevent snow drifts from perishing himself and the little ones. His wife being nigh her confinement, he for her sought shelter in his sister's house, but the farmer on whose croft the sister's house stood was instructed by the Factor to turn the sister out. The wife and family were removed, and the woman, while being driven in the cart, by the way was delivered of a child, as no one would be allowed to shelter her during the time of her delivery.

Another man, Hugh McLean, was blind, and was disgracefully served an order to quit, but having no house to go to, he was still in his own home. The Factor then sent men to strip the roof off that home by means of instruments of iron. Hugh then removed to the barn, in which lay a quantity of grain. The same men were then sent back with orders to strip the barn too; and the poor blind man, with his crippled wife, and no sons to help him, as they were drowned some time before, and his only other son was insane in the asylum, were cruelly turned out and left at the roadside.

Also there was Neil Black, an old man, who was well-to-do at one time on a farm, and on being evicted could not get even a cow's grass, so died a pauper four years ago. He was so poor and so neglected that when neighbours felt called upon to minister to his necessities and offer him bodily attendance, his flesh was falling off his bones, and he was in so disgusting a state that only stout-hearted men could go near him. The cause was aggravated by there being two sisters in with him, which only added to the distress.

Widow McDonald, also very old, and a pauper, died nearly two years ago, and but for her poor neighbours, would have been dead years previously. They could not prevent all the effects of official neglect, and the woman became diseased for want of attention, and the maggots were alive in her body before she was dead.

Donald Black, at one time a crofter, but being unable to cultivate his land without a horse, gave up, and soon became a pauper. He also died about three years ago, his death having been hastened by want of care, and the consequent filth in and about his bedclothes. He was a prey to heaps of vermin, insomuch that those who in desperation visited him wondered why he was not being carried out of his bed by the parasites. His widow died shortly afterward, and such was her state of body and bedding from the same causes that she besought the neighbours to bring her nettles that she might relieve herself from the irksomeness of vermin with their stinging pain.

It is these things that we discussed as we thought what to do about the Laird's regulations. When the Factor came round among us again, holding a paper in one hand for us to sign and a notice to quit in the other, he told us that unless we signed this paper agreeing to the regulations, the effect of which was that we would require to be obedient to anything and everything which either he or the proprietor would order us to do, or we would have to quit the place.

We said that we would not sign, and that besides, the good Lord had only ten commandments, and these were hard enough to keep, even with the reward of Heaven to behold. The Factor was offering us much less than that. But in the end we all signed, and we would all chop off our hand rather than sign it now.

Since that time, his mode of procedure has been to raise our rents excessively each Whitsunday, in hopes that we would follow our neighbours to foreign places and give up our crofts for sheep. Our rents are now double, the hill pasture has been taken away, and we are impoverished and in debt. Some of us were sent to the shore last year, and now a notice to quit will be delivered to the last of us, and so here we are in the wind and rain by a fallen-down wall. It is a wonder that poor people were allowed to breathe the air of heaven and drink from the mountain stream without having the Factor and the whole of the county police pursuing us as thieves.

But what does it matter if we go ten miles or a thousand miles? It's the same. Whatever is left of our stock, the valuation will be less than the fines we owe the Laird for poinding. We are now sojourners, only citizens of the world. Instead of gathering to pay our rent on Martinmass, we are being gathered together to be expelled like sweepings to the four corners of the world. We should have strayed abroad last year, with some of the others who emigrated to Canada. That was the choice then: go to the bog next to the shore, go to Canada, or stay and harvest the crops we had planted, and tend our animals on the good grass of summer, before their valuation. We chose to stay because we hoped that the Laird would change his mind and allow us to remain. But that did not happen. Our crops were trampled, our animals starved for lack of grass, and as fugitive inhabitants, we are only a cloud of living witnesses to the destruction of our homes.

Against us are a combination of landlords and Factors, and also one clergyman of the established church of the parish, who also made himself useful on these occasions, threatening us with punishment here and hereafter, if we refused to bow our necks to the oppressor. According to this man, all the evils inflicted upon us were ordained by God, and for our own good, whereas any opposition on our part proceeded from the devil, and subjected us to not just punishment here but eternal torment as well.

Last summer when many were evicted, Angus McLeod had recourse to an expedient that annoyed this minister very much. He erected a lean-to on his own ground in the churchyard, on the tomb of his father, and in this solitary abode he kindled a fire, and endeavoured to shelter and comfort his distressed family, and show a determination to remain, notwithstanding the wrath and threats of this minister and the Factor. He said that at least he can claim the land on which his father is buried, if no other. After several days, the Factor's men knocked down his shelter and threw his belonging in the ditch next to the church.

Support for the Crofters

Not everyone is against us. There have also been those who took an interest in our suffering, especially since there have been disturbances between Factors and crofters. This past spring there was a gathering on a Saturday in the local school that was organized at the request of a group from Edinburgh, who were travelling in the Highlands and Islands with the expressed purpose of gathering information on the social conditions of the crofters. No one among the visitors could speak Gaelic, so they relied upon the local Free Church Minister to give them some understanding of the history of the area and to provide some communication with local people. The visiting group was called the Society for Propagating Christian Knowledge and their fact-finding mission had brought them to a number of sites in Lewis after crossing the Minch from Skye.

On one of the afternoons during their stay, the group gathered in the local school to hear the Factor give his views on the plight of his charges. There had been enough concern expressed in various circles to bring the group here to assess the domestic situation of the inhabitants with regard to whether petty tyranny secludes the natives of the Western Hebrides from the benign influence of the British laws and government.

The Factor began his talk by outlining the three reasons for the current crofting system: to support enlistment in the military, the kelp manufacture, and improved fishing. "As opposed to the previous clan system where the Highlanders were spread throughout the glens, this new system afforded ample opportunity for the crofters to choose military service as a way to better themselves, or, if they were to stay at home they could make ready money cutting and burning kelp, although that was not as profitable as it once was, and also by prosecuting the fishery, either here in Lewis, or by going off to the herring fishery in Wick.

"As for the current agricultural prospects of the ever-increasing crofter class, there are too many of them and the quality and quantity of the land and the extremities of the weather are against them. The only remedy for the deterioration of the land is, I think, for the crofters to go where they can get land, that is, America. Go to Manitoba and various parts of America and Canada, and they can get land there very cheap. But instead, they cling to the soil here in Lewis, and it is very difficult. The Proprietor would give £500 today if all the crofters on the estate went away. He would keep the paupers. Out of Christian charity, he would not ask the paupers to go away.

"In order to shed light on the cause of these evictions from the land that you have heard of, I may state that with regard to this township, when the old common hill pasture in the north became valuable, in consequence in the rise of the value of sheep, the crofters were unable or unwilling to stock them or to pay anything like the rent offered for them by others from the south. The operation of this cause, combined with the fact that many crofters who were evicted were deprived of their holdings on account of non-payment of their rents, can be seen as the chief causes of them having to go away.

"Currently I draw rent from 28 households, 26 of which are aborigines of the place. They have their own habits, customs and sympathies. They are clannish when they get among strangers, and they fight a good deal among themselves. I have to say that after much encouragement and direction, there was nothing that could be done for them because they can be, I am sorry to say, indolent and lazy, and they marry when they are young. As a consequence, there are too many of them and they do not want to work. They say that they cannot pay our high rents, but I would go so far as to say that in many instances, if even the small tenants got their land rent free, their comfort would not be substantially increased, for if industry disappeared with rent, the tenants might not be much the gainers. For they are more indolent about their own land than they might be. There are no better workers or more faithful servants for others, but I am afraid they are a little indolent at home. Laziness and discouragement have led to many insolvencies in the crofter class.

"The crofters also complain that the pay for their labour is low and it is not worth it for them to sell it at such prices. But let me say that whenever there is labour required for a property, crofter labour is of less value than the labour of parties living solely by a week's wages. It is for this reason, that at the time their services are of the most value to the employer, they leave to attend to their own crofts. As you can understand, it makes an immense difference to an employer of labour that he can command the labour at the time when it is of the most value for his purposes. And another thing, within the last twenty or thirty years there has been so much improvement made in working land with regard to even cutting hay or corn, or gathering it in, with horse rakes and so on, that the great advantage is to economize hand labour and make use of implements to lessen the cost, as far as possible, of working the land.

"That being said, there is plenty of work going on just now on the estate, but the crofters like to work as it pleases them. A year or two ago, I had to bring a crofter from the east coast to do a job for me. I knew of two crofters from here who could take it. The one man from here declined the place because he wished to work when it pleased him. I then offered it the other man from here, but he said he would not clean a cow on the Sabbath, and I thought animals required to be cleaned as well as fed daily. Now there are those who say that asking a person to work for pay reduces the crofters from the status of crofters to labourers. But I think that someone who is able to work and make their own livelihood is in a far nobler position than a crofter who, every five or six years, has to go and cry out, 'I am destitute and want help.' Where is the dignity and status there, when you hold out your cup and expect a gift?

"To conclude, this holding tight to the land is only a matter of sentiment, a feeling of sentiment for the past. I happen to come from the east coast, where the sentiment is not quite so extreme. I don't see the crofters in the light of sentiment, when it is really a question of subsistence. I see it as an issue regarding the overall improvement of the efficiency of the estate."

With this, the talk by the Factor ends, and the Free Church Minister rises and thanks him for his description of conditions as he sees them, and he then turns to the gathering and also thanks them for coming so far and for taking an interest in the crofters. The Minister then invites questions for the Factor. After a short silence, one of the members of the group, an older man, rises from the small school chairs with difficulty, his knees tipping the table in front of him forward, which he holds with the flat of his palm as he steadies himself.

"I too wish to thank you for your well-informed opinions. You have certainly made our sometimes difficult journey worthwhile, which I have to say, was seriously in question as we crossed the Minch yesterday." There is some mumbling among the other members, as well as some laughter from the two women in the group. "Let me ask this of you. Are there old people who are unable to work?"

"Yes, there is one. I know one old man who gets something from the poor rolls, and he gets something from me now and then. He exists really, and that is all."

"It is very sad. We heard about his plight from the Reverend. You must recognize that that is a very sad thing for a man who formerly kept several cows?"

"I think he is quite incapable of that now. He had an acre and a half which he was unable to farm, and his wife is dead and he has no relatives."

"What is his name again?"

"Black Donald."

"In the case of a man who falls into that position, I suppose when he dies his house will just be swept away?"

"Well, there have been one or two swept away, because they were inclined to sweep themselves away."

The answer is followed by more silence, so the Minister steps forward from his position near the window.

"Do you propose by and by to remove the people from their present houses to a barrack?"

"That is my idea. It may or may not be a barrack. It is a castle in the air in the meantime, and may or may not come about."

"But that is the idea in building the place?"

"Yes."

"What is the object of consolidating the dwellings of the labouring people?"

"First, it is because I want the place as a residence for myself in the meantime and, second, because it is a more economical way to build."

The Minister turns back to the gathering, and a woman rises. "You mentioned times of destitution. Do you give them any special assistance in these times of want?"

"Yes, I gave them seed oats and seed potatoes."

"Was that in the form of an advance or a gift?"

"Certainly in the form of an advance. I should never lend myself to spoiling them by giving them gifts."

The minister pushes himself from the wall into the centre of the room and faces the visitors. "Do not expect such a thing as charity. No. Instead there is the scanty hand of those who have been the means of reducing the crofters into their present state, and the pitiful mite of relief obtained with so much labour and ceremony that comes from interested and caring souls such as yourselves, is doled out by pampered underlings with more than the usual insolence of charity, and will after all be paid for in the end by the crofters themselves. Such is the state of our whitewashed world where the desperation of the poor is exaggerated and the oppression by the powerful is left out of sight. The Laird can offend the hand of God and nothing happens, but the crofter breaks one of the Factor's regulations and it is an unpardonable sin. What the overlords can't ascribe to Providence, they lay at the door of the crofter's improvident character, who live in a state of nature, and are continually in need of handouts. What is expected now, it seems, is that the crofters should dutifully starve in their own homes, or slide off into some corner of the world where they will not inconvenience anyone as they die in silence."

The Factor does not respond, but stands silently, looking toward the window.

After a time one of the guests rises to his feet. "There has been mention of outside agitators coming in to stir up the crofters, and that you have accused the crofters of reading newspapers. Is that so?"

"I never accused them of that." The Factor pauses and stares at the Minister before continuing. "I may have put them on their guard against reading certain literature, but since few of them are literate it is not an issue. But I may say that the influence of evil doctrine on the general body of the crofters, through hearsay, can easily be imagined when people, whom I knew to be previously friendly and respectful, are carried away to be most insolent and offensive. I can only say that I am much astonished that a person of seeming intelligence should be carried away in the stream of rebellion, and I believe this has all arisen from the evil influence of agitators. I myself have of late been maligned by anonymous writers of articles in radical newspapers and other like publications. My principal reason for bringing this matter forward is to try and show who have been the chief movers in abusing me and stirring up the township to rebellion."

"We have heard in other places that the current crowding in townships such as this one is caused by crofters insisting on marrying when they are young?"

"I agree that is the case. Would it not be better for a young man or woman to go and try their fortune away from home, than to sit, and marry, and beget children on a miserable bit of land here?"

The Minister steps forward. "It would be better to have a good comfortable living at home than to risk the chance of straying abroad. It is not for everyone to make a living by shifting about in that way."

The other woman in the group raises her hand, and although the Minister is set to continue on, the Factor nods in her direction. "Please."

"If you find a person for some years following a certain profession—the pursuit of agriculture in their own way, let us say—and you of a sudden put a stop to that which they have been accustomed to, what is the result for these crofters? Can they at one moment turn their attention to another profession?"

The Factor smiles. "I am not aware those crofters have a profession."

"Have they not the profession of agriculture?"

"I am not aware they have land in their possession except a garden and a cow's grass. I don't know what profession you call that."

"They said themselves that in the past they were happy and contented with their lot and made a living. Is that not a profession?"

"They are always that, and yet periodically they are also in great destitution, and every now and again, as the Proprietor told me himself, subscriptions have to be got up to assist them."

"And that being the case, the estate thought the best thing for them would be to deprive them of what they have?"

"I cannot say what the proprietor then thought. I am merely giving you the information I have. I cannot state what the proprietor thought when I was not made aware of it."

One of the other members stands up. "Would it be possible to leave local issues for a minute and discuss more general topics that have come up as we have travelled about? For example, we have been hearing all over the country that people sixty years ago were better off than they are now. What have you to say about that?"

"It is my opinion they would be better today were it not for their folly. Money is more plentiful amongst the people than it was in my first recollection. For example, I am sure if you compare the condition of the people in your own township where you grew up sixty years ago with the condition of the people there now, which are the better off?"

"There are no people in my township today. It is only sheep and deer." An uneasy silence follows.

The visitor continues with another question. "There have also been many opinions expressed on the general character of the Highlander. Would you mind offering us yours?"

"Well, I mentioned earlier that we do not value crofter labour as highly as that of those who work for a daily wage. In general, I attribute it to intermittent availability, and to a certain extent climatic lassitude, the cause of laziness of which the west-coast Highlanders are accused. Away from home they become excellent workers, but on their return to their homes they become infected by the indolent surroundings, and especially during the winter months. Inactivity is a matter of course with them, what some have called inglorious self-content. Uneducated Highlanders also have a strong attachment to localities and hence their antipathy to emigration. They would rather suffer starvation than leave their homes even for a season's work. Accordingly, the knowledge of agriculture among the crofters is far behind the age. Highlanders are naturally imitative, and are more apt to follow leaders either for good or evil than to think for themselves."

"So the people have proved less skilful and more thriftless on the west-coast farm?"

"Yes."

"As a result of your observation and experience, do you think there is a decided difference in the character and habits of the west coast and islands, and the east-coast people?"

"I do."

"Have you any definite information or theory on the subject?"

"Yes, there are two reasons. One is that they are quite a distinct race."

"In what respect?"

"They have not the same intermixture of Scandinavian and Saxon blood in the west, as on the east coast."

"You think they are more Celtic in the west?"

"Yes, they are. Another reason, and the principal one, is that they are kept so much to themselves—they do not mix with people on the east coast to gather information. They do not associate except among themselves, and consequently they cannot acquire so much knowledge. I know from their habits and their mode of thinking that they would not suffer any strangers among them, for the stranger is looked upon as an oppressor among the native Highlanders. They hate them. The same feeling exists in those unbroken parts of the Highlands as it did two hundred years ago."

The minister raises his hand and steps forward again. "I am sure you are not saying that all the unrest regarding the strangers who have come among the crofters can be put down to a matter of insularity and disposition. Surely there is the issue of current conditions that plays a role in the unrest?"

"As a consequence of the agitation, and unreasonable expectations of a crofter's situation by well-meaning but injudicious counsellors, who wish them well on the one hand, and by disloyal socialistic demagogues on the other, a tendency to exaggeration and misrepresentation has seized the minds of the people, who are evidently under the impression that the worse the case they make out, irrespective of its truth, the more they are likely to get as a result of their complaints, so that people have come forward who really have no cause or right to do so. Much of the poverty of which they complain of is, as I have said, undoubtedly of their own making, for they too commonly spend, in entire idleness, time during which they might earn money enough to improve their circumstances very materially. Another active factor in their life of indolence is the facility with which large sums of money have been raised for Highland destitution, so they have come to expect handouts on a regular basis."

The Minister expresses exasperation as he flings down his arms. "Before God, you cannot be saying that the current plight of the crofters is all exaggeration and indolence. You must accept that there is something injudicious in the tenant at-will relationship with the proprietor that has caused all this suffering. What we see around us is not how God would wish it. This is not punishment for sins, surely."

Rather than looking toward the Minister with his reply, the Factor turns to the visitors. "All ministers must take an interest in keeping their flocks together."

"I am afraid the flocks you look after are the four-legged kind."

"I think I take as much interest in my work-people as any Factor or Proprietor has ever done."

The Minister moves to the front of the room. "It is the Factors and the capitalists that have a controversy with the people, and not the Almighty. The crofters have always been a religious, a devout, and a praying people, and now their oppressors, and not Divine Providence, have made them a fasting people."

"I entirely disagree with your characterization of our relationship with the crofters. From my knowledge of the country,

I am satisfied that the influence which landlords and Factors exercise over crofters is salutary—nay, is absolutely necessary to prevent the injustice with which crofters, when they have the power, treat each other. It is only one who has lived amongst them, and has a practical knowledge of their ways, who can understand the difficulty of keeping them in order. Highlanders are generally not as elevated as they ought to be. Highlanders want elevation." There is mirth on the Factor's face, and a murmur of reluctant laughter passes through the visitors, further exasperating the Minister.

Emboldened, the Factor continues. "But what is most to be regretted is that the worthless croft provides an inducement and an excuse for the occupier to stay at home, and waste time that would be so much more profitably spent in regular employment at fair wages."

Sensing that he has lost ground, the Minister's voice warbles with intensity. "Is there any use in beating about the bush? Is it not the fact that those people were removed from their holdings solely and entirely because they were in the way of the sheep?"

"Certainly not."

"If not, what other reason was there?"

"It would have entailed very considerable expenditure upon the proprietor to have built houses and put up fencing to separate the crofters from the sheep farms."

"That is what I say. The people are in the way. The Proprietor does not choose to spend that money, and therefore the crofters must go and make room for the sheep. Is not that so?"

"I have given you all the facts that I can. But if I think on it a minute, I would say that children of the Caucasian race came into the world without any covering. Let us examine his wardrobe. Is it too much to say that for every person born a certain number of sheep must be lambed. Thus does Providence in his wisdom and kindness give certain districts to yield clothing to man. In such matters, I say that we cannot oppose nature without placing ourselves in a false position, which is punished by diminished profit, as well as the increased suffering of mankind. With good conscience, we therefore grow wool on these hillsides, and by doing so are a benefit to humanity."

"And so your idea of charity and godliness, which you so value, chafes against the objectionable sentiment of the crofters clinging to their native soil, and who are made sinners for doing so?"

"Well, it is objectionable in one way, because so long as the crofters remain, they will be a burden to themselves and to others, but if they have the moral power to go away they would be a benefit to themselves and a relief to others. It is the raising of the moral character, the elevating of the moral character, that would make them think for themselves, and overcome the attachment to their home place that is so strongly implanted in the breast of every Highlander."

With that, the discussion ends. The Factor shakes the hands of the members of the society and then excuses himself and goes outside to the carriage that awaits him. The Minister hangs back, and then proposes to the group that they take a walk through the township, or what is left of it at least.

Crofter Demands for Change

Soldiers are now camping near the Laird's house. This is their second visit to the township in the last year. They also came last Whitsunday after we sent a petition to the proprietor setting out our complaints about the rack-rents and the loss of the hill. We ended our petition with the statement "We most respectfully request a reply in writing, so that we may consider what steps should be taken so as to secure our object. Ever your humble servants." We felt this was necessary because our previous requests for consideration had gone unheeded.

When the Factor read the petition, he did not like it. The next day he went to Edinburgh to meet with the Proprietor. He returned with the Proprietor's response, along with a band of soldiers. This statement we had sent him was taken by the Proprietor as a threat of violence against the laws of the land. He accused us of treason, and so he requested a force necessary to put down a possible rebellion. Two of our own were put in jail for their trouble, until supporters from the Highland League worked to gain their release.

Notice of Meeting
We, the tenants on the estate, do hereby warn each other to meet at the Free Church on the 7th day of July for the purposes of stating our respective grievances publicly. The Ground Officer is requested to attend. The meeting will be moderated by the Free Church Minister.

Word of the meeting planned for tomorrow has brought more soldiers sent by the Proprietor who are now setting up camp near the Church. The notice has also brought supporters of the crofters from Glasgow and Edinburgh, as well as journalists, who have come to hear what the crofters have to say. We are informed by the Ground Officer that the Proprietor dismissed our meeting as the work of outside agitators who are promoting rebellion, and he repeats the offer that that he made last year: that anyone who is unhappy on the estate could apply to have their way paid if they chose to emigrate.

With the soldiers here again, we are now also considered rebels, and the fangs of the law are forcing us to leave immediately because we are a threat to the social order. In our defence, we can say that we are urged on by fearless want. First, they ruin us and make us paupers until the very stones cry out, and now they want to get rid of us because we remind them of what they have done to us. The very individuals who have been the authors of all our woes, are now our vindictive persecutors.

How I wish for the older days. Things are not so quiet as they used to be. The crofters have been of late years irritated to such a degree that a rebellious spirit has arisen in the minds of the people. In former years we were as quiet, and as good a people, as could be found in the whole of Great Britain; and when I sometimes go and listen to the feelings of irritation they give expression to, I simply am surprised, and wish myself back in my own home. When I look around now, there is a great deal of confusion and upset in what is left of the township. Many feel that it is too late to save us no matter what. The arrival of the soldiers confirms this, especially when there is also talk of a boat coming to take us away, while others see hope with the arrival of the Highland League.

Because of the poor state we are in, some of our own at first wanted the moral courage to come up to the occasion of having a meeting. If anyone showed symptoms of weakness in this way, they were encouraged so that on the appointed day the clansmen could meet and deliberate on the situation. In the time leading up to the meeting, it was resolved that, as a body, we should adopt a united course of action. We are all similarly situated. Each person and each town has a grievance, and it was decided that no individual will be called upon to make a separate claim. Each township or combination of townships is to make one demand, and if any punishment should follow on such an act of temerity, it should not be allowed to fall on any one person, but on the united body as a whole. To guard against any backsliding, and to prevent any chicken-hearted leaguer from falling out of the ranks, we, one and all, subscribe our names in a book, pledging ourselves as a matter of honour to adhere to the resolution thus arrived at.

The Highland League has met with representatives of our township and has helped us organize the meeting so as to discuss what the crofters want to do next. The sympathizers also brought news that several Members of Parliament had, that day, raised issues related to the crofters with the Prime Minister, and to reassure us that there is support for us among the general population of the United Kingdom. All this seems a mockery to many of us who are starving and past hope. When

I think back to the appointed day of our destruction, the Ground Officer had come to our camp with a pail of water and extinguished our fire, and a great steam arose; and what with the noise of the roof being torn off and the denseness of the steam, my wife went out of her senses. She is beside me now, huddled under the sail, but she is not herself. It grieves me so to hear people now speak about what can be done for us, when we are phantoms merely, gone as the steam from our fire.

As the meeting begins, the Minister welcomes everyone and then introduces the visitors in the room and thanks them for making the trip to hear the concerns of the crofters. He then salutes those who had earlier in the year been taken off to jail, for whom there is a rousing cheer. One of them steps forward and thanks again those who had secured their release from jail, as well as thanking the authorities in Edinburgh who "were so kind to us, that we were not out of lodgings till we came home."

The united statement of the grievances of the crofters is much like the earlier one that had been sent to the Proprietor as a petition, but more clearly laid out. A young scholar from the place looks to her father, who stands beside her. She begins to read in a wavering voice:

1. We ask that those who have lost their land should have it restored, and that the whole of the township should return to the allotments that existed in the time of our fathers, with the hill fields of our shielings restored. Sheep have been the ruination of us. There is plenty of good land for all concerned, if it would only be reallocated properly. God made the land to be a benefit to all, not for the profit of the few.

2. There is no tenure of land. The crofters hold their land from term to term. Leases have been hitherto unknown in the township. This situation has led to many families being served with notice to quit. We ask

that their lands be restored to these families and that they be allowed to live in peace with enough land to serve their needs. We want leases, provided adequate lands are given, sufficient to support a family, and pay a fair rent. By having leases, we can improve the land and have a certain stability given us.

3. Rack-rent, or such high rent on the land, which, in turn is insufficient, or of such poor quality, that we cannot support our families. The land for which we are paying these unreasonable rents is of singularly poor quality. The best arable and grazing land is now in the hands of sheep farmers. Crofters have been sent to the inferior lands only because it is unsuitable for the large sheep farms.

4. The return of our hill pastures. This was taken away many years ago and let as sheep walks, and we were never compensated for this loss. We need the hill pasture for the summer grazing of our animals, which allows our crops to ripen unhindered. Otherwise we have to buy feed for them, which further impoverishes us. This destruction of the commons has carried on and expanded over the last forty years, despite our repeated requests for its restoration.

5. Cottars who are thrown in upon us from other districts are a cause of great distress. These families do not have a cow's grass, or a patch of potato ground, and are living on whatever piece of bog that is available. Although we try to help them, there is much suffering among them, which also drains our reserves.

6. No public works toward improving the property or the land of the crofters. Although we pay road money, we see no improvements in our district. That money is spent on the proprietor's projects, with no benefit to crofters.

7. No compensation for improvements. We are discouraged from improving our land and our habitations

because it will only lead to increases in rent, and there will be no benefit paid to us for improvements should we be evicted.

8. As regards emigration, we can frankly state that we have no interest in emigration. Why should we emigrate when there is plenty of land available in our own township, if it were not under sheep? Those who wish to go can do so, but we are against forced evictions. We want land granted to us which will be evaluated by impartial judges and a reasonable rent based on the goodness of the soil.

9. The poverty of the crofters. We are yearly getting poorer and those of us who have not already been cleared from our land, are hemmed in on all sides. The land is not allowed to rest, as we yearly plough the same exhausted and unproductive ground. We have been deprived of seaware to replenish the land since the time of kelping and have not had it restored. We only produce enough meal for half the year, and so having to spend, we are impoverished.

There is a general murmur among those present as the young scholar finishes and her father clamps his hand gently on her shoulder.

One from the place rises to speak. "We therefore consider it a great grievance that we, being loyal subjects of Her Majesty, living under what we are taught to believe to be the glorious British Constitution, living in a country which is supposed to be the best governed in the world, should be left so much to the mercy of landed Proprietors, and, still worse, their Factors, that we can scarcely call our souls our own." The man then sits down.

Others look around amongst the crowd. Another man from the place stands up. "The Proprietor led us into poverty, and that then became the excuse for sending us to the far-flung world. Those who could were obliged, of their own accord, to go away; and those who were not able to go were only able to creep into such small corners as they might until their means failed, and then they had to go away too. I, for one, have never seen that emigration gave more room to people, though it did to sheep. I would leave if I thought it would make more room for my neighbours, but it will only make more room for sheep."

Another stands. "The result is that from being poor we have become poorer, and our case is truly pitiable. That is not something like the stuff the Highlanders are made of. It is an easy matter to say that we are lazy, and to say every other bad thing about us, if we are in your way and you want to get quit of us. These are the arguments used against the Red Indians of America. The Highlanders are not lazy, but we refuse to be serfs, and insist on being persons, and as good at least as our oppressor."

A stranger then steps forward, who had been leaning against a far wall. "The present conditions are due to the insecurity and insufficiency of the crofter's holdings, and the deprivation of their hill pastures, and the huddling together of large numbers of them on unproductive land, to make room for sheep and deer, as was duly pointed out in your list of grievances. The chronic poverty prevalent in the land is mostly, if not wholly, due to the unequal distribution of the land, the most and the best of which is in the hands of a few. All that is necessary to remedy this sad state is the redistribution of the land, giving each family as much arable and pasture land as will keep it in comparative comfort, and then to apply the principles that have been proposed in Ireland for fixing fair rents and giving security of tenure. Nothing short of this will allay agitation, restore contentment, and satisfy the just demands of the people. Why speak of emigration as a cure? Among all the Acts passed by the lords of the soil, I am not aware of one to preserve the people, but there are many on the statute books to preserve game and deer. I think it a mistake, however, to consider the crofter question as a mere local question affecting only the crofter population, and that can be settled by remedies that have only a local application. It involves the great social problem of modern civilization, as seen in the institution of private property in land, the ownership by some of the people of the land, on which and from which the whole must live. It is this system that produces the destitution in the Highlands and the hideous squalor of our city slums; and it involves the problem of the overall distribution of wealth."

An older man rises now to speak. "I am no longer a crofter, I am only a sojourner. I was a crofter on the estates many years ago, and then I emigrated to Australia, where I remained for twenty-seven years. I have come back now to get a consecrated grave in my native country. I remember the failures of the crops and the destitution that followed at the time of my leaving. At an early age I was obliged to work on my father's croft—a great part of which was actual quagmire—filling drains and removing stones, for which we got bad oatmeal in payment from the Laird. This meal, I always understood, was "destitution" meal. This meal was kept in the cellars, until, as was said by the people at the time, it "became alive;" while many of those for whom it was intended were on the verge of starvation. It was a common saying in the parish among those who had come for their dole ten or twelve miles across the hill, that they might have stopped at home and whistled for this meal, for it could walk to the township. Ultimately it was put into the sea because it had spoiled utterly, and, it being a calm night, it floated on the surface, and next morning a border of meal could be found along the shore, while the people were still in a state of semi-starvation. Before I left for Australia, the wood of our house was burned as firewood by the shepherds who came into the estate, and the careless feet of the shepherds still trod upon our roofless hearth. If I was a young man again, I would surely prefer to put five thousand miles of the salt water between me and this estate, as I did in my youth. The reason is this. I would prefer emigration so that I would not be annoyed, because it is not easy for a spirited man to put up with what he feels. For injustice and tyranny are vindicated and the people are made prey. And the demon of sordidness has assumed the shape of the angel of civilization."

A woman from the place sets aside her knitting and stands. "I have something to say about our houses. They are built on the shore. We built them ourselves, for the proprietor gave us no assistance. We had to pay for the wood that we got from him for the purpose. We spoke to the Factor about a change of site for the houses, and as an answer he asked us whether the sea was coming over the roofs of them. We said it sometimes did; and he told us then that we should put back doors upon them, and when the sea came in, then we could run away. That is right. That is what he said. Nearly the whole of the crofters' population, and all the cottars are like so many half-water, half-land plants studded over the poorest parts of the slopeland, often flooded by the tide, and never properly drained for seed. The last time we met with the Factor at the schoolhouse, he also made fun of us, telling us to take crops out of the rocks, and to imitate earthworms who are splendid drainers."

One from away rises now, seeing no one else ready to speak. "The grievances we hear today are examples of the natural tendency of the system under which we are struggling to place at the disposal of the owners of lands a great deal of power. There is excellent land lying waste in the hands of the Proprietor, that is ready for the plough; and he does not allow the people who are willing to work it, to take a living out of it, and add to the wealth of the nation. It is a good enough reason why we should add our voices to those of others who have suggested that the Government should take the land into their own hands, and make sure that it is applied to the purposes for which God created it. There are those who want only two classes of people in the world: capitalists and day labourers who have only what their labour acquires on the passing day, and who have no independence or property. What we want instead is a world organized for the free cultivators of the soil."

The visitor next to him stands. "I want to assure you that your voices are being heard by those who support you. And when you state your grievances, your disappointments, your hopes, and your own ideas for the redress of what troubles you, you reveal a good deal of the character of your minds, and give us a glimpse of the sort of men and women who have been lying so long under the burden of wrong which has at last compelled you to make your voices heard. It has been alleged that the crofters have been moved and primed from without by the opinions and creations of what the young man writing in Edinburgh to the *Scotsman*, called certain "cowardly and unscrupulous agitators." Now, it so happens that I am, from direct personal knowledge, in a position to remove much of this difficulty. The weightiest part of the work of these pioneers, or agitators as they have been called, is mitigating the adverse influences of the men who have for so long kept the crofters in a state of unworthy fear. It is but right to say that the warping influences that have operated to defeat the objects of the Government and the Crown in any measure, are those exerted by the very class who have objected to all preparation on the part of the crofters. We are charged with putting complaints into the mouths of crofters, and we are abused as agitators because the peeled and evicted people are at last encouraged to state their grievances.

"On another more general point, I am quite ready to admit that education may be so perverted and applied so as to promote emigration, to promote a taste for clerkships in the large cities, and make the pliable youth grow up into superficial creatures who think themselves superior to the tenders of those who take their living out of the soil. But this is a false education, or mis-education; and I admit also that under school boards composed of Factors, sheep and cattle farmers, and others who are not in sympathy with the native people, young people are being educated into cosmopolitans, who care not for the things and the duties which lie nearest to them, and instead are schooled into being mere verbalists that do not think the language in which Fingal spoke, and Ossian sang, worthy of their study and care. This, and much more, I know is being done by the means of the machinery of education. But that is not education. In so far as the means of education are thus perverted, they are operating from the same source and in the same direction with all the other alien forces that have gone to set aside the instincts, the language, the intelligence, the common sense, the feelings, and the interests of the native people.

"When a person is convinced that their language is a barbarism, their lore is filthy rags, and that the only thing good about them—their land—is, because of their general worthlessness, to go to someone of another race, and another tongue, what remains to struggle for? Every word that is said against the Highlander is really evidence against their so-called superiors who have done their utmost to stop the education of the race, and substitute for it the godless economies of 'the greatest good for the smallest number.' It is a systematic attempt, carried out with public money, to distort and debase the minds of the people, and have the schoolmaster as the co-labourer with the Factor and the Ground Officer in destroying all chance of the people in ever raising their heads in their own country.

"The first thing wanted in the Highlands is the revival of the spirit of the people. The second, the calling forth of their intelligence, common sense, and enterprise. The third, definite legislative protection from interference with them by the petty deputies of absentees and aliens as have kept them so long in a state of slavish uncertainty and fear."

A swirl of emotion circles the room, people stand, then sit, raise arms and voices, shove each other. Some of them run outside into the night, and as quickly come back in, slamming the door. There is the wrench of desk legs pushed across the rough floorboards. The Free Church Minister raises both arms, and calls out, "In praise of our Lord, we thank him for his many mercies, and we pray that he has heard our call tonight, and that he looks down upon us now and blesses us and our calls for justice. That he sees our travails and knows that in our hearts we worship him and desire to do his bidding. In the name of the Father, Son and Holy Spirit. Amen." By the time the minister finishes his prayer, the room has calmed down, as one after another bows their head. The people of the place go quietly into the night, and shift toward home, if they have one to go to. Those who have come from Glasgow and Edinburgh stay behind and answer questions from the few journalists who have made the trip with them. The Ground Officer has come forward from his spot at the back of the room. He is ignored by those who remain.

Confronting the Soldiers

Over the following days, the soldiers continue to camp near the church. Word has spread that more soldiers are coming, as well as a boat to take us away. This is confirmed when the Ground Officer stated that everyone in the township will be served with a notice to quit, as soon as the papers arrive from Edinburgh.

On the appointed day, the soldiers assemble outside the Proprietor's house to prepare to deliver the final notices to those who remain. Two old men dressed in the torn plaids from their former highland regiments watch the proceedings. The soldiers in their red tunics ignore them, as they silently make preparations. The two old men begin to speak, first to each other, and then gradually turn and gesture to the nearby soldiers.

"My grandfather went into the army—at least he was forced to go—and his bones are bleaching on a West Indian island. My brothers served fifteen years in Her Majesty's Navy, and now his grandson is being evicted from this bare rock that has been uninhabited until recently."

The other then begins. "There is not a family in the whole of this island where there are two sons, but one of them at least has been in the service of the Crown, and neither they nor their fathers can now obtain a foot of the soil upon which they could live. It would appear that when Britain becomes involved in a struggle with another nation in the future, they must send for the sheep and deer, as well as its young men, and then they can see which is the best bargain."

The other man steps forward again, louder this time. "I remember four who fought at the Battle of Waterloo. Three fell on the field, and one of them died in hospital afterward. Instead of the widows of these men being looked after, they were driven to the wild woods of Canada, and the land they possessed was placed under sheep. That was the justice meted out to them. It was the general talk since I recollect that if they served in the military their families would not be put out, and I have seen some of the soldiers when they came home, going to the reduced stances where their families now lived and shedding tears, and saying they would go and pull down the Laird's manor.

"We went through many a war for Britain. Three of us again went through the whole of India. In Afghanistan we were represented by one of our number, and he was killed in the last battle. That is the last person belonging to our place that was in Her Majesty's Service. We complain bitterly that we cannot get the houses that our families paid for. In days past, the old Waterloo men came home and told stories, and the young men would be delighted to be connected with the army. We went because others came home, and we saw them dressed in the kilt, and when we saw that, our hearts went into it. I went to Edinburgh to enlist, and others followed me. There was the feeling that they would like to be in one of the Highland regiments."

The Sheriff emerges from the Laird's house with a sheaf of papers and the soldiers begin to fall in. This at first gives the appearance that the soldiers are lining up for the two old men, who happen to be standing in the spot near the Sheriff's appointed place.

The two old men stand straight in response and face the group. "But it does not happen that way now. All life is crushed out of the people. The real facts connected with the raising of the regiment are not so glorious now. The general is sent to every parish, and calls every tenant, with their sons, to the parish minister's parlour, where they are met by the Factor with his rental book on the table, and every tenant who would not give one of his sons to the general had his name scored out of the rental book. This general got in this way about five hundred young men, thus forcibly enlisted, rather than see their parents and relatives reduced to beggary. This is after having been promised that their leases would endure forever."

One of the old gentlemen now squares his shoulders and points toward the soldiers, who could do aught but listen. "There was just such a man, like you are, harassed out of his country when he was trying to speak of these things, so much so that on one occasion when he happened to be away seeing a friend at the time his military pension fell due, the parish minister, who was drawing the pension money, returned it back to London. You know what it is when a pensioner's money is returned. He is considered a dead man. This man was obliged to go to London and represent himself as a living soul before he got his pension. That was done by the man right in there." He points to the Laird's house.

"If you want to fight a war now, 'Send your deer, your roes, your rams, dogs, shepherds, and gamekeepers, to fight the Russians, for they have never done us any harm.' Should the Czar of Russia take possession of that house there, we would not expect worse treatment at his hands, than we have experienced at the hands of the family of this Laird for the last fifty years. How could your Grace expect to find men where they are not, and the few of them that are to be found among the rubbish and ruins of the country, have more sense than to be decoyed as chaff to the field of slaughter."

The Proprietor comes out his front door and is conferring with his Factor and Ground Officer. The old man continues: "All modern history, from the rebellion of 1715 onward, teems with the record of Highland bravery and prowess. What says our Highland-evicting Laird to these facts, and to the treatment of the Highlanders?" He points at the Laird. "What reward have these men received for saving their country, fighting its battles, conquering its enemies, turning the tide of revolt, rescuing women and children, and establishing order, when disorder and bloody cruelty have held their murderous carnival?" He points directly at the soldiers. "And we ask, in the name of those who have served ere now. How can you come here to fight against your own?"

He points back over the hill, to which the Proprietor turns and absently looks. The old man jabs his thumb again in that direction, where now only the remains of a graveyard are visible. "And those who proudly planted the British standard on the heights of some far hill, how are they, their fathers, brothers, and little ones treated? Is the mere shuttlecocking of an irrepressible cry of admiration from mouth to mouth, and the setting to music of a song in their praise, all the return the race is to get for such noble acts? We can fancy the expression of admiration of Highland bravery at the Dunrobin dinner table, I heard of recently, when the dukes, earls, lairds, and other aristocratic notables enjoyed princely hospitality. We can imagine the mutual congratulation of the Highland Lairds as they prided themselves on being proprietors of the soil which gave birth to the race of Highland heroes.

"Alas for the blush that would cover their faces if they would allow themselves to reflect that, in their names, and by their authority, and at our expense, the fathers, mothers, brothers, wives of 'the invincible 78th' have been remorselessly driven from their native soil, and left to starve and to die in the open field. Alas, more than fourteen thousand of this same 'race of heroes' of whom you so proudly boasted, have been haunted out of their native homes; and that where the pibroch and the bugle once evoked the martial spirits of thousands of brave hearts, razed and burning cottages have formed the tragic scenes of eviction and desolation; and the abodes of a loyal and liberty-loving people are made sacred to the rearing of sheep, and sanctified to the preservation of game. Yes; we echo back the cry, 'Well done, brave Highlanders!'

"But to what purpose would it be carried on the wings of the wind to the once happy straths and glens? Who, what, would echo back our acclaims of praise? The cry might startle a timid deer, or frighten a covey of partridges, or call forth a bleat from a herd of sheep, but people would not, could not, hear it. We must go to the backwoods of Canada, to Detroit, to Hamilton, to Woodstock, to Toronto, or Montreal. We must stand by the waters of Lake Huron, or Lake Ontario, where the cry 'Well done, brave Highlanders' would call up a thousand crofters, and draw down a tear on a thousand cheeks.

"Or we must go to the bare rocks that skirt the sea coast of this island, where the residual population were generously treated to barren steeps and inhospitable shores, on which to keep up the breed of heroes, and fight for the landlords who dared—dared—to drive them from houses for which they fought, and from land which was purchased with the blood of their ancestors. To what purpose did their fathers climb the Peninsular heights, when their families are rewarded by the toleration to starve, in sight of fertile straths and glens devoted to beasts? We were but a reservoir of blood to be profitably spent in British wars, and as it is clear to all now, you have exhausted the source."

The dismal brigade of soldiers shuffles, and then turns in unison as the neat coterie of superiors, including now the Proprietor, the Factor, the Ground Officer, the Sheriff, and the Sergeant, gather before them. The new group had not deemed to listen to what the old men have said, and are conferring with each other about the plans for the day.

One of the old men pushes forward to the edge of the group. "Proprietor, Sir, you may think that you are right, but we know that you are wrong in what you are doing. There is an element of sentiment in the situation that is impossible for his lordship to understand. But for that we do not blame you. It is not your fault, but your misfortune, that your upbringing and outlook are such that a proper understanding of the position and point of view of the crofters is quite outwith your comprehension. You have spoken of daily wages and employment and emigration to new kingdoms in tones of veneration, and that is no doubt what you believe, and in the view of those unfortunate people who are compelled to live their lives in smoky town or foreign land, steady work and steady pay are very desirable things. But in Lewis we have never been accustomed to either, and, strange though it may seem to your lordship, we do not greatly desire them.

"We desire to attend to our crofts in seed time and harvest, and we follow the fishing in its season, and when neither requires our attention, we are free to rest and contemplate. You have referred to our houses as hovels, but they are our homes, and I will venture to say, my lord, that poor though these homes may be, you will find more human happiness in them than you will find in your castles. You own the land, but you do not own us. You say you cannot give us our land back. We say we refuse to be bond slaves. We want to live our lives in our own way, clear of the fear of the factory bell."

His partner steps forward and pats the shoulder. "That's yourself, boy." The Proprietor pauses to take note of the two old men and then turns to commiserate further with his assembled underlings.

When the Proprietor finishes, he goes back inside his manor, and the Sergeant moves over to address the troops. "Now, men, it is of the utmost importance that order be kept at all times.

Our job is to accompany the Ground Officer and the Sheriff throughout the township. There have been threats of rebellion, and there are foreign agitators among them, so it is very important to keep our heads. Spirits will no doubt run high, but it is our job to maintain the peace."

The soldiers lead the procession over the hill, followed by the Factor, the Ground Officer, and the Sheriff, who has the notices to quit in his hand. Across the hill and above the road leading to the township, the crofters begin to gather, having received reports that the soldiers are marshalling. People can be seen coming from all directions to join the group on the side of the hill.

The crofters cheer as the soldiers mount the knoll, where they are then saluted with volleys of sarcasms about their voyage from Glasgow. The women, with infuriated looks and bedraggled dress—for it has started raining heavily—are shouting at the pitch of their voices, uttering the most fearful imprecations, hurling forth the most terrible vows of vengeance against the enemy. One of the women of the place steps directly into their path as they approach the first hovel and points at the Factor, saying: "We will not let you destroy the last of our ancestral homes. We demand the restitution of our inalienable rights as Highlanders to live freely in this place. It is a satanic imposture, that the stewardship of God's soil is freely convertible into a mischievous power of oppressing the poor. It is better for landowners to have been born beggars, than to live in luxury while causing the wretched to want and weep. The people would prosper, and nothing would be lost but hunting grounds for the younger branches of the aristocracy and English snobs, and that could be easily supplied by Her Majesty directing the attention of this cruel cowardly class to the Hudson Bay and Northwest Territories, where they might have plenty of useful sport."

The Sheriff attempts to carry on with the business at hand. He confers with the Ground Officer who points out the crofters whose names are on the notices to quit. The group of women in their soaked home-spuns gathers next to the dwelling and blocks the Sheriff's way. The soldiers respond by raising their bayonets. One of the women grabs the papers from the hand of the Sheriff and proceeds to tear them to shreds. What she does not trample into the mud, she flings back at the Sheriff, while gesturing at the Ground Officer and Factor. "There are your orders to quit. Now it is you who must quit and go back to your barracks. You may think we will yield but we will not. The strong side knows the law better than the weak side, and can put it in force because they have plenty at their backs to do it with." The woman points to the torn papers on the ground. "Now, we may be the weak side, and we may have very little at our backs to spare, but that does not mean we are not as independent as the master is with regard to what we take in hand." A cheer goes up as more mud and rocks are hurled at the Sheriff and soldiers. At that point, the Sergeant of the troops signals for his men to come forward. The soldiers gather around the officials and face out toward the women, who continue to hurl threats. The Sergeant then orders his men to "reverse course" and return to the Laird's house, followed by a howling crowd of children.

On hearing that his notices to quit were so disrespected, the Laird pronounced, "Let them go to hell, but they must leave our boundaries." In the days that follow, more soldiers are expected to arrive, along with new notices to quit, as well as arrest warrants for women charged with de-forcing the Sheriff. News spreads that a ship is coming and will moor in the bay for the purpose of taking the crofters away. There is much consternation and agitation in the township, and many want to go and see the Proprietor and ask if they can take up the offer of a place on the shore that was put to them the year before. Others want to flee before they are arrested for participating in the disturbance.

Two days after the confrontation, a group of crofters gather outside the Laird's house. The door is blocked by several of his men. Eventually, the Ground Officer appears to hear their request.

"What is it that you want?"

"We would like to see the Laird."

"I think he is hoping he has seen the last of you."

"We have a petition for him."

"I am sure this one will be greeted with the same response as the last."

"We have come to apologize for our previous petition, and for the disturbance, and to ask for a lot on the shore, or at least to be allowed to stay another year so that arrangements can be made for emigration to Canada. It is too late in the year to set out now."

"I think you will find that you are beyond consideration."

Further entreaties follow until the Ground Officer agrees to take the petition to the Laird. The Ground Officer returns a short time later to say that legal proceedings are clearly under way and cannot be stopped now, and that the crofters should prepare to leave.

〜〜〜〜〜〜

More soldiers arrive with the ship in the following days, and are added to the first group. Soon after, they accompany the Ground Officer and his men as they go round, not just with notices, but with faggot and iron. They tear the roofs off whatever habitations they come upon that still remain, throwing what furniture there is out in the mud, and burning what is left of the rafters and thatch. From house to house, from hut to hut, and from barn to barn, the Ground Officer and his menials carry on the work of demolition as the soldiers watch, until there is scarcely a human habitation left standing in the district. When they set fire to a house, the Factor's men watch for any of the domestic animals making their escape from the flames, such as cats, hens, or any other poultry; and they are caught and thrown back into the inferno. The box of meal from one habitation is thrown down the cliff. All over the township, smoke ascends from horrid places, and able-bodied men who, if the matter would rest with the mere trial of physical force, could have bound the Ground Officer and his party hand and foot, and sent them out of the district, now stand aside as dumb witnesses, while children run to and fro dreadfully frightened. No opposition is offered by the inhabitants as this destruction takes place, no hand is lifted, no stone cast, no angry word is spoken.

Once this desolating work is done, the inhabitants are gathered up and herded together by the soldiers, who begin to lead them down toward the shore, where the ship is moored in the harbour. Several crofters break free from the group, chased by soldiers. They run back to their hearths, fall down among the stones and clay, and fill their pockets with the earth of their ancestors, before being dragged back to the road by the forces of the Crown.

CHAPTER VI

Shelburne County, Nova Scotia, 1993

History from Above

With the perceived failure of the UN Conferences on the Law of the Sea in the 1970s, coastal states unilaterally declared in 1977 that they would extend the Exclusive Economic Zone to two hundred miles offshore, thereby internalizing the control of coastal waters within the structures of nation states. The rationale for this declaration was that high sea voluntary regulation failed to control exploitation of the international fleet and that the regulatory capability of the nation state could better guarantee economic prosperity and environmental health in the fishery.

As a result of a program of grants, subsidies, and licensing provided by the Canadian government, the Canadian dragger fleet was more powerful by 1981 than the international fleet that was expelled in 1977 for being unsustainable. This program of industrial expansion led to a clear split in the Canadian fleet between the more traditional artisanal inshore longline and handline fleet and the highly mechanized offshore dragger fleet. Within five years, there were clear concerns—first raised by the Newfoundland inshore fishery—that the stocks were as dangerously close to collapse as they were in 1972. Despite these warnings, the industrial interests driving the collapse were the ones who continued to be rewarded with licences and quotas by the federal Department of Fisheries and Oceans. The massive program of modernization of the fishery, as set out in the Kirby Task Force of 1982, was interrupted only by its complete ecological collapse in 1992.

In the context of shrinking quotas, there was inevitable conflict between the offshore dragger fleet and the inshore artisanal fishers. Into this strife-ridden world sailed the Russian ship in July of 1993, the blockade of which by the inshore fishers is the focus of the following narrative.

My own life mirrored the challenges faced by the inshore fleet. In the years just before the blockade, I was fishing when there was money to be made, and in off-times I went to work construction in central Canada. I had built a new boat just before the fishery began its complete ecological collapse and so was in considerable debt. Given these grim realities, I decided to sell the Laura Elizabeth *to my friend David Stewart the year before the blockade and used the money to enrol in graduate school at York University. My partner, Laura, was also a graduate student there and so we went from living in our home in Nova Scotia to residing in a graduate residence in Toronto with our baby son, Lauchlan. This all felt like a desperate enterprise that was full of uncertainty, a high-wire act without a net. The drive from Nova Scotia to Ontario—which we have made over one hundred times—always felt monumental, loaded down as we usually were in the Joad-mobile. But at least I had identified a place where I might be able to land. This was not the case for many inshore fishers and their families, who faced considerable grief over the way of life they were losing, and the hard choices that lay ahead.*

History from Below

> *Some people may ask, "Why rake up all this inquiry now?" We answer that the same laws which permitted the cruelties... are still the laws of the country, and any*

tyrant... may legally repeat the same proceedings when-
ever he may take it into his head to do so.
                                    —*Alexander Mackenzie, 1883: viii*

Thick fog hangs from the stay wires as the vessel makes
its way toward the calm of the eastern passage into the
harbour. The dull green of the land hovers insubstantially in
the mist. After navigating through the passage and turning
up into the wide harbour, the vessel changes course and heads
north. Fifteen minutes later, the large squareness of the government wharf comes into view and, when it does, the vessel swings its bow to the east'ard, cuts its engines to an idle,
eventually sliding into reverse with a clunk before revving up
again. With several more bursts, the boat comes almost to a
standstill. The transmission thumps into forward again and
the stern of the boat swings around until it is only about ten
yards from the abutment. The transmission drops into reverse
one last time, and the vessel idles slowly back alongside the
wharf. The lines are thrown down onto the wharf to waiting
hands and are secured to the bollards along the capstan.

After idling for ten minutes while the gangplank is pulled
aboard, the main engine of the *Pioner Murmana* falls silent.
As it does, the engines of six Cape Island longliners start up
and steam out from behind the other side of the wharf. The
Shelley Dawn II, the *Darren and Adam*, the *Joyce and Boys*,
the *Leonard and Ryan*, the *Rusty Scupper*, and the *Portuguese
Prince* idle alongside the vessel on the water side, throwing
lines to each other and tying them to their deck staples, hem-
ming the *Pioner Murmana* in. At the same time, a line of half-
ton trucks moves out onto the wharf and occupies the space
along the capstan. The truck engines are shut off, and the
doors are locked, making it impossible to unload the vessel.
The Shelburne Blockade of July 1993 has begun.

The *Pioner Murmana* is a freighter and supply ship out
of Murmansk, a city in northwestern Russia on the Berents

Figure 7   The Russian ship blockaded in Shelburne Harbour.
Photo by Ray Rogers.

Sea, containing almost eight hundred metric tonnes of frozen cod and haddock that is to be off-loaded into the freezers
of Continental Seafoods, just up from the wharf, for trans-
shipment to markets in the United States. The "business as
usual" decision to allow a foreign ship into Canadian waters
containing huge amounts of a fish species that the Nova Scotia longline and handline fleets are themselves not allowed to
catch due to quota restrictions, and to unload this cargo while
the domestic longline fleet remains tied to the wharf nearby,
is to illustrate vividly the failed management decisions made
by the Canadian Department of Fisheries and Oceans (DFO)
and to stoke the anger of the inshore fleet that has been made
to feel like spectators in their own lives.

The fact that the fish in the hold of the vessel have, in all
likelihood, been caught in the Barents Sea north of Norway
does not prevent the Canadian fishers from regarding the
Russian ship as guilty of the many offences they associate
with the Department of Fisheries and Oceans. Aside from the

all but complete management failure that led to the collapse of the fish stocks less than a year before, there is a deeper and longer anger against DFO regarding the ongoing marginalization of the inshore longline and handline fleet, for whom the presence of the foreign fleet in Canadian waters is a potent symbol of their own displacement. The shunting aside of the small-boat inshore fishery in favour of the large foreign and Canadian dragger fleets has been, in the minds of those who live in the small communities along this coast, emblematic of the whole of Canada's management of the east-coast fishery since the declaration of the two-hundred-mile limit in 1977. And it seems that nothing has been learned in the immediate aftermath of the collapse of the fishery. The federal government has continued to grant quota to those most responsible for the destruction of the fishery.

Although I was no longer a fisher, I visited the wharf most days to see how the blockade was going. The collapse of the fishery went from being a central reality in my life to an area of academic study. I had recently read through every policy document the Department of Fisheries and Oceans had produced on groundfish management over the last twenty years. During the time of the blockade and in its aftermath, I wrote a series of articles for the local newspaper, *The Shelburne Coastguard*, on the systemic failures in fisheries management and the marginalization of the inshore fleet. Leonard Pace was the editor of the paper and, as a journalist, had written on fisheries issues for years. During that brief and intense time, it felt as if inshore fishers' views were finally being heard, even if only for a brief moment, and social relations that were leaving the world were contending and in conversation with the forces that were strengthening their hold on that world.

All of this conflict had come to a head the day before the blockade began, when five hundred fishers attended a meeting in Yarmouth organized by the Fisheries Resource Conservation Council. The mistrust and antagonism boiled over for all to see. The fishers arrived at the meeting head-up, because earlier in July the council had released scientific recommendations calling for reduced groundfish quota in District 4X, the western Scotian Shelf. The scientific advice was to lower the current 4X quota from 26,000 metric tonnes to 7000 metric tonnes the following year. The pollack quota would have to be cut at the same time, as would the cod quota on Georges Bank. Already tied to the wharf because of catch restrictions, the inshore fleet regarded this further cut to their quotas as threatening them with annihilation.

The Conservation Council meeting was chaired by Herb Clarke, vice-president of Fisheries Products International, which is a large corporation based in Newfoundland. In his opening remarks, Clarke emphasized that "our mandate is conservation." He went on to describe the council as a "partnership between government, the scientific community, and industry, bringing together fisheries and scientific expertise to make formal recommendations to the Minister of Fisheries and Oceans on total allowable catches and conservation measures for the Atlantic fishery." Sensing a level of agitation in the crowd, Clarke spoke of the recommendations he planned to make to the Minister in October for catch levels for the 1994 fishery and added: "If council feels adjustments are necessary to the 1993 groundfish plan, it will make more short-term recommendations to the Minister in the coming weeks. We are here to listen."

The floor was then opened for questions. "We have no fish to give away," asserted James Mood, a plant owner in Woods Harbour. "We need it for the Canadians that have their boats tied up. If you want to talk about rebuilding the stocks, you need food in the ocean." Mood was referring to the silver hake fishery caught largely by foreign boats.

"It's no secret the fishery is in trouble," said Grand Manan fishers' representative Klaus Sonnenburg, "but to go from 26,000 tonnes to 7000 tonnes is not responsible management."

"The real problem must be addressed now. The foreign fleet is not being properly monitored," claimed Noble Smith, Executive Director of the Nova Scotia Fixed Gear Association. Smith came armed with a box of juvenile cod, hake, and haddock that were five to seven inches in length and had been taken off a Cuban vessel fishing in Canadian waters. He held them up as he stood at the microphone. "This bunch can't be controlled, whether they are inside or outside the two-hundred-mile limit. They are using illegal gear that catches fish like these. We are already in tough shape, and this kind of thing only guarantees it will get worse. Nature can't stand it."

"Those fish of Noble's, we have fifty-pound frozen blocks of them," said Gary Dedrick, chairman of the Fixed Gear Association. "They were hidden among the squid when they were landed in Shelburne. You talk about draggers and long-liners misreporting. What about the foreign misreporting? And don't tell me you have 100 per cent observer coverage. That's one person working eight hours a day. What is going on the other sixteen hours? How is one person going to work twenty-four hours a day for a month straight? Can't be done. So there is not 100 per cent coverage on the foreign fleet. There can't be. There is only one observer.

"And it is not just the foreigners who are destroying the fishery. We all know that. Why, there are humps on bottom that we used to fish that are gone now. You think hook and line destroyed that? Dragger doors, chains, and rock hoppers did that. There's a plant owner here today who told me that he took 15,000 pounds of spawn out of 86,000 pounds of cod caught by draggers last winter. So how long is a fishery going to last when draggers are decimating fish that are schooled up and getting ready to spawn? That's what the draggers look for. You could set fifty tubs of longline gear down through that school and you wouldn't catch one. They're not feeding. But that is what the draggers prey on.

"Meanwhile the fixed-gear fleet is facing a reduction in haddock bycatch at the end of this month from a thousand pounds per trip to 183 pounds per trip. You can see the frustration in this room today. We have no hope of making a living, and all around us we are seeing what is going on. And on top of it all, we are being lied to and ignored by the government." Shouts filled the room, clapping and whistling, and raised fists.

"Order, please. Order." Herb Clarke raised his open palm. "If we are going to be able to listen to your input, we need to have a civil conversation. Myself, and I think I can speak for the rest of the council, are clearly not ignoring you. We are here to listen, and have no intention of lying to you. Next person at the mike, please."

"If you feel the skepticism in this room, it is because nobody knows the fishery better than the fishermen," stated Roland Deveau of Clare County. "The one thing the council should do, if nothing else, is set up a meaningful ongoing consultation mechanism to deal with issues as they come up, not just when you decide to roll through town. Before we have even had our say, we are eating the dust from your tires as you pull out of the parking lot."

"We don't even know what gets sent in for a recommendation," said Ricky Nickerson, from Cape Sable Island. "We want everything on the up and up. No more privileged information. There's too much of this 'behind the door' stuff. Let us see what you recommend to the Minister before it is sent. None of this 'We'll get back to you later.' Later is now. Something has to change or we're all done."

Another man stepped up to the mike and held up a document. "What I want to know is: Where is the provincial Minister of Fisheries Ron Barkhouse? When we met with him a few days ago, he said he would be here to support our concerns. The Eastern Fishermen's Federation presented this conservation plan here to him at that time and he said he supported it. For those of you who haven't seen it, it calls for banning all fishing for cod and haddock if the TAC [total allowable catch] falls below 5000 tonnes. Up to 6500 tonnes only hook and line fishermen would have access to the stocks. Above that, the smaller draggers would be allowed back in. Only when the TAC reaches 26,000 tonnes would the large offshore draggers be allowed to fish for cod and haddock. This plan is a true conservation plan because it recognizes that hook and line fishing is the most ecological way to go and is a precautionary approach to the health of the stock."

"When we met with Barkhouse last Monday, he called our proposal 'a conservation-minded plan, nothing unreasonable about it. I will support it.' And he promised then that he would be here today to say so. But guess what? The big boys got to him in the meantime and he's in the weeds somewhere licking his wounds. And now the Premier comes out and says he could not favour one gear sector over another. So we are right back to square one. Everything is going to hell, and we are out here on our own when push comes to shove. And you bunch up there on the stage will be no different. The big boys will tell you what to do and that will be the end of it. No offence to you up there, I know you mean well, but everyone in this room knows how it is. Business as usual will be the ruination of us." A roar erupted in the room, and at the back a few chairs were thrown around as people get to their feet to cheer.

Talk at the meeting ranged across a number of issues, including a proposal to ban dragger fishing. Concerns were expressed about the privatization of shares of the fish in individual transferrable quotas (ITQs), the threats of foreign fishing, and, of course, the lack of respect shown to the smaller-boat fixed-gear sector. At the end of the meeting, the idea of eliminating the foreign fleet from Canadian waters received unanimous support. A number of dragger fishermen and their crews were in attendance, so issues related to banning the draggers or stopping the privatization of quotas in ITQs were met with debate and challenge, and the RCMP had to be called in to make sure that fights did not break out. "We are at the point now when we have nothing to lose. Look out when a man has nothing to lose."

Whatever ill will the inshore longline fleet feels for the Canadian draggers, far more of it is reserved for the foreign fleet that is permitted to fish in Canadian waters. As one of the longline fishers stated, "The foreign fleet has a bycatch [non-targeted species] fishery that lands more fish than our total groundfish catch." But the most extreme indignation is reserved for the Department of Fisheries and Oceans itself, universally regarded as a bunch of pencil-pushers who deserve to be set adrift in the poisoned sea of their own ignorance, a shoreless misery of infinite extent. "These DFO people can walk around Ottawa feeling good about themselves, go to the sports store and buy their kids skis, go out for dinner, 'Oh, aren't we the upstanding sort.' Go to work well dressed, be courteous to everyone, work hard even. This may pass for a reasonable use of one's life in Ottawa. The same way, I'm sure, it makes sense to work in Indigenous Affairs. But the sum total of all this attentiveness, when their decisions play out, is complete disaster. It is an obliterating, scattering cyclone from start to finish."

<hr/>

The first few days of the blockade of the Russian ship witness a steady stream of trucks and boats making their way to Shelburne from the communities along the southwest shore of Nova Scotia. In time, over one hundred inshore boats arrive to tie alongside the Russian freighter, and fishers' trucks continue to fill the wharf. Local businesses shut down in support of the fishers, and a canteen of donated food is set up to feed those participating in the blockade. The longliners are demanding a larger share of the haddock quota, as well as participation in the decision-making process concerning quotas allocated to the foreign fleet. In terms of alterations

Figure 8 Inshore boats participating in the Shelburne blockade.
Photo by Ray Rogers.

to the overall management structure, these demands were
not extreme, given the devastation that had occurred in the
industry as a result of government's failure to manage the
industry sustainably.

The first response of the federal Fisheries Minister Ross
Reid to the blockade in Shelburne was that it was clearly a
criminal issue best dealt with by the Mounties. As the protest
strengthened and took on a life of its own, Reid proclaimed
that he would not negotiate "with a gun to his head." The
fishermen had to end the blockade before any conversation
between government and fishermen could take place. The
current atmosphere, he said, was "not conducive" to reasonable negotiation.

"Now you tell me, who the hell is the one with a gun to
his head? You sitting up there on your fat arse in Ottawa with
your cushy office and your big salary and your pension for
life, or me down here with debts up the yingyang, crewmen

with families to feed, and all of us one step from losing the house and boat and being chucked out in the ditch? Eh, you tell me, who has a gun to his head? All we want to do is go fishing like we have always done and we can't go, while the big boys just keep on truckin' like there's no tomorrow. Now, who the fuck has a gun to his head? And whose finger is on the trigger? He's got some bloody nerve, that fella. Not conducive, you're goddamn right it's not conducive, and it's going to get a hell of a lot less conducive, you watch."

There is a wariness and edginess in everyone, as the fishers await a response to the blockade. What will the Russian crew do? What will the Mounties do? What will DFO do? At the same time, there is the need for them to make their case to the media, as well as to identify who is speaking for the fishers. And it is not as if this was all planned out ahead of time. It was more like, "We gotta do something. Chain ourselves to a flag-pole. Occupy DFO offices, and throw all the furniture out the sixth-floor window of Purdy's Wharf. Anything. Because it's clear we are going down. No doubt about that. Another season of this, and we'll all starve. So we either take a stand now or pack up the truck and head for out west or somewheres. But our future is not here, that's for sure. Not the way we are hemmed in on all sides by the draggers, the foreigners, and the quota restrictions."

By the end of the first day, the fishers have put out a statement listing their demands. The Mounties say they are there only to observe and to keep the peace. The Russian crew throw up their hands and look to the skies. And DFO goes silent after stating they will not negotiate as long as the blockade continues. By the second day, there is an easing of tension. The weather is fine. There is a lot of local support for the protesters. Tables are set up to feed those on the wharf. More people arrive to see what is going on, out for a drive, that's all. "Man, it's a bit like a funeral. You get to see people you haven't seen in years." Groups of fishers sit on the tailgates of the rows of trucks, or lean against the side of the box, hands in their pockets, and the talk ranges over topics of all kinds, just like it would on any other summer day on the wharf.

Amid all this chat and milling about, every once in a while voices would be raised, and a larger group would gather, many times accompanied by the media and their cameras. "Well, it has just gone beyond. That's all there is to it. It's just gone beyond. This foolishness has got to stop sometime and it may as well stop now. We have seen our way of life destroyed, and those that destroyed it—the bureaucrats, the big companies, and the draggers—are carrying on now just as brazen as ever. They still have their jobs, and here we are with the ass out of our pants. What's to be had, and what's to be lost, are never put together. It's just load and go, load and go with that gang. I spent fifteen years on the draggers before I went back to longlining, so I know what I'm talking about. It was pitiful to watch. Tow after tow coming back with ten thousand pounds of ping-pong haddock no more than fifteen or sixteen inches long, while the crew spent most of our time shovelling rocks over the side. We would just shake our heads as we steamed for home loaded to the doors. We knew it couldn't go on like that for long. Nature can't take that. No way. So here we are now—them smug and us desperate. We aren't the ones who destroyed the fishery, but we're the ones paying the price. A few offshore draggers have half of the quota, sixty forty-five- to sixty-five-foot draggers have a quarter of the quota, and four hundred or so inshore longliners and handliners have what's left. That's all you need to know about how screwed up things are. The one's who destroyed the fishery are the ones controlling it."

Another man steps forward. "You try and do what is right in life, and then you look around and see that the ones that are getting ahead are the ones who don't give a damn. They just brace both feet and let 'er go. No thought for tomorrow. Why, the big companies are buying dairy farms in Georgia. That's right. Taking the profits out of collapsing the fishery and buying dairy farms in Georgia. They shift their ground, and we're left here holding the bag. You can shit in your hat and put it back on your head, and after a while it stops stinking. But that doesn't mean you don't have shit in your hat. Well, no way. No more. Enough. Time to take a stand."

The crowd ambles around the government wharf, cup of coffee in hand from one of the church groups, listening in on conversations. "Don't get me started. Those educated idiots in DFO. My. My. My. Why, they would make a mess of the Lord's Prayer, they would. Not two clues. They don't know north from south and they are put in charge of a fishery. They are lucky if they can find their way around 200 Kent Street, let alone find Shelburne on a map. I was visiting family once up in Ottawa. So I went down to the DFO offices one day just to see what was going on. Man, they were terrified of me. My God, a real fisherman is here. No wonder we are in this mess. Well, now, everything is on fire, everything's for sale."

"The system is collapsing, and there is nothing left for us but to beat on each other, which is what we are doing here. All this noise for nothing. Things aren't going to change. It's too late now. The big boys behind all this will see to that. They won't quit till they pull the last fish out of the ocean. No siree, they won't quit until they pull up that scrawny cod with a tag on its tail that says 'Last fish in the ocean.' They've gone to ground, where once they did abound. It's the mutiny of the bounty."

Gary Dedrick climbs up into the back of a half-ton, and fishers gather around, as do the media. "I just wanted to let you know what is going on. We have not heard back from the Minister of Fisheries about our demands, but I have been talking to the local MP, Peter McCreath, and he has been passing along our concerns to the Minister. So there is the beginning of some kind of dialogue. I think we have managed to convince McCreath that our concerns about the foreign fleet are worth looking into. That is all I have to report for the moment. I also want to be clear that the blockade will stay in place until we get some concessions from the government." A small cheer goes up from those gathered.

Later in the day, Peter McCreath's office releases a statement saying that he has outlined the fishers' concerns to the Minister of Fisheries and that McCreath believes there is persuasive evidence that issues with the foreign fleet needed to be examined more closely. McCreath also states that "until a solution can be achieved that fishermen can live with, there is no point in a meeting between them and DFO taking place at this time."

Because he has to be seen to do something, and the Mounties aren't willing to be that "something" by arresting people, the Minister of Fisheries agrees after four or five days to send some government representatives to hear what the fishers' concerns are and to see if common ground can be found for discussion. But he reiterates that he will not negotiate until the blockade comes down. Tim Nickerson responds, "We have been burned too many times. This is DFO, remember. The blockade stays until we get a deal." In response to claims by DFO that the foreign fleet is closely monitored, Gary Dedrick tells journalists that the government is just "baffling you guys with figures. It may add up on paper, but not on the ocean. The foreign fleet is taking more than their quota and they are doing it with irregular gear."

An older gentleman, in tartan house slippers, stands in a group of fishers. "Well, I didn't expect to see this. Frank was down at the wharf in Little Harbour and he said he was coming up here to have a look at what was going on. I said I may as well come along for the ride. Fine day, not much doing. Why, quite a sight, you. All the boats and trucks. And the people. Why, I've seen some fellas I haven't seen in twenty years. Old-timers like me. Mates from the old salt bankers. We had a good yarn and got caught up. I guess everyone is feeling the same. Fed up with what has gone on. Not sure how this kinda thing will work out. Not too sure at all. But there are some good fishermen involved, I see that—younger ones who know what is going on with the quota. I don't pay too much attention, not like I used to. I just tinker around with a few lobster traps now. Anyway, a couple of the fellas said I should talk to the media. They said there's no point in letting a few drunks rave on about this and that, without someone saying something sensible. Well, I don't know about that. No doubt some of the fellas are all wound up. Understandable, yes it is. Just back in from fishin'. It's hard enough going out on the ocean to make a livin' without having to come back in and have to fight a battle on the land as well. It would get to a fella after a while."

"Why, it is hard to believe all that has taken place in the last while. You come down to the wharf and you look out across the water, and then you realize you've been told you can't go fishing. No quota. Why, that is a strange feeling, for sure. I have been going out on that ocean for sixty-odd years in all kinds of weather and in all kinds of rigs. But there was never such a thing as a fella telling you that you aren't allowed to go at all, no matter what. That is a strange feeling for sure.

"'Course, we saw it coming, I guess. Coming for years. We knew nature couldn't stand it. But we kept hoping it could, what with everyone getting new boats and gear and the fleet expanding. Longlining would never destroy the fishery. Never in a hundred years. Especially in a thirty-five-foot boat like ours. We could never hurt the fish with what we catch; day boats fishing on the shore in the summer time. The dragger fleet made a mess of everything, that's for sure. As soon as they got going, you could see it in our catches. Any time a school got gathered up, they would pound it until there was nothing left, back and forth across the banks. Yes, sir, pounded 'em flat.

"After a while, there would be nothing left for us at all. Hundred pounds to a tub, maybe. All that saved it was that the prices were up. So, really, by the time they shut 'er down, you were hardly making any money anyway. Hard to believe, though, just the same. As I say, there have been ups and downs all along, no doubt about that, especially when the Russians were in our waters in the early 70s, but never a complete collapse like we have now. And we can't blame the Russians. This is all our fault. We are the ones with the hook in our mouths this time. We caught up all the fish and now it's us in the slattin' pen, on our way to market.

"It's a strange thing to know something only when you have to kill it. That's the way it is with fish. You know it only when it is flopping around on the deck. Otherwise they are invisible. They come from the nether regions, as the old fella used to say, come from far away. Look out on the wharf there. All of the people we know who have come here are protesting in the same way a haddock protests as it gasps away on the deck. So it is the death throes as much as it is a protest. Now as it all comes to an end, we see who we are. Yes, it's us out there in the new air."

Support for the Fishers

A man stands up in the back of a half-ton with a microphone. "As you may have heard, the Minister of Fisheries has backed off in his comments about not negotiating while the blockade is on and is sending down his Interim Deputy Minister to 'see if there is some common ground and to find out what our concerns are.' We are waiting for details on the meeting. So we are making some progress. Keep up the good work. Keep the blockade going. Keep everyone safe. At this time, I'd like to thank all the people who have donated food. I also want to thank the crew of the Russian ship for their cooperation." He points to the vessel and everyone on the wharf waves to the crew as they lean on the upper rail of the *Pioner Murmana*. The Russians look at each other and then wave back and laugh. "All the support is very much appreciated. Gary Dedrick, Tim Nickerson, and the rest will be meeting with DFO over the next few days. We'll let you know if there are any developments. They asked us to end the blockade now that negotiations are under way and we told them 'No way!' We've seen in the past how that story ends. But not this time. The blockade stays until we get what we want." The people on the wharf clap and whistle before turning again to those they have been speaking to, and a hundred different conversations resume.

The blockade has become its own little town. Led by Elaine Hemeon and Bernice Goodick, a group has organized a canteen to feed those on the wharf. Next to their table is a bulletin board listing all the businesses that have donated food, as well as a freezer truck to store the food. The fire department has set up a public address system for any announcements, and portable toilets have been provided by a local contractor.

Farther along the wharf, someone plugs in a guitar and strums away as darkness sets in and the dampness and fog return. The warmth that still radiates from the concrete of the wharf creates a buffer of clear dry air above the crowds that mill about. "Here's a song I wrote about Bubby Thorburne. We all remember when he and six crew members, including his son, were lost on the *Johnny and Sisters II* on December 3rd, 1989, steaming back from the east'ard. I fished with Bubby for three or four years, but then I lost my nerve. Too many times coming back from the Grand Banks with six inches of freeboard. Scare you to death. Not to say it was his fault they drowned. That was one terrible storm that took them, and it came up quick and they had no warning.

"But, my God, the man could catch fish, that's for sure. I remember once we sank the boat on a fine day while hauling gear. Just kept shacking off everything but the steakers until we went under. Spent eight hours in the life raft that time. Yes, the man could catch fish. That's for sure. So here's a song for Bubby and his crew and their families. It's called 'Swamp Loaded in a Hurricane.' We may not be swamp-loaded these days, but we sure feel like we're in a hurricane. A lifetime of work and it's a broker, I guess. No way we are going to fish our way out of trouble this time. So here we go."

Swamp Loaded in a Hurricane

Brother's up the mast
Having visions of the deep
The fish have come to take us
Home to Davy Jones
Home to Davy Jones
Fill up the cud
And load up the lifeboat
We'll sleep with the fishes
The last thing that I wanted
The one thing that I fear, is to be

Chorus:
Swamp Loaded in a Hurricane
Winds are picking up
And we're nor'east of nowhere
There's six inches of freeboard
But the cod keep coming
We've started to pray
And it ain't for rain
We've started to pray "Oh, not again"
Swamp loaded in a hurricane

Bubby looks over the side
It's smother white
All the way down
We're making money now, boys
We're making money now
There's not much for it
But to keep on coiling
Oh, what could be better
Oh, what more could you wish for
Than to be

Yes, it's more than you can ask for
It's more than you can dream
There's a fish on every hook as big as a man
Roll that steaker in
Roll that steaker in
And get ready for the next one
It's moments like this I know who I am
It's moments like this I know who I am
I know I swore I wouldn't
I know I promised that I'd never
But it looks like we're gonna be

By the end of the song the crowd is singing along and clapping. When it is over, there are dozens of spontaneous and simultaneous storm stories being told among those assembled.

"Why, sonny, we fished all them kind of days."

"That reminds me of the time we broke down next to the ledges."

"Yes siree, took the windows right out of the windshield. Green water everywhere. We thought we were done for."

"I swear she rolled upside down that time. I was in the bunk when it happened. Once I gathered myself up and looked around, I could smell something burning in the engine room. I went down there and everything was pitched around and some hydraulic oil had spilled on the exhaust. I happened to look up as I was rearranging one of those big truck and bus batteries that was next to the engine, and there was the imprint of it on the overhead beam. How we stayed afloat, I have no idea."

"Remember Edwin Brewer, steaming his new boat the *Polly and Robbie* to try to save the *Maureen & Michael* in 100-mph winds. Captain Fiander said not to come, it was too rough for anything but laying to, that they had put out a sea anchor and would make out fine. But Brewer kept coming. He told Captain Fiander, 'If the boat can't take this, she's no good to me.'

Well, that was the last we heard of Brewer. The next day the Coast Guard picked the crew off the *Maureen & Michael*. All they found of the *Polly and Robbie* was part of the wheelhouse and a life ring with the boat's name on it. My. My. My."

On the sixth day of the blockade, negotiations continue in a hotel in Bridgewater, an hour away. There are reports of increased tension and raised voices, with people walking out in protest. On the wharf, by contrast, a pattern of normalcy has settled in. The same people run the food tables each day. Most of those involved have known each other for years. Many of the fishers are sleeping aboard their boats and so would come up in the morning for coffee and breakfast. Instead of fearing reprisals from the Mounties, they now have a conversational relationship with them. Someone, somewhere, is fuming about all that is going on, but it would not have been apparent to anyone who walks around among the trucks on the wharf, as country music wafts out from radios in the cabs, all tuned to the local station in case there are updates on negotiations.

Around lunchtime, an ambulance rolls out onto the wharf and two young medics in their starched uniforms get out and walk over to a group of men leaning on the back of a truck. "Well, look at that, would ya? Gumpy in a uniform. Who would have thought?" There is a general rattle of laughter as one of the young medics blushes and shakes some hands. "Glad to see that course paid off. At least you're not fishing." Everyone laughs.

"Neither are you, by the look of it," replies the young man.

One of the men from the other side of the truck turns around. "Well, there it is, our last line of defence: Gumpy. Imagine that, all that stands between you and death's door in your last moments is Gumpy and his gear. That's a scary thought indeed." Another joins in. "I'll tell you what. If I am in some big head-on collision out on the nine-mile and there's trucks and bodies everywhere and I'm lying in the ditch, Gumpy, you just let me go, you hear? 'Cause if I come to, and look up, and all I see are those big wet lips of yours hovering above me, why, with my last ounce of energy I'll reach up and strangle you right there on the spot. So you hear me, just let me go, 'cause I do not want to slide off out of this world, the last thing I see being those big red lips of yours, and you all dewy-eyed."

Another group. Another truck box. "You see that out there? Over on the west side of the harbour? Those are fish pens. Just put them in there. Going over to fish farms now, they are. Can't fish the ocean anymore, not with the technology they have today. They have to start farming it now. Need to have 'inputs,' as they say. Unadorned nature won't do anymore. No, sir. It's jack it and whack it. That's where we are now. More aggressive all the time. One approach fails, so they try another. So fish farms become the solution to draggers. You just up the ante. So the old problem of ecological collapse will be gone and the new problem of pollution from the poop and the feed everywhere will take over. Yes, sir. Don't stick around, this is a fuck-up."

~~~~~~~~~

Shelburne has seen its share of boom and bust over the years. The settlement was created overnight in the aftermath of the American Revolution, when shiploads of Loyalists arrived from New York so they could continue their life under the British flag. As the tide turned in the war in favour of the rebels, those who remained loyal to Britain gathered in New York, where arrangements were made for them to be transported to remaining British colonies in North America. Although at the time there was little European settlement in the area around Shelburne, it was identified as a site for a new town and also as the possible future capital of Nova Scotia because of its excellent harbour, its forests, and its potential arable lands.

As a new town, Shelburne was entirely planned. Surveys were done and streets and lots were laid out in preparation for the arrival of its new citizens, the Port Roseway Associates.

These loyal subjects were made up of respectable families "who for their attachment to Government, and after numberless fatigues in supporting the Royal Cause—have been obliged to quit their All and take refuge within the King's lines." Amid the chaos at the end of the war, any person who asked to join the association was carefully scrutinized. A person had to be recommended by one of its members and then face a committee's questions regarding background and suitability before joining the expedition to Port Roseway, the original name for Shelburne. The land immediately surrounding Port Roseway harbour was reserved for the Associates, while the less fertile outlying areas were allotted to the rank and file of decommissioned members of the British Army—many of them Highland regiments—as well as to former slaves who had responded to the British offer of freedom if they agreed to cross the lines and fight on behalf of the Crown.

Things did not go well for the new citizens of Nova Scotia. There was a great deal of bickering over allocation of the town lots as well as debate about how the town should be governed. By way of criticizing the Loyalists for having brought the republican sensibilities of their enemy with them, the surveyor Benjamin Marston complained: "This cursed levelling spirit must be crushed by every means or we shall be for rebellion soon." Along with the conflict over lots, there were many vehement pleas to Governor Parr in Halifax about increasing the meagre provisions to be supplied by the British.

A majority of the Associates were merchants and traders, and their skills were poorly suited to homesteading. The land turned out to be very rocky and unyielding to the plough. After a flurry of work during the first years of town construction—and when it was for a time one of the largest settlements on the east coast of North America—Shelburne quickly began to shrink in size as members of the Association moved on to more benign sites in His Majesty's Empire. This process was accelerated when over five hundred "Black Loyalists"—who were doing most of the work as hired help or indentured servants or slaves in clearing the land and building the new town—decided to leave their hovels in nearby Birchtown and accept the offer to go to Sierra Leone and "a situation so advantageous as to make them some atonement for the injury they have suffered" in Shelburne, where they had "sunk to the lowest pitch of wretchedness." Through the efforts of humanitarians such as William Wilberforce, the Sierra Leone Company was set up and financed by the British government to give these Black pioneers a new home in Africa.

So in short order, the grand houses of Shelburne were abandoned and fell into disrepair, and weeds grew in the new streets. This decline continued until the middle of the nineteenth century, when the community began to revive with the expansion of shipbuilding and the fishery, which had become part of the triangular trade, providing the indentured labourers on the plantations in the Caribbean with salt fish in return for the molasses and rum produced there and taken back to England. Meanwhile, the other, less privileged, Loyalists—front-line troops from twenty-three different British regiments, among them Donald McDonald—who had been granted land in the bays and inlets to the east and west of Shelburne, and who had much less grand schemes in mind but more appropriate skills, had carried on making lives for themselves in whatever way they could, grateful to at last be free of government edicts. These are the families who, several generations later, are gathered now on the wharf in Shelburne.

⧉⧉⧉⧉⧉⧉⧉

Journalists move among the fishers, doing backgrounders as they wait for developments in the story of the blockade. Perspectives that would normally be of no interest to news reporters provide colour commentary and balance for their stories. "Well, Florence came in with me today. She dropped me off and has gone to do some grocery shopping. Not sure what will happen with negotiations. Those DFO people never cared much for the inshore fishery. We were backward, as far as they were concerned. They liked the big boys best. They'd rather ride around on John Risley's yacht than go to some meeting hall where they would be insulted and abused by a roomful of inshore fishers. They don't speak our language, and we don't speak theirs. That's about the sum total of it.

"We think they are a bunch of educated idiots, and they think we are a bunch of dumb hicks. Well, we've gotten a lot dumber lately, that's for sure—newly stupid, I guess you could call it. All the things we knew before are useless now. All the places we used to fish are no good to us. The lifetime of figuring out wind and tide and learning the ocean bottom are like some language on the tower of Babel. Compass and a watch, that's how we used to get around. Courses and times. You had to pay attention. Longlining is all about getting your gear where you want it. Middle of the night, thick fog, old chop on, and you steaming offshore an hour or so, trying to find some hump not much bigger than a sheep pasture. Depending on which way the tide is running, it can take you miles one way or the other, so you have to take account of that. It's all experience when it comes to finding fish. Or at least it used to be. Of course, now it's all technology. It's a push-button world now. There is so much electronic gear in the wheelhouse you can barely see out the window. Make a genius out of anybody. Divides the ocean into city blocks and takes you right back to the place you were the night before. Pretty soon you will be able to lie at home in your bed and send the boat out on its own. Remote control. Except that there's no fish now. Ha! That's a problem the new gear won't solve.

"It's a far cry from the old salt bankers I went on. You could be gone a month or more, accordin' to. You had to stay until you filled 'er—300,000 pounds, lots of times. Go all the way to the Grand Banks in them days. You feel like you're halfway to England out there. I was only there the once. Just a kid. My dad was down there fishing many a time. Gone all summer. By the time they swung her around for home, they could be on the Flemish Cap.

"But in my time, we would stay this side of the Cabot Strait. That's a long enough pound back in a sailing vessel against those sou'west winds. Lots of times we would go to Banquerro or to Sable Island Bank or Emerald Bank. Good fishing there up in the shoal water in the summertime. That was important when you are jigger fishing out of a dory. Hard enough on the hands without yarding those big steakers up from forty fathom down."

A man walks by and waves. "Listen to the old fella. He was born in a compass box. He knows his way around, that's for sure."

"Hey you, Myers. Anyways, back to fishing off Sable Island in the old salt bankers. As I was saying, you like to jig in shoal water if there are any fish around, because it's easier on the hands. On that trip we had fifteen dories aboard. Two men to a dory. As the old fella says, early in the trip two men could haul their own dory aboard on the ropes and pulleys, but by the time the trip is over, your hands are so dried out and cracked from the salt and wet and guts that it takes well-nigh the whole crew to get a dory aboard, your hands are so sore.

"We are out there jigging in the shoal water. Thick fog, not a draft. Out to the east'ard of Sable Island. It starts to breeze up during the day. Thank God the wind cleared up the fog some and we were able to gather everyone up and get back to the vessel. It took some time for us to find George and Allan, who had drifted well to the west'ard by the time we swung around and found them. It was blowing thirty knots, and we had a heck of a time getting them alongside, but we did. Drifted down onto them and hauled 'em aboard on the leeward side of the vessel. The glass had begun to drop, and we knew we didn't have a lot of sea room where we were, so we headed further to the south'ard hoping to get out beyond the shoals of Sable Island, so that if we had to, we could drift to the west'ard.

"It kept breezing up through the rest of the day, and throughout that night as well. We had a sea anchor out and only a small riding sail in the stern to keep 'er head to it. The next morning it was blowing sixty knots and we could see breakers to the west of us, so we knew then that we had not made it far enough to the south'ard to avoid the southern end of the sand bars. Pretty soon we were in the foam and the vessel began to wallow and bottom out in the sand while in the troughs, and the tops started coming off of the waves. Man oh man, what a sight. Each wave lifted us up and carried us to the west'ard, and then in each trough we would come down with a thud in the sand. We were side-to-it half the time, waves breaking over us. The boat would lay over on the lou'ward side when the wave hit her and the water would fill 'er up to the rails on that side. The ocean was so churned up by the storm, that the waves were full of sand, and as the waves drained off through the scuppers, sand began to build up on deck, which meant we were laying lower and lower in the water. It was only a matter of time before the next wave that came would bury us rather than lift us up. And that would be the end. There was nothing for it but to lash ourselves to the lou'ward side of the deck and hang on as the wave broke over us, then shovel the sand over the rail for dear life until the next wave came.

"Throughout the rest of the day and the following night, we shovelled and shovelled. My God, what work. I thought every wave was our last. Thank goodness the storm carried the Gulf Stream onshore and warmed the water up. Otherwise we would have perished for sure, just from the cold, instead of being just half drowned. By that next morning it was still blowing hard, but every once in a while we would not bottom out in the sand between waves, and by and by we were afloat again in the deeper water to the west'ard of the island. We put out the sea anchor, and a riding sail kept us up in the wind again.

"Of course, now that we were afloat, she leaked like a sieve after the pounding she took. So we had to man the pumps to keep her from heading straight to Davy Jones. After a while the wind started to die down, and we swung her around, set her sails, and jogged for home, never letting up once on the pumps. We managed to salvage a good part of the catch, although some of it was so full of sand we threw it overboard, which helped to lighten the load.

"That was some welcome sight when Lockeport came into view. We had all said our goodbyes to each other when the storm was at its worst, and here we were now, waiting to see our families again. We were some glad to be home and, after greeting everyone who came down to see us, we half sunk at the wharf. Thank God some fellas from town came down aboard and took over the pumps. It was all we could do to crawl up the ladder. We were done. Man oh man. The works. The works. That was my last trip down there."

"You're darn right it was."

"This here's Florence. She's back from getting the groceries. That didn't take you long."

An older woman with glasses and a tight perm of grey curls moves in beside her husband. "If it was left to you, you'd sit here all day and yarn. I just caught the tail end of the Sable Island story."

"Well, get in here and have your say. I know you want to. Then we can go home."

Florence turns to those assembled. "He never went back on the vessels after that because I wouldn't let him. I had to put him to bed for a month after that. He just lay there and shook for a good long while. The rest of them were about the same. Of course the vessel was so beat up, it spent a couple of months in dry dock anyway. But when it was time to go again, the captain came around to see him. I told you straight, didn't I? 'It's either him or me. Take your pick.' Gone for months at a time, I was half a widow anyway. But I didn't want to be a whole widow. And there's so much work around home with the garden and the animals and everything. It was okay when the boys were still around, but they have their own lives now. It's lonesome, I tell you. If it keeps up, I'll be watching the stories every day and taking pills like the rest of 'em. So I told him, 'You find something to do closer to home or find yourself a new wife. One or the other.' Well, when Mitch and Lawrence Taylor's boats were lost a while later, that really capped it. Between captains and crew, there were fifty kids in Lockeport who had lost their fathers. That was rough, let me tell you. A person couldn't get one foot in front of the other for a while." Florence looks out across the wharf. "I'm not sure what to make of all this. It brings to mind the Lockeport Lockout. I was a young girl in 1939, just out of school and working in the plant, cutting fish. It takes a lot to get people riled up around here, and that was one of the few times. The Catholics are a lot better at this sort of thing. Moses Coady and their bunch would work together way better than the Protestants. It takes it all for people around here to get together to push a boat off the slip.

"Well, the first thing I always think of when I remember the lockout is the picket line us fish cutters set up outside the plant. Bessy was right out there front and centre. She was a large woman, in every way, and she wore this sandwich board that only partially covered her ample figure. The sign on the board said: 'This is what starvation wages have done to me.' God bless her. She was gone the following year.

"Times were very tough in the 1930s around here. Hungry! They were lean times for sure. Lots of the husbands would go away to work—Boston, mainly—to fish on the boats out of there. That fishery was better organized and you got paid way better prices for your fish. Up here, all the companies would get together and decide what they were going to pay for fish. If I remember rightly, we were getting a cent a pound for haddock, while in Gloucester, they were getting five cents. On top of that, most of us were in hock to the companies, so it's not like we could shop around, especially when they put in facilities like bait freezers and all. Why they even had a Royal Commission look into price fixing at the time.

"My uncle was working at Swim Brothers Fish Plant in Lockeport. He got me my job there and I was working with him on the splitting table one day when Black Norman came to see him. Black Norman ran the plant and we called him that because he was so mean. The almighty dollar, that's all that mattered to him. Anyway, he came to ask my uncle about being skipper on one of his vessels. He had turned the previous skipper ashore for letting the crew take home a few of the smaller fish for their families. So Norman comes to see my uncle in the plant and he keeps having to walk around the splitting table to try and get close to him. My uncle keeps moving around to the other side of the table. It was not so much that he was afraid of Norman, although he was that, it was because he was embarrassed that he was working barefoot because he couldn't afford a pair of rubber boots. When my uncle finally agreed to take the vessel, Norman asked how much he wanted to be paid for the trip. 'I don't need to be paid anything. Just cover the grocery bill for my family while I am gone.' Norman looked at him aghast. 'I can't do that. You've got seven kids, for mercy's sake.'

"Because things were so tough, we tried a number of times to get organized so we could get better wages. Moses Nickerson tried for a while and so did the bunch from Antigonish, and that didn't work out either. Then the Canadian Seamen's Union came down from the Great Lakes and began to organize both the fishing fleet and the plant workers in Lockeport. The new union tried to negotiate a contract with the plants, but Blanchard Swansburg from Lockeport Company and John Swim from Swim Brothers said they wouldn't deal with unions, and if any organizers were seen around the plants, they would be arrested.

"But when they saw we were serious about starting a union, and that we didn't back down from their threats, they just locked the doors. All we wanted was enough to live on, but for the companies, that seemed like too much. While others in Canada were crowing about the achievements of their new democracy, we lived in a tyranny down here. The old company store was all we knew. So Lockeport Company and Swim Brothers paid us off the wages they owed and told us our services were no longer required. They said it was our own fault for listening to outside agitators like Pat Sullivan and Charlie Murray. That was the start of the lockout. It was a terrible shock, not just for us workers, but for the whole town, and for the fleet as well, because there was nowhere to sell the catches. It was the fall of the year, and it looked like a bleak winter ahead—bleaker than we knew, as it turned out.

"Anyways, when word came round there was going to be this big meeting at the theatre in Lockeport after they locked everyone out, we went to hear what they were saying, and what the others were thinking. We knew Ben Mackenzie. He'd fished all his life and been over to Boston, and here and there, and he had the doings of it, and said the union was a good idea and would help the plant workers and the fishing fleet. Strangers spoke up as well—Sullivan and Murray, I believe. We didn't know them then. Most everyone figured, How much worse could it be? So we may as well give the union a try. It was either that or go back to work with our tail between our legs.

"Although the province had recently passed a Trade Union Act, it was not very popular with the powers that be, especially if Communists were involved: not the Premier, nor the Minister of Fisheries, not the newspapers, not the Mayor of Lockeport, nor the Mounties. But we stuck together through it all, and after they locked the doors we set up a picket line on the railway tracks near the cold storage. We figured that as long as there were some frozen fish to sell in the plant, we had some power, but if we let them clean the place out, they'd just shift their ground to another plant down the coast. So we stopped any trucks or trains going in or out."

"Lockeport Company then said they were going to disman-
tle the plant and move it somewhere else to get away from the
'illegal interference' of the fishers and workers. The Mounties
came down and tried to scare us by taking down the names of
everyone who stood on the tracks to stop the train. We didn't
worry too much about being run down by the train. The engi-
neer was Happy Lennox and he was a good union man, and he
would always sound his whistle a good way off to make sure
there were lots of people down there when he arrived at the
plant. So things were peaceable enough on that front. In the
meantime, we got the co-op running in Whiteman's old plant,
which created some work for us cutting fish and gave the fleet
a place to sell their fish. So people started to feel like 'My God,
we might change things after all.'

"Then Tom Maclean, a manager at Lockeport Company,
ran his car into the picketers and hurt a bunch of people.
That's when things started to turn bad. The Police Chief saw
what Maclean did but refused to arrest him. Later that day,
a handful of workers turned in their union cards and asked
to go back to work. When some of us women in town heard
about this, we gathered up what eggs we had and down we went.
Well, what a mess we made of them fellas. That was the last we
heard tell of anyone turning in their union cards for a while.

"After that, the Lockeport town council passed a motion
condemning us, saying we were interfering with business.
You're darn right we were interfering with business. It was
down and dirty now. The government said what we were
doing was illegal, and the whole system started to rain down
upon us. We had another big meeting at the theatre and Pat
Sullivan bucked us up, saying we were as solid as ever. There
was even a choir of young girls singing union songs. I tell you,
it warmed your heart to be there after all the misery we had
put up with. I remember one song they sang. It was called 'The
Padlock on the Door' and was written by Jimmy MacKenzie's
wife, Betty. I remember the chorus:

'Twas in the year of '39 Pat Sillivan came to town
With him was Charlie Murray to help the man that's down
They organized a union to help a poor man out
And so began the initial round of that historic bout.
Hurray for the union with three big cheers we roar
To you we'll prove we can remove the padlock from the
    door.

"But, as I say, winter was coming on and people were getting hungry. We didn't have much at the best of times, and after a couple of weeks supplies were running low. We sent a letter to the clergy of Nova Scotia asking for help, saying our kids were hungry, and what we were doing was the right thing. The fish companies wrote their own letter saying if we wanted some food, all we had to do was to come back to work, and to stop listening to outside agitators.

"A few days later, Mayor Locke asked the Attorney General to send down Mounties to clear the tracks. Trucks and freight cars were lined up as if a shipment was ready to go. People came from everywhere to help out us picketers. I think there were about seven hundred of us by train time. Fifty more Mounties had showed up in town, booked into the local hotels. When the time came, the Mounties walked along the tracks in front of the train and ordered us in the name of the King to disperse. We stood our ground. There was some pushing and shoving as the Mounties moved to clear the tracks. Rocks from around the sleepers started to fly and pretty soon there was a melee. But we didn't back off, even though some of us took a pounding from billy clubs. I remember this one Mountie was coming to move a group of us women off the tracks. This person I didn't know stepped in front of me. I think she lived with Miss Celie, I believe, and she just stood her ground. The Mounties weren't sure how to use her. They didn't want to throw her off the tracks like they did the men. So they were having a little tussle with her to move her along.

She got one hand free, and she had on this straw hat, in winter mind you, and she pulled this long hat pin out of it and gave it to the Mountie right in the arse. He went about six feet in the air. They dragged the bunch of us off the tracks after that.

"My. Oh. My." Florence shook her head. "In the midst of it all, one fella even climbed up on the boxcar with a Union Jack and we all sang 'God Save the King' and 'O Canada' in the middle of it all. My goodness. The works, the works. After a while, Happy backed the train up the tracks and left, and the Mounties went back to the hotel.

"It snowed the next day and not much went on. Just two Mounties came down to the tracks. But the day after that, 150 more Mounties arrived in town. But there were no further attempts to clear the tracks. Our union sent a telegram to the Premier, protesting the use of Mounties as strikebreakers. We bore those young fellas no ill will personally: 'We feel that these RCMP boys are only being used as a tool by those who have ground us down to the conditions we have lived in, and wish to keep us down to a bare existence.'

"Although we backed them off, that confrontation with the Mounties really hung there in the air. We felt like we were in no man's land now. We were never much for standing up to authority. We always just wanted to get along. And it seems like it all got to be too much. A couple of days later, the companies agreed to recognize the fish handlers' union but not the fishing fleet, who they regarded as co-adventurers. Most of us workers were offered our jobs back, except for those who were seen as union organizers. Those ones went off to war. And Charlie Murray went to jail. Then the old familiar whistle at Lockeport Company went off again as usual, and we made our way down the hill to the plants.

"Anyways, things did get better some, even if there was a war on. There was more money around than there had been. So that took the edge off our misery, but the whole thing still hurts when I think about it. The same thing happened up in

Canso in 1970. They were on strike there for seven months. No one could have been tougher than that bunch and they stuck it out together. But what chance did they have? It seemed like the whole world turned against them: the Mounties, the politicians, the courts, the newspapers. My. Oh. My. They had it rough. They got about the same as we got in Lockeport. A lot of grief. Make a little noise and the world changes. I doubt it. Well, my butter is going soft."

Another place on the wharf. "Now that fella Paul Watson and his Sea Shepherd Society. He's got the right idea. I see on the news he's out there on the Grand Banks right now running down those Cuban ships that are overfishing on the Nose and Tail. That takes guts and that's what we need these days. No more of this letting bureaucrats sift some paper and destroy our lives, with the law behind them too. Destruction is legal these days. So we have to go outside the law to protect ourselves. Same as that Watson. He's upholding a higher law than the one DFO abides by. That's what he claims and more power to him. According to what they say on the set, that Watson has a pirate flag on his ship. That's the only one worth flying these days.

"Just got in today. Been out fishing on Georges. We heard on the set what was going on. So when we got unloaded, the crew jumped in the truck to come up and have a look. 'Course the fact that the liquor store was nearby didn't hurt. Ha! Well, at least things are being talked about now. All that secret backroom stuff is out there for everyone to see."

The End of the Protest

Negotiations between Acting Deputy Minister Maryantonett Flumian and Regional Director Neil Bellefontaine and Gary Dedrick, Tim Nickerson, Noble Smith, and Cliff Fanning continue on into Thursday at the Wandlyn Inn in Bridgewater. Terry Demings provides regular reports on the wharf as the talks drag on.

"Just to let you all know, negotiations have gone on all day in Bridgewater. They are still at it and some progress is being made. Things blew up a couple of times and people stormed out. But they are back at it. No final agreement yet, but they are still talking. DFO claims everything is closely monitored, and they say our protest is based on faulty assumptions. We are out there on the ocean, and we know what is going on. The foreigners are taking way more than their quota and their allowable bycatch, and we know they are doing it with illegal gear because we have seen it. Our quota for cod and haddock is gone, and they are still out there catching them. That's what we have to sort out. There have been some rumours that DFO is going to call in the Mounties to break up the protest, but we have been assured that they are only monitoring the situation. So let's keep it orderly and civil so they don't have any excuses to come down hard on us. When we hear anything else, we'll let you know. So hang in there."

Among the boats a number of signs have appeared, painted on the sails, or hanging from the masts of the boats tied around the *Pioner Murmana*:

"Whose country does our government work for anyway?"

"Farewell to Nova Scotia."

"We are here till Christmas if that's what it takes."

"Ross Reid is no Santa Claus."

"Ross Reid has spoken. This is our answer."

"I remember last year working down at the shore with the other fisherman when John Crosbie's announcement came over the news on the truck radio about the shutting down of the cod fishery. 'I am making a decision based on the desire to insure that the northern cod survive as a species.' He was in this hotel ballroom in St. John's and he hadn't let the fishermen in to hear what he had to say. Can you imagine? Anyway, it was too much for them and they tried to batter the door down to get in. It rattled you right to your bones to hear it. The shouting and the banging and us standing there around the truck on a fine day, doing what we usually do.

"Man, it was a sick feeling. We just kind of stood there and looked at each other, like we were almost strangers, after all these years of fishing alongside. We knew the collapse was not happening only in Newfoundland. We knew the whole Scotian shelf was in the same shape. I had an old wrench in my hand that had belonged to my father. He had made it especially for tightening up the water-cooling pipes where they go through the hull. I looked down and I wanted to apologize to it. I wanted to apologize to my hands."

〜〜〜〜〜〜

Farther down the coast in Lunenburg, those on the wharf hear an announcement that today 120 workers will be laid off due to lack of fish to process. More layoffs are expected in the future. Up in Cape Breton, fishers in Bay St. Lawrence have blocked the mouth of the harbour to protest the fact that some fishers in the harbour have crab licences and are earning a good living, while others are having trouble making ends meet because the fishery has collapsed and lobstering is poor.

And farther out to sea, the vessel *Cleveland Amory*, captained by Paul Watson of the Sea Shepherd Society, has been impounded after colliding with a Cuban vessel and endangering a Spanish Vessel on the Nose and Tail of the Grand Banks. The Coast Guard is currently towing the *Cleveland Amory* into St. John's. When contacted by journalists, Watson states that he is subject to a higher law of protecting nature from human exploitation and he does it because governments such as Canada's have failed to implement proper conservation measures. In response, the Canadian government states that it regards Watson as an outlaw who does not have the support of fishers or the Canadian people and that he is endangering lives on the high seas and is breaking marine navigation laws.

Standing on the wharf in St. John's later that day, a defiant Watson states that he has already leased the *Cleveland Amory* to a local environmental group. This group is headed by lawyer Owen Myers, who intends to use it to challenge not only the foreign fleet but also Canadian draggers, a group Myers believes is responsible for bringing the northern cod to the point of extinction. Myers stated, "The only way to get the government's attention is to carry out the type of activities Paul Watson and his crew are engaged in." The cost of leasing the *Cleveland Amory* is a loonie and a bottle of screech. With regard to the lease agreement, Paul Watson states: "We have other things to do. We are a very busy organization."

≋≋≋≋≋≋

Saturday morning, day eight of the blockade. Chairs and microphones are lined up on the flatbed of an eighteen-wheeler. A large crowd is gathered on the wharf—not just the fishers that had been involved in the protest but many of the townspeople, as well as media outlets. Climbing a makeshift set of stairs set at the rear of the trailer, Garry Dedrick, Tim Nickerson, Noble Smith, and Cliff Fanning, as well as Neil Belfontaine and Maryantonett Flumian, line up in front of the chairs. Garry Dedrick steps to the microphone.

"I want to thank everyone for all their support. It has been a very hard few days, for you here and for us negotiating. We didn't get all we wanted, but I think we sent a message to DFO and the main thing is that the foreigners are leaving and we can go back fishing. At this time, I want to thank Neil Belfontaine and Maryantonett Flumian. One of these times I'll get her name right. We didn't always agree on issues or on the numbers, but we stayed at it and worked out a compromise. So I thank them for all their hard work. Hopefully, they can take our message back to the other folks at DFO.

"It is also very important for us to thank the captain and crew of the *Pioner Murmana*. We made it clear from the beginning that we had nothing against them. Our beef was with the Canadian government. Throughout all this, the crew have been very patient. To show our appreciation to them, we will be gathering up a collection of food and clothing for them to take back to their families in Russia." The crew wave from the upper deck, and the crowd on the wharf claps and whistles.

"Now to the agreement we have reached. First: by the end of August, all foreign vessels will have left Canadian waters. Second: foreign vessels, I know, have already left the Hake Box, and more will be leaving soon. Any new agreements to let foreign vessels fish in Canadian waters will be subject to stricter regulations, and we will be consulted before any of these agreements are signed. That issue is very important for the future of our fishery. Third: we worked out an agreement where our boats have enough quota to keep fishing for the rest of the year. There was a lot of debate over how accurate DFO numbers were regarding how many fish have been caught already, and it became clear that we were nowhere near catching our quota. Fishermen have the choice of haddock by catch: either 1000 pounds per trip, 2200 per week; or 5500 pounds three times a month. We also put in place new monitoring procedures so that we have a more accurate tally on how many fish have been caught. So, in a nutshell, we have an agreement. The blockade is officially over, and fishermen can get on with their lives with fish to catch, and without worrying about the foreign fleet."

One by one the half-ton trucks start up and manoeuvre their way off the wharf as the crowd begins to disperse. The stalls where food has been served are loaded away. The protest signs are taken down. The camera crews pack their gear into vans and head back to Halifax.

The fishers crawl from boat to boat as the fleet gets ready to sail. Engines start up and lines are untied. With a wave, the boats swing to the south'ard, a flotilla of vessels that will gradually fragment as each boat makes its way to one of many small harbours along the shores of Shelburne County. The throb of the engines leak up into the fog that hangs offshore, so that the sight of the boats disappears, and then the sound of them gradually dies away.

Eventually, the Russian ship sits alone at the wharf. With a groan and a shake, its mighty engines start up as its hatchways are opened. The forklifts from Continental Seafoods squirrel out onto the wharf to begin the unloading. A whistle sounds in the distance.

<hr />

The inshore longline/handline fleet has entirely disappeared from the Atlantic fishery. If there is any longline gear left at all, it is being eaten by mice in the back of a shed somewhere. After twenty-five years, the cod have not "come back." Collapse is a stable state. When was the last time you saw someone come back from the dead? There have been a few signs of recovery in the schools of haddock on Georges Bank over the last few years, and if they had been protected there would now be, in all likelihood, haddock along these shores. Instead, the drag-gers have pummelled these stocks into a precarious state once again. Department of Fisheries and Oceans officials should be in jail for overseeing this decimation.

Southwestern Nova Scotia continues to depopulate, as it has done for the last seventy years. As the fishing industry col-lapsed, the incidence rate of family breakdown and domestic abuse increased. Despite the successes of the blockade, many longline and handline fishers had their boats repossessed by the loan board in the years that followed and had to go away to find work.

And for those who stayed behind in the aftermath of collapse, there are persistent threats from outside because your area is seen as vulnerable and therefore under threat of becoming a sacrifice area. American interests tried, and failed, to build a toxic-waste incinerator. While it is illegal to ship toxic waste across state lines, the plan was to barge the waste up the eastern seaboard across the fishing grounds to Nova Scotia. These types of schemes were followed by the massive expansion of mega-fish farms that threatened lobster habitat

Figure 9 The launch of the *Laura Elizabeth* in Little Harbour, 1985. Photo by Laura Jane McLauchlan.

and polluted local bays, and by an exponential increase in the clear-cutting of forests in the area, all of which were supported by the Nova Scotia government. These same kinds of initiatives dominate development in the Global South: industrial interests make a great deal of profit, governments earn tax revenue, local people are offered a few poor-paying jobs, and the natural habitat is devastated. The South in the North.

As with the industrialization of the fishery, these agendas are underwritten by the naive conception that nature "bounces back" after being over-exploited—that if left alone it will return to its pristine state, as if nature is a mechanism that is outside of history. But like any other assault that is experienced, nature does not emerge unchanged. You go on by necessity, but you are different. The cod ocean has not returned. The area off southwest Nova Scotia is now a lobster ocean. One of the main predators of juvenile lobsters was codfish. When the cod were wiped out, lobster stocks went up 500 per cent. This surge in lobster numbers was a surprise, and has, at least for now, brightened what had been a very dismal outlook for coastal fishing communities.

Such rapid shifts in ecological relationships are rarely stable. Lobsters are showing up in places that have never been fished before. Whereas lobstering has historically been a shoal-water, rock, and kelp kind of fishery, boats are now catching them in ninety fathom of water and on the muddiest of bottom. Despite the large catches, prices have stayed up because of the influx of Chinese buyers, who are now taking over many of the lobster pounds and processing facilities in Nova Scotia. Boats are getting bigger and bigger, as fishers go farther and farther to catch more and more lobsters. It is not unusual for a fisher to be up to a million dollars in debt after buying a licence, boat, and gear.

These new outsized economic realities make it all but impossible for a small-scale fisher to get into the industry now. It is made all the more precarious because the pressures of climate change could mean this ecological blip is short-lived. The oceans are warming and lobster stocks in southern New England have already begun to collapse. There is an assumption that the lobsters have moved north to colder water. The same argument was made twenty-five years ago, that the cod had moved north into the Labrador Sea.

The mutiny of the bounty. This is how it feels. Tyranny and grief, amid the waste of something wonderful, heartbreaking for what could have been and now for what is. We have slid down the hill like mud in the rain and the dew is on our heads. We came to the ebb and then pushed passed it. Our pursuit of the "finny race" has seemed like a curse, an exile that has pulled us down into a murky and unfathomable territory where we joust with the unknowable, when we should have been up with the animals, feeling the warmth of the sun.

EPILOGUE

Little Harbour, Nova Scotia, 1831

There is a gale blowing as dark comes on. Donald McDonald stands out beyond the house, which rests on a low rise along the Western Shore amid the chewed bushes and tufted grass just beginning to turn green. Buffeted, he leans to wind'ard as he goes down the hill past the well to make sure the sheep and the cow are safe and the barn doors are closed. On his way back he stops, despite the wind, to look out at the waves as they build and crash against the eastern side of Ram Island. An easterly gale and a southerly sea. Storm going by outside. Black Rock is smother white. The previous winter, the ocean had set a boulder the size of a hay wagon on top of the rock. Maybe this storm will take it off again. Below the bank, there is the hollow periodic roar from the beach, as rounded rocks repeatedly chase the waves seaward in their temporary retreat.

Salt air layers his eyes. He catches himself, and through the grey of the mixing, he sees a light in a horrid place, in the range of the Emulous Breakers beyond Ram Island. Then it is gone. And as he stares out, he thinks he hears the refrain of a familiar tune from his childhood amid the clatter and guff of the wind. How can that be? Donald stands and listens, and after a while his senses are once again saturated by the storm.

Donald goes back to the house and tells Jane what he has seen and heard. She has just come downstairs after putting Agnes to bed and blowing out the lamps. They both go back

267

outside but neither of them can see or hear anything beyond the roar of the elements.

The next morning it is still blowing a gale, and the drowned can be seen in the surf as they begin to wash ashore. On the rising tide, the breakers sweep up across the field into the trees. The body of a woman and her two children, lashed to a makeshift raft made of fractured pieces of deck, are tipped up on edge where they have been shoved into the branches of a stunted cat spruce.

Just before dark, the tide drops somewhat and Donald and Jane wade out into the surf and cut them free of the ropes. They carry them up to the field and lay them down, side by side, on the grass. Agnes watches from the doorway of the house. Donald then props open the barn door with an old anchor against the gusts of wind. The cow lows and the sheep shuffle in the corner as the bodies are carried in, the dog staying close at Jane's heels on the trips back and forth. They pick the kelp from their hair and their woollen home-spuns, and then roll the three into a remnant of old sail and lay them in the straw, the animals attending. Jane stands over them and makes the sign of the cross.

The next day, as the storm subsides, British soldiers come down from Shelburne on horseback, along with sailors from the British navy ship that is in port for repairs. The people of the area walk the beach from the Madd Rocks, along the Western Shore, around Hemeons Head, and out across Black Point Beach. A trunk is found below the burial mound and is loaded into a horse-drawn cart. When the trunk is opened later, it turns out to be the Captain's chest, with details about the passengers and crew, amid the soaked papers and charts for places the Captain will no longer go to. The ship is a 160-ton brigantine named the *Billow*, on its way from Bermuda to Halifax with 137 passengers. The *Billow* had left Bermuda on 3 April, under the command of James A. Dennis. The passengers were made up of thirty-nine discharged soldiers from the 81st Regiment under Lieutenant Listen, along with their families; in total twenty women, sixty-eight children, eight crew members, and one passenger, John Bond of Yarmouth.

Donald's uncle had told him of crossing those southern waters. "You leave Hamilton Harbour and you haul her due north for Halifax. Drift along in the Gulf Stream most of the way. When you are in the range of Cape Cod you have to haul the vessel to the westward more because the current will carry you offshore as the Gulf Stream heads out across the Atlantic." A storm must have surprised the skipper. If he'd sensed the storm coming, he would have headed farther offshore when he had the chance, to give him more sea room when the easterly came on. An old square-rigger is not much good when you try to beat back into a gale. Especially when it is a twenty-five-year-old tub that is worm-eaten and rotten from sloshing around in the tropics.

After four days of searching, twenty-nine bodies are recovered: eight soldiers, five women, and sixteen children. When the authorities are assured that there are no next of kin nearby to claim them, Donald and Jane are then ordered to bury the three they have in the barn. Names unknown, no marker required.

They find a space in the grass near the shore and begin to dig. Donald and Jane decide on one large grave for all three of them. Agnes goes down onto the beach nearby to gather up some flat beach stones, while the parents take turns with the spade. First the turf is set aside and then there is a foot of black earth, then six inches or so of rusty clay, followed by the yellow clay with the tightly packed stones in it that makes for slow digging. By the time there is a large mound of earth, Agnes has made a number of trips back and forth with the beach stones, which are now stacked and ready for use.

Donald and Jane go to the barn and each carry a child up onto the grass. Between them, they wrap the mother in the sail and slide her along on the grass. On the trips back and forth, the animals follow along to where the bodies are laid out. The sail is used to line the grave and the mother is lowered, with the children above and on either side. Water has already begun to seep into the hole as the first shovelfuls of earth are used to hold the flaps of the sail in place. The sediment and rocks are then filled back in, with the turf tamped in gently on mounded-up hummock. The head- and foot-stones are then tipped up into notches that were made for them. "Blessèd are thee and blessèd are we, for thee are commended unto thy hands forever."

The family of the passenger from Yarmouth walks the shore for weeks after. He had been a preacher, and on behalf of the church had gone to the West Indies to inquire into the conditions of the workers on the plantations there. Now and again, family members stop by the house to ask if Donald or Jane have seen anything, their eyes moving reluctantly out across the field to the new mound of earth near the bank.

After an offer of tea is declined, Donald and Jane watch as the preacher's family make their way along the ebb. Here and there are remains of the *Billow*, around which they gather, as if this bit of ruin brings them closer to their grief. The procession then moves on, picking at what they find among the rocks and sand.

Little Harbour, Nova Scotia, 1994

Wilbur and Norman Harding stand out on the wharf in Little Harbour. They have arrived separately on similar morning rambles. Not another soul around. Boats are hauled up, with weeds pushing up between the skids of the slipway. The remains of the freezer building and the baiting shed are rank and mildewed in their dereliction. The two men lean against the concrete abutment and look out over the armour rock toward the Can Buoy.

"My god, you'd die of loneliness around here these days."

"You got that right. Die of loneliness for sure."

"I see you got a shovel in the car. You taken up gardening or what?"

"I'm going out to straighten up Donald's tombstone. It's starting to lean some."

"You mean the one out on the point?"

"Donald McDonald. He's a relation of mine. I thought I'd straighten it up before it falls over and disappears in the grass."

"Well, you and I are related back there, so he must be a relation of mine too. All us Hardings go back to Jasper Harding. His grave is over in Little Port L'Hebert."

"I've been there many a time. They say there's a new development going in. Some American has bought it up. He knocked down what was left of Andy McDonald's house."

"There goes another lobster mark. I used to set a string of traps with Andy's house lined up with the rock on the outside end of Harding Island."

"Well, if you want to come along, we'll go in my car. Road's so bad."

"One shovel and two men. That sounds like a plan."

"The other can hold the bottle."

"Why, that's a plan and a half."

They drive around the beach and pull off the gravel and into what was a lane, although it is now overtaken by alders.

"Man, this used to be one of the nicest views on a summer evening, looking out across the water over Western Wharf Rock to Black Rock and Ram Island. Now it is so overgrown, you are hard-pressed to know there is an ocean at all." Wilbur and Norman work their way through the rose bushes and alders to the openness at the edge of the bank.

"Well, size it up, you. That's a big gravestone. And granite too. Built to last. When you drive by and see it from the road, you wouldn't imagine it is this big."

"Sent over here from Scotland."

"God bless him. And look at the bank. It gets closer every year. This will all tip into the ocean one day."

"Well, that will be long after we're gone. Did you ever hear tell why Donald wanted to be buried out here, and not in the churchyard? You'd think he would want to be with his own kind."

"I guess this was his request to be buried here. Why else would there be a stone, if this wasn't what he wanted? I think his wife is buried here with him. There are other stones hereabouts, so maybe others are buried here too. See them there." Wilbur kicks around in the grass to reveal a number of beach stones turned up on their edge. "Accordin' to, he wanted his grave to face across the water toward Lewis. But this can't be the Donald who got the original land grant, not according to the dates here on the stone. This was the nephew of the first Donald, the soldier."

"That neighbour of mine, the fella from the States who comes up in the summer, said that Donald was buried here because he came ashore in a shipwreck."

"That's just nonsense. The first Donald was in the army and came here with the Loyalists after the American War. He was an original grantee. This was his fifty-acre lot. I've seen his name on the map."

"Which war was that?"

"I'm not too sure. But he was a Loyalist, so it must have been the War of Independence, far as I know."

"Too bad about the house there. It was a beauty. Robert tore it down to build a shop." Near where the house used to be is a patch of smoothed-over earth on which sits an eighteen-foot aluminum trailer with a temporary electrical service hooked up to it. "Some American has this land now. Put that trailer in and has never been back."

"The young go away and the summer people show up. What can you do?"

"Well, the lean times haven't exactly ended, have they. So what are we doing here?"

"We're going to dig out the dirt on the high side, as much as we can. Then straighten her up into the space we made, and fill the dirt in behind her to keep her upright. Maybe throw a few stones in for support."

"Good enough." They commence to digging, taking turns, and sharing a drink.

"We're both going to have to push. You ready? She's a heavy one. Let's get our asses behind us." They stand the stone and pack earth and small rocks around its base.

"Good for another ten thousand miles, Donald. Say what?"

"Have a drink, pard'. Job well done. Pour a shot on the grave while you're at it. There you be, Donald."

They both turn and look out to sea. "Not a boat in sight. Hard to believe on a fine summer day like this."

"In the good times, there would be sails up and they would be hauling gear on the outside edge of the Flat Ground all the way along. Remember the time we were out and the German sub surfaced and came up alongside?"

"You shook the gaff at them."

"Them were the days. But, my God, hard to believe, isn't it? Not a boat. Some forlorn. The animals used to be all around us. Here and abouts. Even the poor gulls have starved."

"Lonesome is right. You know, they say you can sometimes hear that song from the wreck on the breakers. Especially when it is thick fog. You'd catch it on the wind. I forget the name."

"Of the vessel?"

"No, of the song. It's by Burns, though. I know that for sure. My mom used to sing it in the old days."

> A Highland lad my love was born,
>   Tha Lalland laws he...;
> But still he was faithfu' to his clan,
> My gallant, braw John Highlandman.
>
>   ....
> We ranged a' from Tweed to Spey,
>   An' liv'd like lords...;
> For the Lalland face he feared none,-
> My Gallant, my Braw...
>
>   ....

Comments on Sources and Other Theoretical Considerations

> Oral tradition, [Innis] argued, permits continuous revision of history by actively reinterpreting events and then incorporating such interpretations into the next generation of narrative. Its flexibility allows...a given narrative to make sense of a confusing situation.
>
> — Cruikshank (2005: 62)

Emphasizing the similarities in the arcs of historical change in the crofter and fisher communities has been the main goal of the work, and the commonalities between these anatomies of dispossession are set out in the views expressed by those who experienced these transformations first-hand. The book is meant therefore to be an invitation into a larger conversation about the fate of rural communities such as my own in Atlantic Canada that are subject to economic stagnation and depopulation, punctuated at times by social unrest, and understood in the national media of Canada as being caused by "a particular resistance to change" (Ibbitson). In order to achieve that goal, the book is organized so as to commemorate ways of life that are being lost in these historical transformations, and also "to make the present strange" by using voices "from without" modern economic realities in order to highlight the historic specificity of the relations in which we are currently enmeshed and thereby contribute to an alternate history of Canada. This alternate history is based not on the triumphant-settler story but on one that highlights the way a staples economy marginalizes Indigenous peoples and casts aside others it has made use of in the exploitation of resources.

The eyewitness accounts of the Scottish crofters are derived from sources such as the four thousand pages compiled in the minutes of the Napier Commission, which was set up by the British Government to inquire into the causes of social unrest brought on by the expulsion of the Scottish crofters from their ancestral homes. The Commission travelled throughout the Highlands and Islands so as to hear directly from the crofters. Although a great many of them lived in an oral culture, were illiterate, and spoke only Gaelic, the translated descriptions of crofter's lives and their views of the changes they saw occurring around them provide a corrective to the "culture of improvement" and "progress" perspectives that dominated political discourse then and continues to dominate it now.

As can be seen in the endnotes that follow, I combined the comments of crofters from different communities into a single narrative that can be seen as representative—as a narrative that details the demands and conditions inflicted on the many communities affected by the Highland clearances. Given that the recollections of the crofters reflect a consistency across a wide number of locales—and despite that some commentators at the time claimed this consistency reflected coaching from outside agitators—I trust that in creating a unified narrative I have not undermined the veracity of the crofters' experience of those historical realities. With regard to the sections based on my own life experience, I have recreated what I believe to be reliable proximations of conversations that occurred during, for example, night fishing (in "Hemmed-In Communities") and living in the Long Spruce work camp on the Nelson River (in "Remittances Home").

Another consideration I dealt with in relation to the dispossession of communities was the issue of time. The Napier Commission was appointed a generation after the vast majority of the clearances took place. The crofters' demands, as recorded by the Commission, are framed in terms of how things used to be, and so there is a continual reference to the past as a way to understand a present that was, for them, foreign and incomprehensible. As James Hunter states, "the enduring significance of the crofters'[Arcadic] view of the past is not to be found in its historical accuracy or lack of it, but in the fact that it enabled crofters to set the grim realities of the nineteenth-century present against a vision of an older order in which material plenty was combined with security and social justice" (93). The remembered past therefore became an analytical tool to make sense of the threats of the present. Similarly, Walter Benjamin argues that "history is the past recalled in a moment of danger" (257). The danger Benjamin refers to is the threat of being incorporated into, and destroyed by, dominant structures.

This book is an attempt to make use of the personal narratives of the past as an analytical tool for understanding how we make meaning in the world today, recognizing that, at the same time, this present is shaping our understanding of the past. For me, as a former fisher, the present is informed by the collapse of the cod and the disappearance of Atlantic coastal communities, and these realities generate a particular kind of past in which enclosure and dispersal shape the way I understand my world. That understanding links Donald McDonald's world with my own in a specific way. The book therefore casts both a wide net in terms of years and locales, and yet it focuses very particularly on social and economic enclosure and the grief, pain, and social unrest that accompany it.

As the focus on the experience of dislocation emerged in the process of writing this book, my approach to the research shifted from a peasant or working-class history and environmental history to one that included narrative and life writing as another way to embody the "rough and plenty." As David Craig states in *On the Crofters' Trail*, "we can recover the events but not the emotions of the people's history from the documents" that underwrite academic research (3). In this book, "depersonalization and abstraction" are set aside in favour of a submerged history made up of collective voices in the landscape, of "feeling oneself alive inside the past" (Karr, 36), with a focus on "understanding narrative's role in exploring intersections among knowledge, power, and ideology" (Cruikshank 2005, 62).

Any resonance that the work has is not so much in the individual decisions that drive a narrative along, but rather in the recognition of the extent to which we are all historicized beings who are dealt a script that is not of our own making. In the case of the crofters and inshore fishers, the script is an especially painful one of economic transformation, leaving in its wake transformed subjects, and the odd stone remnant, like Donald McDonald's grave.

By focusing on this "cloud of living witnesses to the destruction of our homes" (MacLeod, as reprinted in Mackenzie, 67), I hope to contribute to an alternate history where— rather than seeing our history in terms of a triumphant story of settlers taming the wilderness—the focus is instead on the way a staples economy reinforces neo-colonial structures that continue to marginalize local people and decimate the natural world. In less determined contexts in the past, modern forms of economic exploitation were more clearly seen as the cause of dislocation and injustice. Today, by contrast, these dominant realities increasingly frame the very assumptions under which debate takes place, thereby rendering themselves largely invisible. Making the present strange, by including the voices of the rough and plenty, presents the opportunity to challenge this narrowing of the current realms of discussibility.

Methodological Approach: Personal Narrative and Environmental History

This work operates at the intersection of life writing and environmental history. Making use of Donna Haraway's conception of "situated knowledges" from marginal perspectives as a basis for beholding and critiquing master narratives, I ask the question: How does one explore "moments of danger" in a way that does not in some way unwittingly replicate the assumptions of dominant structures that cause social injustice and environmental degradation? This approach is based on the recognition that, within a range of environmental debates (e.g., on climate change), analytical enclosure has followed political and economic enclosure.

In broad terms, these economic transformations in modern society reflect what Karl Polanyi refers to as the movement from embedded to disembedded relations. For Polanyi, embedded relations are those where the economy is embedded within wider social institutions and serves social ends in strengthening communities. By contrast, capitalists markets create a disembedded pattern of integration where market relations are autonomous from social relations. Social relations are then reduced to serving the economy, rather than the economy serving society, so that humans and nature became adjuncts to the dictates of the market. It is the tyranny of markets, and their accompanying champions as well as their disciplining mechanisms, that can be described in terms of inversion: when the world is turned upside down, and where commodities and capital have the dominant social relationship, and humans and nature are reduced to playing the role of the passive material (human resources and natural resources) that serve the dominant market relationships. It is this transformation from embedded relations to disembedded relations that frame the moments of danger for both fishers and crofters, as their worlds are turned upside down and this new alien world denigrates and disciplines them. The ramifications of inversion are wide-ranging, especially when it comes to the normalization of these "strange" arrangements as the only way to discuss issues such as social justice and environmental degradation.

One way to get analytical purchase on the tendency to universalize present economic relations is through personal narrative. William Cronin contends that narrative storytelling is central to environmental history because it can give the discipline "its moral center" in any examination of historical transformation. Cronin states: "As storytellers, we commit ourselves to the consequences of human actions, trying to understand the choices that confronted the people whose lives we narrate so as to capture the full tumult of their world. In the dilemma they faced we discover our own, and at the intersection of the two we locate the moral of the story" (1370). This approach to storytelling is not open-ended but is instead, for Cronin, circumscribed in three ways: (1) our stories cannot contravene known facts about the past; (2) our stories must make ecological sense; and (3) narrators are not isolated beings but instead tell their stories from within communities. The "moral center" of this work is the attempt to present the voices of those who saw modernity "from without," so as to generate analytical and emotional space for those within modernity to recognize that they live in a strange and sometimes brutal world.

As an academic who focuses on political economy and environmental history, I was inclined at first to let the "rough and plenty" speak for itself and to be suspicious of inserting what could be seen as a colonizing academic voice that acts as guide and provides ongoing interpretations and summations of what is taking place as I "make the case." I have dealt with this tension by confining academic contextualization to the few comments in this section, while in the main body of the work I foreground the first-hand accounts, with the caveat that there are always issues of selection and emphasis, as there are with all forms of representation.

The kind of life writing I am aiming for is therefore one that is collective and situated, rather than individualized and reflective. I felt that this approach drew closer together the historical accounts of crofters and my own experience of life in a fishing community. Individual qualities and individual acts had little to do with the transformations that took place in the text. Therefore the focus on the individual as a lens into historical narrative was, I felt, less appropriate than the focus on collective experience. Most crofters lived in an oral culture and were largely illiterate. The only reason they are in the historical record at all is that their oral testimony was transcribed and translated by others. So the starting point for this kind of life writing is different from that of conventional life writing and provides an alternative basis for a narrative about their lives. Without a great deal of contrivance, I do not think there is the extant material available to convey these lives in a more deeply personalized and individualized form. By contrast, there are readily available the many voices in the historical record to convey the views of "the cloud of living witnesses."

I also wanted to emphasize the dimensions of landscape and collective experience that were shared by communities as they were being dispossessed, rather than privilege the experience of either myself or a created historical personage on which the narrative would concentrate. Because I have focused on communities that were without modern economic processes, it may also be that the narrative distance is necessarily part of this record of transformation into capitalism. The usual entry points into a narrative told in a more "proximate" and accessible way are not always there as a result.

Similarly, I recognize that the descriptions of longline fishing are quite detailed—a how-to manual of sorts, if one wished to take it up. No inshore longliners are left in Atlantic Canada, and what I have presented here could be one of the last descriptions of the practice in the historical record. An example of this kind of situated narrative that comes to mind is *The Wheelwright's Shop*, by George Sturt, which conveys rural nineteenth-century life in England as seen through those involved in the making of wooden wagon wheels. In a book that centres on anatomies of dispossession, the grief of fishers and crofters would be incomprehensible if there were no strong invocation of their attachment to particular land-scapes and to collective ways of life. Therefore, I believe that the inclusion of landscape, and the activities that take place in that landscape, such as kelping and fishing, provide a context for that grief.

This work is therefore informed by an integration of nar-rative and memory. As Leyshon and Bull state, "Memories are crucial to our construction of place. They simultaneously offer an anchor for identity and different temporalities to encounters in the landscape" (159). By "re-spatializing the here and now," Donald's grave acts as an anchor for the tem-poralities of the crofters and the fishers in this particular land/seascape, so that I come to understand my home in terms of what Leyshon and Bull refer to as "self-*in-situ*" or a "bricolage of the here" where memory and narrative combine to create an "interplay between materialities of space, and the social, cultural and historical positioning of human lives" (165). In this context, narrative "is an active process through which coherence is woven through the complexities of everyday life" (165) and is "key to understanding how the past reverberates in the present, how history is always 'contemporary'" (180).

But this is a coherence that is not based on a stable sense of selfhood. By describing the lives of pre-capitalist communi-ties, I seek to challenge ideas related to the individualization of experience. In these terms, McCooey states that "life writing of [marginalized and diverse] subjects was seen to deconstruct the supposedly secure limits of selfhood and auto-biograph-ical expressions of selfhood" (277). This work is therefore informed by a perspective that sees particular kinds of inte-riority as emblematic of an increasingly alienating world, where modern humans have been driven indoors as a form of self-preservation. The entrenching of increasingly hard-ened self–other dichotomies based on an identity that is skin-encapsulated and oppositional are symptomatic of modernity itself. In archaic societies, life is lived more out in the open and in collective terms, and is centred on participation rather than individualized reflection. An oppositional consciousness is essential for members of marginalized groups if they are to resist exploitive structures. What I have attempted to create here is a collective oppositional consciousness grounded in participation in ways of life that have largely disappeared.

In these strife-ridden narratives, my fidelity to crofters and fishers has created some reticence in this work ("you don't want to hear from me"). This reticence may be understood in terms of Lucien Goldmann's characterization of tragic literature, where incommensurability and refusal are central to the tragic vision, as they capture the crisis inherent in the shift from rural societies to urban merchant societies as seen, for example, in seventeenth-century England. The crisis is engendered by beholding two worlds at the same time—one that is quickly becoming the past and the other appearing as an ominous and painful future—and "the complete refusal to accept this [new] world as the one in which one could live..." (33). Therefore, the "moment of danger" has two elements within it: first, a sufficient number of relations remaining of the previous embedded social formations that these relations retain deep resonance; and, second, the emergent disembedded relations that pose a great enough threat to be seen in all their alien power. These realities underwrite the grief of refusal, as well as the social unrest, that accompanies these transformations. Hunter makes this case in terms of the crofters, who were regularly referred to as "aborigines" by their "social betters" (90): "[The crofters] had not been born into a culture familiar with the capitalist order in which they found themselves, for that had come from outside—insidiously, through the operation of economic forces of which the crofters had no comprehension and over which they could exercise no control."

For the crofters and the fishers, the spectre of spiritual grief in an alien universe is central to this threat of economic transformation, as is the loss of home and community, offering no path forward, after their protests were met with resistance. It is a crisis-ridden, painful, and horrifying world. This version of economic transformation highlights a profound incommensurability as mediating the shift from embedded relations to disembedded relations. As Goldmann states, in tragedy "the conflicts are necessarily insoluble" (4). This is because the world of disembedded relations has "destroyed the two closely connected ideas of the community and the universe," which were then replaced by "the concept of a collection of free, equal and isolated individuals, whose relationships were largely those of buyers and sellers" (27). The struggles of Indigenous people all over the world are rife with this kind of incommensurable horror and are underwritten by a version of the world that saturates one's entire being as, at the same time, it evaporates into a cloud of grief. This moment of danger is conveyed in the heartbreaking statement by the Crow Chief Plenty-Coups: "When the buffalo went away the hearts of my people fell to the ground, and they could not lift them up again. After this nothing happened" (Linderman 311). This "environmental grief" has come to be referred to as "solastalgia," as it describes a more general condition that is affecting more and more people in the face of waning biodiversity and the seeming intractability of environmental problems (Albrecht S95).

In charting the experience of the enclosure of the commons in Scotland and New Scotland, the present work reconceptualizes Hardin's version of tragedy of the commons. For Hardin, the tragedy of ecological collapse was driven by the inevitable over-exploitation by a community-less, genericized, and selfish peasant. For my purposes, tragedy is understood in terms of the grief-stricken specificity of particular peasants who experience the loss of their socially embedded worlds at the hands of the disembedding forces of capital. The tragedy is based on a social crisis brought on by a world being turned upside down in a "moment of danger." This version of tragedy overcomes the massive shortcoming in Hardin's universalization of human behaviour as selfish by nature. In its place is an analysis that makes clear that this selfishness is a social creation of modern economic relations and needs to be problematized rather than universalized, and is at the root of social injustice and environmental degradation.

If this were a history told from above, there would be clear patterns of intensifying forces of capital and technology that would link the historical periods of commons enclosure. Analysis would focus on the similarity between the realities that led to the expulsion of the Scottish crofters from the Highlands and Islands in the nineteenth century and, over one hundred years later, the marginalization of the inshore fishing fleet in Atlantic Canada. An extensive historiography on the commons could be called upon to make the case for the parallels between the fates of the crofters and those of the inshore fishers. Many other examples of enclosure would support this thesis, drawn from other contexts across the world, especially in the Global South, as can now be seen in the current literature on "land grabbing."

Beyond the specifics of particular enclosures, the expansion of the private realm and the consequent shrinking of the public realm are identical with the growth of capitalism. The enclosure of the commons is widely recognized as an event in this process, as are the current neo-liberal calls for privatization, deregulation, and free trade that support the politics of austerity.

The dominant structures that churn away above this submerged history that is presented here appear only occasionally, and almost always through the eyes of those who are being dispossessed. As voices in the landscape, these historical subjects are a dematerializing "cloud" chorus that is commenting on the deeds of powerful actors in a play in which most of the action occurs offstage, in the salons of London or the boardrooms of Ottawa. The grief is obvious only to those whose hearts are being broken.

Toronto 2019

> This then... is the representation of history. It requires a fal-
> sification of perspective. We, the survivors, see everything
> from above, see everything at once, and still we do not know
> how it was.
>
> — W.G. Sebald (125)

I am near the end of my academic career now and my partner, Laura, and I are looking forward to returning to Hemeons Head full-time, while our son, Lauchlan, who works in social media, remains in Toronto. He was wise enough not to ask me for career advice. Laura was the one who first encouraged me to go to Nova Scotia so many years ago, having been there herself on a holiday. We had been high-school sweethearts but were no longer together. It could be that going there myself was a strategy to win her back. If that were the case, it worked.

This book is an attempt to bring my life full-circle, to knit together the applied and the practical, the analytical and the theoretical, and at the same time highlight a refusal to enter modernity as anything other than a permanently recent immigrant. Given the stories I tell about displacement and dispossession, my deep ambivalence seems justified, in line with the collateral damage that Walter Benjamin might have seen in the permanent state of emergency that comes with the disciplining from above in late capitalism.

In contrast to this world of denigration and dispossession, theorists such as Norman O. Brown make the case that the initial role of economy was to give sacrificial gifts to the gods so as to overcome alienation, redeem the individual, and reaffirm community. With the emergence of mercantile capitalism in early modernity—what Polanyi would call the emergence of disembedded relations—levels of alienation increased to the point that this debt of guilt was no longer payable, the distance too far to travel for redemption. And so we live in a Faustian world where instead of giving gifts, we keep the goods and swallow the repression and alienation of living in a world gone to the devil. This is the deal modernity makes with each one of us: suck it up and keep the toys. We're hemmed in, in other words.

These realities have never stopped feeling catastrophic to me. Is it not obvious that we live in a gift economy? It is all around us, but invisible and never taken into account when "economics" is discussed. None of us would last five minutes without the gift economy. Our families, the people who love us, the random acts of kindness that keep us all going: these are what give our day-to-day lives meaning.

So the shift from fishing to university, albeit with an extended period in between doing hard itinerant labour in construction, did not feel that dramatic. Universities are medieval communities that have, until recently, resisted being organized around profit. Environmental Studies is especially given to critiquing "the intellectual ruin called development," and with my focus on the cautionary tale of the collapse of the fishery as a main area of study, my academic work kept fealty with the coastal communities I cared about in the land of rough and plenty.

As I entered my academic career, the intellectual work focused on the heavy lifting that would create analytical space for citizens to reflect on how society is organized, recognizing the contingency of these relations and thereby opening up alternate spaces for thinking about who we are as humans. This analysis could then lead to social action against injustice and environmental degradation. When I received the first Ph.D. in Environmental Studies in Canada in the mid-1990s, this emancipatory approach that was generally associated with Cultural Studies was the most popular area of student interest in the environmental field. It has now been entirely eclipsed by management approaches and urban planning. In other words, students now seem to feel they have been swallowed by the monster—it is no longer "over there"—and, as a result, they tend to be more interested in understanding how to live inside the monster.

In the process, mainstream environmentalism has become more technically oriented and has left the intersectionalist social justice battles—like the ones I worked on in the Jane–Finch neighbourhood in Toronto—to marginalized and racialized groups to fight on their own. The first time round, I came to hill field on Hemeons Head as an escape from the grief of settler-society contradictions and my own spent psyche from time in the trenches of care. I am returning to hill field from the trenches of learning that have become increasingly constrained by neo-liberal forces and the politics of austerity.

There is a circle of stones down by the well where I used to have my campfire when I was living in the tent over forty years ago. As I have done from time to time in the past, I will dig down in the turf to find the stones and then gather up some dead branches and light a fire. It's a mark in the landscape, one of many you can find with a little digging in this overgrown land. To do this digging has given me strength, has put me back in touch with the rough and plenty. I hope when you root around in your own life, you too will find markers that give you strength that, by going back, will urge you on.

Notes

The Use of Historical Sources

Among the historical sources I have used on the Scottish clearances that are cited in the notes, I have made extensive use of the first-hand accounts gathered by the Napier Commission. It was set up in March 1883 by the British Home Secretary Sir William Harcourt to "inquire into the conditions of the crofters and cottars in the Highlands and Islands of Scotland" in response to unrest among crofters in places such as the Braes and Glendale in Skye. The Commission was made up of Lord Napier (Chair), Sir Kenneth MacKenzie of Gairloch, Donald Cameron of Lochiel, M.P., Charles Fraser Mackintosh, M.P., Sheriff Alexander Nicolson, and Professor Donald MacKinnon, with Malcolm MacNeill as clerk. The commission visited sixty-one communities throughout 1883, and the committee was satisfied that they had heard directly from the crofters and cottars about their grievances, despite the accusations at the time of outside interference from agitators such as those from the Highland League and the Irish Land Leaguers. In their final report, the Commission stated that they were impressed by "the evidence from even the poorest and least-educated class" from whom there were "many examples of candour, kindness and native intelligence, testifying to the unaltered worth of the Highland people" (I.M.M. MacPhail, *The Crofter's War*, 1989, p. 75). The minutes are available digitally from Lochaber College (renamed West Highland College, Mallaig) at www.highland-elibrary.com.

Abbreviations used in the notes

NC   Minutes of Napier Commission Testimony Napier Commission

NA   Napier Commission Report Appendices

PAGE VI. Epigraph. NC. Roderick Stewart, Inverness, 1 October 1883, p. 2738.

PAGE X. "You don't want to hear from me" by Raymond A. Rogers.

Prologue

PAGES 1–3. The story of the sinking of the *Douglas and Robert* was told to me by Clyde Murphy of Allendale. As a young boy, he walked over to Little Harbour from Rockland to see the wreck. He heard Captain Tanner make the statement about living in hell. The Balish family of Lockeport had a home-movie camera with which they recorded footage of the wreck. It can be viewed on the Web when you search for "Lockeport shipwrecks." I used an abridged version of the description of the *Douglas and Robert* sinking in Raymond A. Rogers, *Solving History: The Challenge of Environmental Activism* (Montreal: Black Rose Books, 1998), pp. 186–87. Pieces of the ship can still be seen on the Madd Rocks, as can coal from the freighter *Brantford City*, which ran aground in the same place.

PAGE 5. Donald McDonald's grave is still situated on the spot described here, on the western shore of Little Harbour, across the road from our home.

PAGE 9. Donald MacLeod, *Gloomy Memories*. Published originally in 1857 and reprinted in *History of the Highland Clearances* by Alexander Mackenzie (Edinburgh: Mercat Press, 1999), p. 67. (The Mackenzie *History* was originally published in 1883.)

PAGE 10. Marlene Kadar, *Essays on Life Writing: From Genre to Critical Practice* (Toronto: University of Toronto Press, 1992).

PAGE 11. Julie Cruikshank, *Do Glaciers Listen?: Local Knowledge, Colonial Encounters & Social Imagination* (Vancouver: UBC Press, 2005).

PAGE 11. Michael Taussig, *The Devil and Commodity Fetishism in South America* (Chapel Hill: University of North Carolina Press, 1980).

PAGE 11. "going backward...the porcupine does." Howard Norman, collector and translator, Introduction to *Wishing Bone Cycle: Narrative Poems from the Swampy Cree Indians* (New York: Stonehill, 1976).

Chapter I   Shelburne County, Nova Scotia, Mid-1970s

The fishing trip described here is based on my own experience as a fisher in Little Harbour, and the night on the water is, I hope, a faithful rendering of those I fished alongside. I was never run down by a freighter, but there were some very close calls. Tugboats and towing barges were the things we feared most. You might drift into a position between a tug and a barge at night and know nothing about it until a one-inch steel cable comes up out of the water and cuts your boat in half.

The remnants of Gideon and Bythinea Hemeon's home is still on Hemeons Head, minus a few foundation stones that I used in my fireplace.

Chapter II   Lewis, Scottish Hebrides, Early 19th Century

PAGE 79. James Hunter, *The Making of the Crofting Community* (Edinburgh: John Donald Publishers, 1976).

PAGE 80. "I would say...extravagantly now." Rev. John A. Macrae, Loch Eport, North Uist, 30 May 1883 in NC, p. 810.

PAGE 80. "I have no faith...kill you in a minute." William Anderson Smith, *Lewisiana: or Life in the Outer Hebrides*, British Library reprint (2013), pp. 93. (Originally published in London by Daldy, Isbister & Co., 1875.) The further details on Malcolm's funeral that appear at the end of this chapter are taken from the same account by Smith.

PAGE 81. "possessed little and enjoyed much." Donald MacLeod, *Gloomy Memories*. Published originally in 1857 and reprinted in *History of the Highland Clearances* by Alexander Mackenzie (Edinburgh: Mercat Press, 1999), p. 126. (The Mackenzie *History* was originally published in 1883.)

PAGES 81–83. "The day we move the animals...arm around our head" (the end of hymn). From Alexander Carmichael's account in the Appendixes of the Napier Report (1883), pp. 469–73.

PAGE 84. "Highland couples...animals and the fire." NC. George Sinclair, Lybster, Caithness, 4 October 1883, p. 2372.

PAGE 85. "Go you must...bottom of the sea." NC. Duncan Sinclair, Balmacara, Ross, 2 August 1883, pp. 1930–31.

PAGE 85. "We have been...on the bog." NC. John McKinnon, Loch Boisdale, South Uist, 28 May 1883, p. 749.

PAGE 86. "Not very long ago...nearly exhausted." NC. Duncan Sinclair, Balmacara, Ross, 2 August 1883, p. 1931.

PAGE 86. "hemmed in on all sides." NC. Angus Peterson, Breasclete, Lewis, 5 June 1883, p. 956.

PAGE 86. "our hovels...by the tide." NC. Archibald Macdonald, Loch Eport, North Uist, 30 May 1883, p. 835.

PAGE 86. "We who are without...I am alone." NC. John McLeod, Tarbert, Harris, 13 June 1883, p. 1170.

PAGE 86. "we do not go away...among ourselves." NC. Dr. W. McGillivray, Factor, Castle Bay, Barra, 26 May 1883, p. 679.

PAGE 87. "I have been obliged...three acres of moss." NC. Donald Gillies, Loch Boisdale, South Uist, 28 May 1883, p. 747.

PAGE 87. "When I open my door...big sheep." NC. Alexander Macdonald, Breasclete, 5 June 1883, p. 926.

PAGE 88. "wallowing in wealth...cannot understand." NC. Donald McNeil, Braes, Skye, 8 May 1883, pp. 30–31.

PAGE 88. "So above us now are the rough hills...they could live." Alexander Mackenzie, *History of the Highland Clearances* (Edinburgh: Mercat Press, 1999), p. 213. Original publication by A&W MacKenzie, Inverness, 1883.

PAGE 88. "called Newland...in a hurry." NC. John Mackay, Edinburgh, 22 October 1883, p. 3221.

PAGE 88. "Misery, danger and want." NC. Statement is from Skye Emigration Committee 1852, read by Dugald Maclachan, Portree, Skye, 23 May 1883, p. 635.

PAGE 89. "I then made my stockyard...should not get the dog." NC. John Nicolson, Braes, Skye, 8 May 1883, p. 32.

PAGE 89. "gallows succeeding the fever." NC. Alexander Ross, Glendale, Skye, 19 May 1883, p. 391.

PAGES 89–90. "What rent do you pay...to take gruel." NC. Allan McIntyre, Castle Bay, Barra, 26 May 1883, p. 684.

PAGE 90. "I am old...promise you much." NC. Roderick Macrae, Balmacara, Ross, 2 August 1883, p. 1971.

PAGE 90. "Sheep...the whole go." NC. Donald Stewart, Glenelg, Inverness-shire, 4 August 1883, p. 2058.

PAGE 90. "I was the father...as I was." NC. John Matheson, Barvas, Lewis, 6 June 1883, p. 976.

PAGE 90. "And I remember...in other places." NC. John Matheson, Barvas, Lewis, 6 June 1883, p. 975.

PAGE 90. "the godless fashions of France." NC. Donald McPhee, Dunvegan, Skye, 15 May 1883, p. 216.

PAGE 91. "All winter long...leave home to do it." Details from Smith's *Lewisiana*. 1875, pp. 60–64.

PAGE 91. "the places I knew...Paul himself to tell it." NC. John Nicolson, Braes, Skye, 8 May 1883, p. 32.

PAGE 92. "It is sad...the fullness thereof." NC. Donald Campbell, Stornoway, Lewis, 8 June 1883, p. 1024.

PAGE 94. "With regard to...bog altogether." NC. John Gillies, Torran, Raasay, 22 May 1883, p. 445.

PAGE 94. "There was one year...passing of vessels." NC. Murdo McLeod, Stenscholl, Skye, 11 May 1883, p. 129.

PAGE 94. "The land above...of the beach." NC. George Mackenzie, Keose, Lewis, 12 June 1883, p. 1139.

PAGE 95. "our places were crowded...among us" and "I hear...till this day." NC. Norman Morrison, Maivaig, Lewis, 4 June 1883, p. 887.

PAGE 95. "the rest were hounded...could think of." NC. Donald McLeod, Torran, Raasay, 22 May 1883, p. 448.

PAGE 95. "This is a thing...land at all." NC. Donald Martin, Stornoway, Lewis, 8 June 1883, p. 1032.

PAGE 95. "I myself was born...she was put." NC. Donald McDonald, Tarbert, Harris, 13 June 1883, p. 1201.

PAGE 95. "The minister asks...are simply cottars." NC. Charles Cameron, Lochaline, Mull, Argyll, 11 August 1883, p. 2282.

PAGE 95. "For the last...from the new croft." NC. Malcolm Ferguson, Glasgow, 19 October 1883, p. 3047.

PAGE 96. "I know that...come through than today." NC. John Martin, Isle Ornsay, Skye, 17 May 1883, p. 287.

PAGE 96. "Those were our times...fault of circumstances." NA. Alexander Carmichael. 1883, p. 473.

PAGE 96. "Eight or ten years ago...Speyside crofters." NC. Magnus Sinclair, Lybster, Caithness, 4 October 1883, p. 2427.

PAGE 96. "Quite the contrary...into a fank." NC. John Smith, Keose, Lewis, 12 June 1883, p. 1135.

PAGE 96. "If any of us...teeth drawn." Alexander McCaskill, Bracadale, Skye, 18 May 1883, p. 351.

PAGE 100. "the fears of...severely wise." NA. Alexander Carmichael, p. 214.

PAGE 100. "The pretended losses of the cruel men." John Lane Buchanan, *Travels in the Western Hebrides from 1782 to 1790* (London: Robinson and Debrett, 1793), p. 161, Kessinger Legacy reprint, 2012.

PAGE 103. "Things are dark...these years." NC. John Macdonald, Ness, Lewis, 7 June 1883, p. 1013.

PAGE 104. "Go to the ebb for whelks." NC. Adam Bannerman, Helmsdale, Sutherland, 6 October 1883, p. 2454.

PAGE 104. "kindly to the sea...sailors entirely." NC. Angus Sutherland, Helmsdale, Sutherland, 6 October 1883, p. 2448.

PAGES 104-5. "For we are accustomed to quiet firths...the peril of our lives." MacLeod in Mackenzie, pp. 45–46.

PAGE 105. "For when we were first moved...would fish for him." NC. Laurence Jarmsen, Lerwick, Shetland Islands, 13 July 1883, p. 1217.

PAGE 105. "fish on the half-catch system." NC. Donald Moar, Balta Sound, Unst, 16 July 1883, p. 1282.

PAGE 105. "he kept half the catch." NC. John Omand, Raefirth, Mid Yell, Shetland Islands, 14 July 1883, p. 1237.

PAGE 105. "thrall of the truck system." NC. Walter Williamson, Lerwick, Shetland, 19 July 1883, p. 1388.

PAGE 106. "Jack was as good as his master." NC. Archibald Patterson, Tarber, Argylshire, 26 December 1883, p. 3369.

PAGE 107. "tailor and a shoemaker...fine nights." Dunlop, British Fisheries Society quoted in A.J. Youngson, *After the Forty-Five* (Edinburgh: Edinburgh University Press, 1973), p. 131.

PAGE 113. "He was the best...in the glen." William Anderson Smith. op. cit., p. 93. Other details of the funeral also come from Smith.

PAGE 113. "we are people...annihilated." NC. Adam Gunn, Bettyhill, Sutherland, 24 July 1883, p. 1613.

PAGE 114. "Last spring we began...our proceedings." NC. Donald Martin, Breasclete, Lewis, 5 June 1883, p. 937.

PAGE 114. "And for aught we know...come upon us also." NC. Donald Martin, Breasclete, Lewis, 5 June 1883, p. 938.

PAGE 114. "our fires were...quenched." NC. Malcolm McPhail, Barvas, Lewis, 6 June 1883, p. 962.

PAGE 114. "we were tumbling...pitied us." NC. Angus Mackay, Bettyhill, Sutherland, 24 July 1883, p. 1617.

PAGE 114. "the land our forefathers...could be found." NC. Angus Mackay, Bettyhill, Sutherland, 24 July 1883, p. 1645.

PAGE 114. "It is like penal servitude...such a place." NC. Donald Mackay, Kinlochbervie, Cape Wrath, 26 July 1883, p. 1677.

PAGE 114. "where hardly a snipe could live." NC. Donald Mathieson, Meavaig, Lewis, 4 June 1883, p. 886.

PAGE 114. "I am lost...provides that for me." NC. Angus Mackay, Bettyhill, Sutherland, 24 July 1883, p. 1618.

PAGE 114. "allowed to gaze...going away." NC. Angus Mackay, Bettyhill, Sutherland, 24 July 1883, p. 1650.

Chapter III   Hudson Bay, Seventeenth to Nineteenth Centuries

PAGE 118. "Enlisting with the Company...their old one." Philip Goldring, "Scottish Recruiting for the Hudson's Bay Company 1821–1880," *International Review of Scottish Studies* 10 (1980), p. 96.

PAGE 122. Login's Well commemorates the time the HBC spent in Stromness and is across the street from the local museum, which has a great many artifacts from the time of the company.

PAGE 123. "This morning was calme...a storme to follow." Thomas Button, quoted in A. Burnett Lowe, "Discommoded by the Cold," *The Beaver* (Winter 1968), pp. 18–21, 19.

PAGE 124. "Jan. 25...severe frost." Jens Munck, quoted in Burnett Lowe, p. 20.

PAGE 124. "He had with him...King of England." Miller Christy, ed., *The Voyages of Captain Like Foxe of Hull and Captain Thomas James of Bristol, in Search of the North-West Passage in*

1631–32, vol. 88–89 (London: Hakluyt Society, 1894), p. 359, quoted in Louis Bird, *Telling Our Stories: Omushkego Legends and Histories from Hudson Bay* (Toronto: Broadview Press, 2005), p. 158.

PAGE 124. "Since the dogs...to the vessel." Christy, pp. 571–72, quoted in Bird, p. 140.

PAGE 124. "so unknown a place." Christy, p. 490, quoted in Bird, p. 142.

PAGES 124–25. "we were loath...subsistence of Man." John Oldmixon, quoted in Burnett Lowe, p. 20.

PAGE 125. "The walls of our houses...as already observed." James Isham, *Isham's Observations and Notes 1743–49* (London: Hudson Bay Record Society, 1949), p. 172.

PAGE 125. "Fort York...rebuilt with fresh timber." Joseph Robson, *An Account of Six Years Residence in Hudson River* (London: J. Payne and J. Bouquet, 1752), p. 18, published as ebook 29 January 2008. Also quoted in Lowe (1968), p. 24.

PAGES 125–26. "Instead of a defensible fort...whose cost it was built." Joseph Robson (1752), p. 14, published as ebook 29 January 2008.

PAGE 126. "My own Place...make it warm." James Knight, *Letters from Hudson Bay 1703–40* (London: Hudson Bay Record Society, 1965), p. 38. Also quoted in Lowe (1968), p. 22.

PAGES 126–28. "They found guns...armourer or smith." Samuel Hearne. Details of the findings on Marble Island can be found in Joseph Stevens's log of the *Success* sloop for 1767 in Hudson Bay Company Archives 42/a/69 and in Magnus Johnston's log of the *Churchill* sloop Hudson Bay Company Archives 42/a/68. The events were later recollected by Hearne in the introduction to *Journey from Prince of Wales Fort in Hudson's bay to the Northern Ocean* (1795). This is cited in *Voyages of Delusion: The Quest for the Northwest Passage* by Glyn Williams (New Haven, CT: Yale University Press, 2003) and in "The House That Knight Built," by Walter Zacharachuk, in *The Beaver* (1973), pp. 12–15. Many issues have been raised about what happened to the Knight expedition. See Owen Beattie and John Geiger's *Dead Silence: The Greatest Mystery in Arctic Discovery* (Toronto: Viking, 1993).

PAGE 129. "looked narrowly into the plan of our route…prospect of return." Sir John Franklin, *Narrative of a Journey to the Shores of the Polar Sea 1819–22* (Salzwasser Verlag). Google Book, p. 10.

PAGE 129. Details about the hardships of the Franklin expedition are from Fergus Fleming, *Barrow's Boys* (London: Granta Books, 2001), pp. 124–53.

PAGE 131. Notice in Stromness newspaper, 1 December 1863.

PAGE 131. "slaves in a savage land." J. Storer Clouston, "Orkney and the Hudson's Bay Company," *The Beaver* (Spring 1937), p. 43.

PAGE 131. On the fight in Stornoway between the Hudson's Bay Company and the North West Company, see Bill Lawson, *Lewis in History and Legend* (Edinburgh: Birlinn, 2011), p. 49.

PAGES 131–32. HBC labour shifts from Orkney to Lewis in the mid-nineteenth century. Philip Goldring, "Labour Records of the Hudson's Bay Company 1821–1870," *Archivaria* 11 (Winter 1980–81), pp. 53–86, 56. See also Philip Goldring, "Scottish Recruiting for the Hudson's Bay Company 1821–1880," *International Review of Scottish Studies* 10 (1980), pp. 83–104.

PAGE 132. Philip Goldring, "Scottish Recruiting for the Hudson's Bay Company 1821–1880," *International Review of Scottish Studies* 10 (1980), p. 96.

PAGES 132–33. "bring home with them…has no compassion." A. Storer Clouston, *The Beaver* (Spring 1937), p. 43.

PAGE 133. Information on York boats from Thomas Blakiston, January 1858, "Travelling by York Boat – York Factory to Red River," Appendix I to *Exploration – British North America*, presented to both (British) Houses of Parliament, 1860. http://ellingtonweb.ca/Hay/TravelByYorkBoat.html (accessed 1 March 2018).

PAGE 133. "white mud banks and toppled trees." Bartley Kives, "Paddling Through History: Few Get to Experience Manitoba's Original Superhighway," *Winnipeg Free Press*, posted 5 September 2015.

PAGES 134–35. "It was now thought…our tolerant people." Robert W. Newbury, "The Painted Stone: Where Two Rivers Touch," *Nature Canada*, January 1974, pp. 12–19.

PAGES 135–36. "On the third day…ceased to be held in veneration." Robert W. Newbury (1974), pp. 12–19.

PAGE 136. "If I knew how to speak... against the Creator." Abel Chapman, "Voices of Hudson Bay: Cree Stories of York Factory," compiled and edited by Flora Beardy and Robert Coutts (Kingston: McGill-Queen's University Press, 1996), p. 57.

PAGE 136. "The white man... as a result." Newbury (1974), p. 247.

PAGE 137. "In cultivating the barren land... enrich them." NA, Appendix A, Isle of Harris, p. 494.

PAGE 138. "In early June... near London." James Hunter *Set Adrift upon the World: The Sutherland Clearances* (Edinburgh: Birlinn, 2015), p. 135.

PAGE 138. "These same two ships... his crew to York Factory." Anthony Dalton, *River Rough, River Smooth: Adventures on Manitoba's Historic Hayes River* (Toronto: Dundurn Press, 2010), p. 227.

PAGE 138. "There were a great many soldiers... nausea, and vomiting." Hunter (2015), p. 136.

PAGE 139. "In early August... a skeleton crew remaining." Hunter (2015), p. 138.

PAGES 139–40 "Many of those... their refractory spirits." Hunter (2015), p. 146.

PAGE 140. "Many crofters died... in the pack ice." Alexandra Paul, "Highlanders' winter journey one of the most heroic feats in Manitoba's history," *Winnipeg Free Press*, 18 January 2014, pp. 1–9.

PAGE 141. "To their surprise... Hudson's Bay Company." Hunter (2015), p. 156.

PAGE 141. "In their sixties now... state imaginable." Hunter (2015), p. 160.

PAGES 141–42. "few poles... rain that fell." Hunter (2015), p. 160.

PAGE 142. "The crofters were... from Red River." Hunter (2015), p. 160.

Chapter IV   Long Spruce Rapids, Nelson River, 1976

The events and characters in this chapter reflect my experience of working in Long Spruce in the mid-1970s. Personages such as Alfred Ronnie and Ford Lady were there during my time. The twenty-four-hour strikes after a worker died were a regular occurrence, and one such event did take place during my time there. The stories that Casey tells about being in Hitler's camps were told to me by friend and neighbour Egon Czerny, who was not in any way like Casey.

PAGE 146. "We are all...Raving Mad." Letter from Ferdinand Jacobs to James Isham, York Factory, Hudson Bay, 27 May 1754. Hudson's Bay Company Archives, Archives of Manitoba, Correspondence book reference code B.239/b/11, folios 8d–9. Thanks to Anna Shumilak at the archives for finding the reference for me.

PAGES 146–47. Regulations for Long Spruce Rapids Camp, Nelson River, set out by Manitoba Hydro.

PAGES 181–82. "Things That Wash Up I Live In." Howard Norman [collector and translator], *Wishing Bone Cycle: Narrative Poems from the Swampy Cree Indians* (New York: Stonehill, 1976).

Chapter V   Scottish Highlands and Islands, Mid-Nineteenth Century

PAGE 184. "would be better...large divisions." James Hunter, *The Making of the Crofting Community* (Edinburgh: John Donald Publishers, 1976), p. 23.

PAGE 186. "About 300 cottar families...strong air." NC. Edward Charles Sandford, Glasgow, 19 October 1883, p. 3057.

PAGE 186. "We are eating...starved to death." NC. Donald C. Cameron, Portree, Skye, 24 May 1883, p. 624. The exact quote is "There were two witnesses from Soay who stated that there had been actual starvation, and that the people in Soay had been obliged to live on a dead stirk..." James Hunter, in *The Making of the Crofting Community* (Edinburgh: John Donald Publishers, 1976) states, "The starving people of Skye were living on the carcasses of cattle which had themselves died of hunger" (50).

PAGE 186. "the dew will be on our heads." James Hunter (1976), p. 92.

PAGES 186–87. "Famished people have blackened...impoverished crofters." Alexander Mackenzie (1999), p. 196.

PAGE 187. "More and more...for their release." Donald MacLeod, *Gloomy Memories* (1857), reprinted in Alexander Mackenzie (1999), p. 41.

PAGE 187. But when the Factor burned our houses...with the houses." Donald MacLeod quoted in Alexander Mackenzie (1999), pp. 12–15.

PAGE 188. "in the open air...former houses." MacLeod quoted in Mackenzie (1999), p. 25.

PAGE 188. "We have lived...wear out our lives." Hugh Miller quoted in Mackenzie (1999), p. 180: "...with its melancholy and dejected people [who] wear out life in their comfortless cottages on the sea-shore."

PAGE 188. "sheep farmers are seen...with hospitality." MacLeod quoted Mackenzie (1999), p. 10.

PAGE 188. List of Regulation taken from Napier Appendix of Reay Estate, Tongue (1883), pp. 297–300. See also Calum Ferguson, *Children of the Blackhouse* (2003), p. 79.

PAGE 189. "Everything set out...forbidden ways." NC. Rev. Donald MacCallum, Arisaig, Inverness, 6 August 1883, p. 2092.

PAGE 189. "grand plans...so changed are we." NC. James Walter, Lybster, Caithness, 4 October 1883, pp. 2401–3.

PAGE 189. "we attended the funerals...of an ass." NC. George Sinclair, Lybster, Caithness, 4 Oct. 1883, p. 2372.

PAGES 189–90. "The man became distant...thirty years before." NC. James Waters, Lybster, Caithness, 4 October 1883, p. 2404.

PAGES 189–90. "distant in the mind." Mary Carbery, *The Farm by Lough Gur* (Dublin: Mercier Press, 1982), p. 109.

PAGE 190. "Neil McDonald...of her delivery" and "Hugh McLean...at the roadside." NC. Donald McDonald, Tyree, Argyll, 7 August 1883, pp. 2142–43.

PAGES 190–91. "Neil Black...stinging pain." NC. Alexander Macpherson, Bunessan, Isle of Mull, Argyll, 8 August 1883, p. 2204.

PAGE 191. "round among us...quit the place." NC. Donald McDougall, Tyree, Argyll, 7 August 1883, p. 2132.

PAGE 191. "follow our neighbours to foreign places...crofts for sheep." NC. Donald McDougall, Tyree, Argyll, 7 August 1883, p. 2132.

PAGE 192. "it is a wonder...pursuing us as thieves." Hunter (1976), p. 156.

PAGE 192. "now sojourners." NC. Andrew Sutherland, Golspie, Sutherland, 8 October 1883, p. 2542.

PAGE 192. "only citizens of the world." NC. Alexander Ross, Kinlochbervie, Cape Wrath, 26 July 1883, p. 1684.

PAGE 192. "strayed abroad." NC. Lachlan Campbell, Tarbert, Harris, 13 June 1883, p. 1202.

PAGE 192. "fugitive inhabitants." NC. George Mackenzie. Keose, Lewis, 12 June 1883, p. 1139.

PAGE 192. "a cloud of living witnesses." McLeod quoted in Mackenzie (1999), p. 67.

PAGES 192–93. "Last summer when many were evicted...ditch next to the church." Alexander Mackenzie (1999), p. 116.

PAGE 193. "natives of the Western Hebrides...and government." John Lane Buchanan, *Travels in the Western Hebrides: From 1782 to 1790* (London: Robinson and Debrett, 1793), Kessinger Legacy reprint (2012), p. 2.

PAGE 193. "enlistment in the military...improved fishing." NC. Dr. Nicol Martin, Glendale, Skye, 19 May 1883, p. 432.

PAGE 194. "The only remedy...paupers to go away." NC. Dr. Nicol Martin, Glendale, Skye, 19 May 1883, pp. 434–35.

PAGE 194. "the cause of these evictions...the chief causes." NC. Alexander Macdonald, Factor, Portree, Skye, 23 May 1883, p. 483.

PAGE 194. "They are clannish...among themselves." NC. John Fraser Sim, Lismore Argyll, 13 August 1883, p. 2350.

PAGE 195. "I would go...much the gainers." NC. Alexander Macdonald, Portree, Skye, 23 May 1883, p. 494.

PAGE 195. "they are more indolent...at home." NC. John Stewart, Portree, Skye, 23 May 1883, p. 541.

PAGE 195. "Laziness and discouragement." NC. Lachlan Macdonald, Portree, Skye, 23 May 1883, p. 557.

PAGE 195. "crofter labour is of less value...working the land." NC. William Henderson Hardie, Managing Trustee of Lochaline Estate, Lochaline, Argyll, 11 August 1883, p. 2311.

PAGES 195–96. "there is plenty of work...as well as fed daily." NC. Alexander Pirie, Proprietor of Lechmelm, Ullapool, Sutherland, 30 July 1883, p. 1840.

PAGE 196. "this holding tight...of the estate." NC. Alexander Pirie, Proprietor of Lechmelm, Ullapool, Sutherland, 30 July 1883, p. 1841.

PAGE 196. "Are there old people who are unable to work?" NC. Alexander Pirie, Proprietor of Lechmelm, Ullapool, Sutherland, 30 July 1883, p. 1841.

PAGES 196–97. "there is one...sweep themselves away." NC. Alexander Pirie, Proprietor of Lechmelm, Ullapool, Sutherland, 30 July 1883, p. 1841.

PAGE 197. "What is the object...way to build." NC. Alexander Pirie, Proprietor of Lechmelm, Ullapool, Sutherland, 30 July 1883, pp. 1841–42.

PAGE 197. "Do you give...giving them gifts." NC. Lachlan Macdonald, Portree, Skye, 23 May 1883, p. 558.

PAGES 197–98. "scanty hand...pampered underlings...out of sight... improvident character." Macleod in Mackenzie, pp. 66–67, 75, 95M.

PAGE 198. "I never accused them of that." NC. Donald Macdonald, farmer in Tormore, Portree, Skye, 23 May 1883, p. 605.

PAGE 198. "the influence of evil doctrine...influence of agitators." NC. Donald Macdonald, farmer in Tormore, Portree, Skye, 23 May 1883, p. 592.

PAGES 198–99. "have of late been maligned...to rebellion." NC. Donald Macdonald, farmer in Tormore, Portree, Skye, 23 May 1883, p. 594.

PAGE 199. "We have heard...when they are young?" NC. Lachlan Campbell, Tarbert, Harris, 13 June 1883, p. 1202.

PAGE 199. "Would it not be better...bit of land here?" NC Sherriff Alexander Nicolson, Commission Member, Tarbert, Harris, 13 June 1883, p. 1202.

PAGE 199. "It would be better...in that way." NC. Lachlan Campbell, Tarbert, Harris, 13 June 1883, p. 1202.

PAGES 199–200. "If you find a person...I was not made aware of it." NC. Mr. Charles Fraser-Mackintosh, Commission Member questioning William Henderson Hardie, Lochaline, Argyll, 11 August 1883, p. 2314.

PAGE 200. "we have been hearing...say about that?" NC. Lord Napier, Chairman of Commission, Balmacara, Ross, 2 August 1883, p. 1966.

PAGE 200. "I attribute it to...a season's work." NC. Roderick Maclean, Inverness, 11 October 1883, p. 2755.

PAGE 201. "proved less skillful...west-coast farm?" NC. Lord Napier, Chairman of Commission, Inverness, 11 October 1883, p. 2763.

PAGE 201. "Another reason...strangers among them." NC. Roderick Maclean, Inverness, 11 October 1883, pp. 2764–65.

PAGES 201–2. "As a consequence...on a regular basis." NA. Reverent Donald Mackinnon, Strath, Skye, pp. 45–46.

PAGE 202. "It is the Factors...made them a fasting people." Donald MacLeod quoted in Mackenzie (1999), p. 62.

PAGES 202–3. "From my knowledge...keeping them in order." NA. Rev. Donald Mackinnon, Strath, Skye, p. 48.

PAGE 203. "Highlanders want elevation." NC. Roderick Maclean, Inverness, 11 October 1883. p. 2760.

PAGE 203. "But what is most...at fair wages." NC. James Mollison, Inverness, 11 October 1883, p. 2916.

PAGE 203. "Is there any use...all the facts that I can." NC. Mr. Charles Fraser-Mackintosh, Commission Member questioning William Henderson Hardie, Lochaline, Argyll, 11 August 1883, p. 2313.

PAGES 203–4. "children of the Caucasian race...a benefit to humanity." John Prebble, *The Highland Clearances* (London: Penguin, 1969), p. 64.

PAGE 204. "of the crofters clinging...think for themselves." NC. Roderick Maclean, responding to a question from Charles Fraser-Mackintosh, Inverness, 11 October 1883, p. 2760.

PAGE 204. "objectionable in one way...every Highlander." *The New Statistical Account of Scotland 1845, Pt. 1-2* (Inverness: Ross and Cromarty), p. 314.

PAGE 204. "We most respectfully request...humble servants." NC. George Mackenzie, Keose, Lewis, 12 June 1883, p. 1144.

PAGE 205. "Notice of Meeting." Used in Glendale, Skye, in February 1882 for a meeting of tenants. Mackenzie (1999), p. 416.

PAGE 205. "fangs of the law." McLeod quoted in Mackenzie (1999), p. 95.

PAGE 205. "urged on by fearless want." McLeod quoted in Mackenzie (1999), p. 47.

PAGE 205. "the very stones cry out." McLeod quoted in Mackenzie (1999), p. 77.

PAGE 205. "remind them of what they have done to us." McLeod quoted in Mackenzie (1999), p. 100.

PAGES 205–6. "Things are not so quiet...in my own home." NC. John Mackay, Golspie, Sutherland, 8 October 1883, p. 2509.

PAGE 206. "it was resolved...thus arrived at." Mackenzie (1999), p. 417.

PAGE 207. "were so kind to us...we came home." NC. Alexander McCaskill, Bracadale, Skye, 18 May 1883, p. 352.

PAGES 207–9. The grievances listed here are from South Uist. NC. Rev. John McColl, Torlum, Benbecula, 29 May 1883, pp. 777–79.

PAGE 209. "We therefore consider...call our souls our own." NC. Dugald McGregor, Lochaline, Argyll, 11 August 1883, p. 2288.

PAGES 209–10. "The Proprietor led us...go away too." NC. John Macrae, Glenelg, Inverness-shire, 4 August 1883, p. 2055.

PAGE 210. "I, for one...more room for sheep." Hunter (1976), p. 80.

PAGE 210. "The result is...truly pitiable." NC. Donald McDonald, Arisaig, Inverness-shire, 6 August 1883, p. 2127.

PAGE 210. "That is not something...as our oppressor." NC. A.S. Black, Commission Agent, Bonar Bridge, Sutherland, 9 October 1883. Example of the myth of the lazy native, pp. 2603–4.

PAGES 210–11. "The present conditions...the distribution of wealth." NC. Hugh Macrae, Portree, Skye, 23 May 1883, pp. 641–42.

PAGE 211. "I am only a sojourner...in my native country." NC. Andrew Sutherland, Golspie, Sutherland, 8 October 1883, pp. 2542–43.

PAGE 211. "I remember the failures...state of semi-starvation." NC. Alexander Mackenzie (author of *History of the Highland Clearances*), Inverness, 11 October 1883, p. 2684.

PAGE 211. "Before I left...into the estate." NC. Alexander Cameron, Lochaline, Argyll, 11 August 1883, p. 2292.

PAGE 211. "careless feet." From a poem by Angus Cameron quoted in Mackenzie (1999), p. 301.

PAGES 211–12. "If I was a young man...what he feels." NC. Donald Simpson, Golspie, Sutherland, 8 October 1883, p. 2541.

PAGE 212. "For justice...are made prey." MacLeod quoted in Mackenzie (1999), p. 101.

PAGE 212. "the demon of sordidness...angel of civilization." Mackenzie (1999), p. 227.

PAGE 212. "I have something to say...could run away." NC. Archibald Fletcher McGillivray, Glenelg, Inverness-shire, 4 August 1883, p. 2028.

PAGE 212. "Nearly the whole of...drained for seed." NC. Alexander Macpherson, Bunessan, Isle of Mull, Argyll, 8 August 1883, p. 2204.

PAGE 212. "natural tendency...God created it." NC. Alexander Macpherson, Bunessan, Isle of Mull, Argyll, 8 August 1883, p. 2204.

PAGE 212. "met with the Factor...splendid drainers." NC. John Macrae, Letterfearn, Glenshiel, 3 August 1883, p. 1996.

PAGE 213. "free cultivators of the soil." Mackenzie, pp. 164–65, 209.

PAGE 213. "your voices are being heard...voices heard." NC. John Murdoch, Glasgow, 19 October 1883, pp. 3069–70.

PAGE 213. "opinions and creations...of this difficulty." NC. John Murdoch, Glasgow, 19 October 1883, p. 3070.

PAGE 213. "The weightiest part...of the crofters." NC. John Murdoch, Glasgow, 19 October 1883, p. 3073.

PAGE 213. "We are charged...their grievances." NC. John Murdoch, Glasgow, 19 October 1883, p. 3081.

PAGES 213–14. "I am quite ready...the native people." NC. John Murdoch, Glasgow, 19 October 1883, p. 3082.

PAGE 214. "When a person is convinced...their own country." NC. John Murdoch, Glasgow, 19 October 1883, p. 3083.

PAGE 214. "The first thing wanted...uncertainty and fear." NC. John Murdoch, Glasgow, 19 October 1883, p. 3088.

PAGE 215. "My grandfather...uninhabited until recently." NC. Alexander McCaskill, Bracadale, Skye, 18 May 1883, p. 348.

PAGE 216. "There is not a family...best bargain." NC. John McLeod, Tarbert, Harris, 13 June 1883, p. 1170.

PAGE 216. "I remember four...meted out to them." NC. Murdo Morrison, Tarbert, Harris, 13 June 1883, p. 1177.

PAGE 216. "It was the general talk...Laird's manor." NC. Hugh Mackay, Lochinvar, Sutherland, 22 July 1883, pp. 1740–41.

PAGE 216. "We went through...Highland regiments." NC. John Campbell, Tobermory, Mull, Argyll, 10 August 1883, p. 2276.

PAGE 217. "The real facts...endure forever" NC. Hugh Mackay, Glasgow, 19 October 1883, p. 3096.

PAGE 217. "There was just such a man...he got his pension." NC. Hugh Mackay, Glasgow, 19 October 1883, p. 3098.

PAGES 217–18. "If you want to fight...field of slaughter." MacLeod quoted in Mackenzie (1999), pp. 144–47.

PAGES 218–19. "All modern history...blood of their ancestors." Mackenzie quoting editor of the *Northern Ensign*, pp. 333–36.

PAGE 219. "reservoir of blood to be profitably spent." John Prebble, *Glencoe* (London: Secker and Warburg, 1966), p. 145.

PAGE 219. "dismal brigade." Mackenzie (1883), p. 427.

PAGE 220. "you may think that you are right...fear of the factory bell." A crofter's challenge to Lord Leverhulme recalled in Colin Macdonald, *Highland Journey* (London: Moray Press, 1945), pp. 145–46.

PAGE 220. "That's yourself, boy." Colin Macdonald (1945), p. 146.

PAGE 221. "volleys of sarcasms." Mackenzie (1999), pp. 427–30.

PAGE 221. "It is a satanic imposture...of useful sport." MacLeod quoted in Mackenzie (1999), pp. 136–37.

PAGE 222. "The strong side...take in hand." NC. John Macarthur, Kingussie, Inverness-shire, 15 October 1883, p. 2946.

PAGE 222. "reverse course." Mackenzie (1999), pp. 96–97, 426.

PAGE 223. "apologize for our previous petition...to set out now." Mackenzie (1999), p. 99.

PAGE 223. "domestic animals...back into the inferno." Macleod quoted in Mackenzie (1999), pp. 124, 268.

PAGE 224. "smoke ascends from horrid places." MacLeod quoted in Mackenzie (1999), p. 51.

PAGE 224. "able-bodied men...angry word is spoken." Mackenzie (1999), p. 268.

PAGE 224. "fill their pockets with the earth of their ancestors." Hunter (1976), p. 84.

Chapter VI   Shelburne County, Nova Scotia, 1993

During the blockade of the Russian ship, I was on the wharf on a regular basis and was writing articles for the local newspaper on the issues that caused the inshore fleet to go to such lengths to protect their livelihood.

PAGES 226–27. "Some people may ask...to do so." Alexander Mackenzie (1883), p. viii.

PAGES 227–28. Details from the initial blockade come from Lewis Jackson, *The Shelburne Coastguard Newspaper Retrospective*, 27 December 1997.

PAGE 230. "The scientific advice...on Georges Bank." Kathy Johnson, CG, 27 July 1993, p. 1.

PAGE 230. "partnership between government...the Atlantic fishery." Kathy Johnson, CG, 27 July 1993, p. 1.

PAGE 230. "We are here to listen." Kathy Johnson, CG, 27 July 1993, p. 1.

PAGE 230. "If you want to talk about rebuilding...not responsible management." Kathy Johnson, CG, 27 July 1993, p. 1.

PAGE 231. "This bunch...fish like these." Kathy Johnson, CG, 27 July 1993, p. 1.

PAGE 231. "Those fish of Noble's...only one observer." Kathy Johnson, CG, 27 July 1993, p. 2.

PAGE 233. "When we met with Barkhouse...I will support it." Harold Hart, CG, 27 July 1993, p. 4.

PAGE 234. "We are at the point...nothing to lose." Harold Hart, CG, 27 July 1993, p. 4.

PAGE 234. "the foreign fleet...groundfish catch." Lewis Jackson, *The Shelburne Coastguard Newspaper Retrospective*, 1997.

PAGE 234. "scattering cyclone." Neal Ascherson, *Stone Voices: The Search for Scotland* (London: Granta, 2002), p. 83.

PAGE 239. "until a solution...at this time." Harold Hart, CG, 27 July 1993, p. 1.

PAGES 243–44. "Swamp Loaded in a Hurricane" was written by the author. The title itself was arrived at with Joe Richman over a bottle of rum.

PAGES 244–45. The Edwin Brewer story is from William Williams Jr. Lockeport, *Tragedies on the Unforgiving Seas* (Seeblick Printing, 2018), pp. 69–71.

PAGE 247. "who for their attachment to government...the King's lines." Marion Robertson, *King's Bounty: A History of Early Shelburne Nova Scotia* (Halifax: Nova Scotia Museum, 1983), p. 33.

PAGE 247. "This cursed levelling spirit...rebellion soon." Marion Robertson (1983), p. 127.

PAGE 247. "Black Loyalists" is in quotation marks because it could be argued that the term provides an appearance of equality with other Loyalists and therefore erases the oppressive conditions under which many of them lived.

PAGE 248. "a situation so advantageous...they have suffered." Marion Robertson (1983), p. 100.

PAGE 248. "sunk to the lowest pitch of wretchedness." Marion Robertson (1983), p. 102.

PAGE 248. "front-line troops from twenty-three different British regiments." Marion Robertson (1983), p. 76.

PAGE 253. "a cent a pound...they were getting five cents." Sue Calhoun, *The Lockeport Lockout: An Untold Story in Nova Scotia Labour History* (Halifax: Oxfam Canada, 1983), p. 3.

PAGE 254. "Royal Commission look into price fixing." Calhoun (1983), pp. 1–2.

PAGE 254. "one day when Black Norman...for mercy's sake." Calhoun (1983), pp. 2–3. This story was also told to me by former dory mate Willie Harding, a native of Lockeport.

PAGE 256. "Happy Lennox...when he arrived at the plant." Calhoun (1983), p. 11.

PAGE 256. "My God...after all." Calhoun (1983), p. 12.

PAGE 256. "Then Tom Maclean...but refused to arrest him." Calhoun (1983), pp. 13–14.

PAGES 256–57. "The Padlock on the Door." Calhoun (1983), p. 14.

PAGE 257. "a letter to the clergy...outside agitators." Calhoun (1983), 16–17.

PAGE 257. "Fifty more Mounties...moved to clear the tracks." Calhoun (1983), pp. 18–19.

PAGE 258. "She got one hand free...six feet in the air." Les Mackenzie in Calhoun (1983), p. 19.

PAGE 258. "We feel that these RCMP boys...to a bare existence." Calhoun (1983), p. 19.

PAGES 258–59. For more background on the seven-month strike in Canso, see Silver Donald Cameron, *The Education of Everett Richardson: The Nova Scotia Fishermen's Strike 1970–71* (Toronto: McClelland and Stewart, 1977).

PAGE 259. "Negotiations...talks drag on." Harold Hart, CG, 27 July 1993, p. 3.

PAGE 260. "Farewell to Nova Scotia...This is our answer." Photo in *Shelburne Coastguard Newspaper*, 27 July 1993.

PAGE 262. "The only way...are engaged in." *Winnipeg Free Press*, 6 August 1993, p. A11.

PAGE 263. "Now to the agreement...three times a month." Harold Hart & Leonard Pace, CG, 3 August 1993, pp. 1, 3. See also, in the same issue, "An Open Letter to Ross Reid," a guest editorial by Ray Rogers on the call for community-based fishery management.

Epilogue

PAGES 267–70. The *Billow* sank on 10 April 1831 and the sinking was reported in the *Yarmouth Telegraph* of 18 May 1832. The wreck is also recorded in J. Murray Lawson, compiler, *Yarmouth Record of Shipping* (1876), pp. 224–25. The discharged soldiers of the 81st Regiment had fought in such places as the West Indies, Guernsey, South Africa, Ireland, Sicily, and Spain. The *Billow* is also referenced by Helen Creighton in *Bluenose Ghosts* because of the stories about the music that is heard in the area of the wreck.

PAGE 273. In "The Wreck of the *Billow*," journalist Arthur Thurston states that the song that was played on the *Billow* as it went down and that is still heard at times off the Emulous Breakers is "The Gay Cockade." I have found no such song, although "The White Cockade"—also called "John Highland Man"—is a traditional Scottish ballad that formed part of Robert Burns's "The Jolly Beggars." Burns wrote new lyrics for the ballad as well and called it "The White Cockade," a potent symbol of Jacobite rebellion. Bonnie Prince Charlie was said to have worn a white cockade at Culloden. *Selected Poems of Robert Burns* (London: Penguin, 1996), p. 11.

Comments

PAGE 275. Julie Cruikshank, *Do Glaciers Listen?: Local Knowledge, Colonial Encounters & Social Imagination* (Vancouver: UBC Press, 2005).

PAGE 275. John Ibbitson, "How the Maritimes Became Canada's Incredible Shrinking Region." *Globe and Mail*, 20 March 2015, F6.

PAGE 277. James Hunter, *The Making of the Crofting Community* (Edinburgh: John Donald Publishers, 1976).

PAGE 277. Walter Benjamin, *Illuminations* (London: Collins, 1973).

PAGES 277. David Craig, *On the Crofters' Trail* (Edinburgh: Birlinn, 2010).

PAGE 278. Mary Karr, *The Art of the Memoir* (New York: Harper, 2015).

PAGE 278. Julie Cruikshank, *Do Glaciers Listen?: Local Knowledge, Colonial Encounters & Social Imagination* (Vancouver: UBC Press, 2005).

PAGE 278. Donald MacLeod, *Gloomy Memories* (originally published in 1857), reprinted in *History of the Highland Clearances*, by Alexander Mackenzie (Edinburgh: Mercat Press 1999). (Mackenzie originally published in 1883.)

PAGE 278. "situated knowledges." Donna Haraway, "Situated Knowledges: The Science Question in Feminism and the Privilege of Partial Perspective," *Simians, Cyborgs, and Women: The Reinvention of Nature* (New York: Routledge, 1991), pp. 182–202.

PAGE 279. Karl Polanyi discusses of embedded and disembedded relations in "The Economy as Instituted Process," *Primitive, Archaic and Modern Economies*, ed. George Dalton (New York: Doubleday, 1968).

PAGE 280. William Cronin, "A Place for Stories: Nature, History, and Narrative," *Journal of American History* 78, no. 4 (1992): 1347–76.

PAGE 282. Michael Leyshon and Jacob Bull, "The Bricolage of the Here: Young People's Narrative of Identity in the Countryside," *Social & Cultural Geography* 12, no. 2 (March 2011): 159–80.

PAGE 282. David McCooey, "The Limits of Life Writing," *Life Writing* 14, no. 3 (2017), pp. 277–80.

PAGE 283. Lucien Goldmann, *The Hidden God* (New York: Norton, 1964).

PAGE 283. James Hunter, *The Making of the Crofting Community* (Edinburgh: John Donald Publishers, 1976).

PAGE 284. Frank B. Linderman, *Plenty-Coups: Chief of the Crows* (New York: John Day and Co., 1964). Plenty-Coups is also discussed in Jonathan Lear's *Radical Hope: Ethics in the Face of Cultural Devastation* (Cambridge: Harvard University Press, 2006) and in Cronin, "A Place for Stores."

PAGE 284. Glenn Albrecht, "Solastalgia: The Distress Caused by Environmental Change" *Australian Psychiatry* 15 (2007), pp. S95–S98.

PAGE 286. W.G. Sebald, *The Rings of Saturn*), trans. Michael Hulse (New York: New Directions, 1999).

PAGE 286. Norman O. Brown, *Life Against Death: The Psychoanalytical Meaning of History* (London: Sphere Books, 1970).

Books in the Life Writing Series
published by Wilfrid Laurier University press

Haven't Any News: Ruby's Letters from the Fifties edited by Edna Staebler with an Afterword by Marlene Kadar • 1995 / x + 165 pp. / ISBN 0-88920-248-6

"I Want to Join Your Club": Letters from Rural Children, 1900–1920 edited by Norah L. Lewis with a Preface by Neil Sutherland • 1996 / xii + 250 pp. / ISBN 0-88920-260-5

And Peace Never Came by Elisabeth M. Raab with Historical Notes by Marlene Kadar • 1996 / x + 196 pp. / ISBN 0-88920-281-8

Dear Editor and Friends: Letters from Rural Women of the North-West, 1900–1920 edited by Norah L. Lewis • 1998 / xvi + 166 pp. / ISBN 0-88920-287-7

The Surprise of My Life: An Autobiography by Claire Drainie Taylor with a Foreword by Marlene Kadar • 1998 / xii + 268 pp. / ISBN 0-88920-302-4

Memoirs from Away: A New Found Land Girlhood by Helen M. Buss / Margaret Clarke • 1998 / xvi + 153 pp. / ISBN 0-88920-350-4

The Life and Letters of Annie Leake Tuttle: Working for the Best by Marilyn Färdig Whiteley • 1999 / xviii + 150 pp. / ISBN 0-88920-330-x

Marian Engel's Notebooks: "Ah, mon cahier, écoute" edited by Christl Verduyn • 1999 / viii + 576 pp. / ISBN 0-88920-333-4 cloth / ISBN 0-88920-349-0 paper

Be Good Sweet Maid: The Trials of Dorothy Joudrie by Audrey Andrews • 1999 / vi + 276 pp. / ISBN 0-88920-334-2

Working in Women's Archives: Researching Women's Private Literature and Archival Documents edited by Helen M. Buss and Marlene Kadar • 2001 / vi + 120 pp. / ISBN 0-88920-341-5

Repossessing the World: Reading Memoirs by Contemporary Women by Helen M. Buss • 2002 / xxvi + 206 pp. / ISBN 0-88920-408-x cloth / ISBN 0-88920-410-1 paper

Chasing the Comet: A Scottish-Canadian Life by Patricia Koretchuk • 2002 / xx + 244 pp. / ISBN 0-88920-407-1

The Queen of Peace Room by Magie Dominic • 2002 / xii + 115 pp. / ISBN 0-88920-417-9

China Diary: The Life of Mary Austin Endicott by Shirley Jane Endicott • 2002 / xvi + 251 pp. / ISBN 0-88920-412-8

The Curtain: Witness and Memory in Wartime Holland by Henry G. Schogt • 2003 / xii + 132 pp. / ISBN 0-88920-396-2

Teaching Places by Audrey J. Whitson • 2003 / xiii + 178 pp. / ISBN 0-88920-425-x

Through the Hitler Line by Laurence F. Wilmot, M.C. • 2003 / xvi + 152 pp. / ISBN 0-88920-448-9

Where I Come From by Vijay Agnew • 2003 / xiv + 298 pp. / ISBN 0-88920-414-4

The Water Lily Pond by Han Z. Li • 2004 / x + 254 pp. / ISBN 0-88920-431-4

The Life Writings of Mary Baker McQuesten: Victorian Matriarch edited by Mary J. Anderson • 2004 / xxii + 338 pp. / ISBN 0-88920-437-3

Seven Eggs Today: The Diaries of Mary Armstrong, 1859 and 1869 edited by Jackson W. Armstrong • 2004 / xvi + 228 pp. / ISBN 0-88920-440-3

Love and War in London: A Woman's Diary 1939–1942 by Olivia Cockett; edited by Robert W. Malcolmson • 2005 / xvi + 208 pp. / ISBN 0-88920-458-6

Incorrigible by Velma Demerson • 2004 / vi + 178 pp. / ISBN 0-88920-444-6

Auto/biography in Canada: Critical Directions edited by Julie Rak • 2005 / viii + 264 pp. / ISBN 0-88920-478-0

Tracing the Autobiographical edited by Marlene Kadar, Linda Warley, Jeanne Perreault, and Susanna Egan • 2005 / viii + 280 pp. / ISBN 0-88920-476-4

Must Write: Edna Staebler's Diaries edited by Christl Verduyn • 2005 / viii + 304 pp. / ISBN 0-88920-481-0

Pursuing Giraffe: A 1950s Adventure by Anne Innis Dagg • 2006 / xvi + 284 pp. / 978-0-88920-463-8

Food That Really Schmecks by Edna Staebler • 2007 / xxiv + 334 pp. / ISBN 978-0-88920-521-5

163256: A Memoir of Resistance by Michael Englishman • 2007 / xvi + 112 pp. / ISBN 978-1-55458-009-5

The Wartime Letters of Leslie and Cecil Frost, 1915–1919 edited by R.B. Fleming • 2007 / xxxvi + 384 pp. / ISBN 978-1-55458-000-2

Johanna Krause Twice Persecuted: Surviving in Nazi Germany and Communist East Germany by Carolyn Gammon and Christiane Hemker • 2007 / x + 170 pp. / ISBN 978-1-55458-006-4

Watermelon Syrup: A Novel by Annie Jacobsen with Jane Finlay-Young and Di Brandt • 2007 / x + 268 pp. / ISBN 978-1-55458-005-7

Broad Is the Way: Stories from Mayerthorpe by Margaret Norquay • 2008 / x + 106 pp. / ISBN 978-1-55458-020-0

Becoming My Mother's Daughter: A Story of Survival and Renewal by Erika Gottlieb • 2008 / x + 178 pp. / ISBN 978-1-55458-030-9

Leaving Fundamentalism: Personal Stories edited by G. Elijah Dann • 2008 / xii + 234 pp. / ISBN 978-1-55458-026-2

Bearing Witness: Living with Ovarian Cancer edited by Kathryn Carter and Lauri Elit • 2009 / viii + 94 pp. / ISBN 978-1-55458-055-2

Dead Woman Pickney: A Memoir of Childhood in Jamaica by Yvonne Shorter Brown • 2010 / viii + 202 pp. / ISBN 978-1-55458-189-4

I Have a Story to Tell You by Seemah C. Berson • 2010 / xx + 288 pp. / ISBN 978-1-55458-219-8